# International Norms and Decision Making

# International Norms and Decision Making

## A Punctuated Equilibrium Model

GARY GOERTZ

ROWMAN & LITTLEFIELD PUBLISHERS, INC.
*Lanham • Boulder • New York • Oxford*

ROWMAN & LITTLEFIELD PUBLISHERS, INC.

Published in the United States of America
by Rowman & Littlefield Publishers, Inc.
A Member of the Rowman & Littlefield Publishing Group
4501 Forbes Boulevard, Suite 200, Lanham, Maryland 20706
www.rowmanlittlefield.com

P.O. Box 317, Oxford OX2 9RU, United Kingdom

Copyright © 2003 by Rowman & Littlefield Publishers, Inc.

British Library Cataloguing in Publication Information Available

**Library of Congress Cataloging-in-Publication Data**

Goertz, Gary, 1953-
    International norms and decision making : a punctuated equilibrium model / Gary Goertz.
        p. cm.
    Includes bibliographical references and index.
    ISBN 0-7425-2589-9 (alk. paper) — ISBN 0-7425-2590-2 (pbk. : alk. paper)
        1. International relations—Decision making. I. Title.

JZ1253.G64 2003
327.1'01'156—dc21

2003041361

Printed in the United States of America

⊖™ The paper used in this publication meets the minimum requirements of American National Standard for Information Sciences—Permanence of Paper for Printed Library Materials, ANSI/NISO Z39.48-1992

# Contents

# Tables

# Figures

# Chapter 1

# Introduction

Man is as much a rule-following animal as a purpose-seeking one.

*—F. A. Hayek*

The form of made things is always subject to change in response to their real or perceived shortcomings, their failures to function properly. This principle governs all invention, innovation, and ingenuity; it is what drives all inventors, innovators, and engineers.

*—Henry Petroski*

The question of order has always played a central role in the study of international politics. The Treaty of Westphalia, for example, conventionally marks the consecration of anarchy and its sibling sovereignty as defining characteristics of interstate relations. In times of little international commerce, population movement, and cumbersome means of communication, sovereign states interacted most obviously through warfare. A major aspect of a king's identity was as commander and chief. Louis XIV certainly saw the conduct of foreign wars as one core aspect of his role as king; even today it is rare for royal males not to hold military offices. Over time, nations have come into increasing contact with each other, and war has now become a remote possibility for many pairs of states and even for some regions. Thus the link between anarchy/sovereignty and war has been stretched if not broken in some areas of the world.

The question arises then with great force about how these increasing—and mostly peaceful—interactions between states are conducted. The classic image of this is the signing of treaties between sovereigns that punctuate the history of states. Even today the signing of international treaties remains a major—and media—event where heads of state gather to solemnly affix their signatures to documents which are to regulate their relationships with each other.

But who is to say that states will observe their treaty commitments? What role do international organizations play in treaty compliance? Do informal agreements play an important role along side the formal ones? In principle all the problems that have traditionally plagued treaties remain in effect in the current era of increased interaction. If there is more order in the international system, we must examine how that order is created and maintained in the absence of centralized decision-making and sanctioning bodies.

This volume analyzes one way in which regularity, predictability, and order can be explained: international norms. These may take many forms with different properties. They can be informal or formal; they can evolve; hegemons can create them. Norms—as well as rules and principles which I shall consider as synonyms for most of this volume—form the cornerstone of my analysis. According to my account the concept of an institution depends on the primitive concept of a norm: institutions are structures of norms. This volume hence strikes out immediately in a different direction from the literature by putting the concept of a norm under the analytical microscope.

We can ask after all: why do governments invest so much time, energy, and money into the negotiation, wording, and details of international institutions? I think the answer quite clearly is that international norms and rules have direct relevance for their behavior. By signing an international treaty a government commits itself to do some things, not to do others, or allocates rights to do things. Hence this volume focuses on international norms and institutions in connection with behavior and choice. Chapter 2 argues that institutions are just words—i.e., do not include any actual behavior—but that they issue directions about government action.[1] Certainly norms must be interpreted and have meaning, but I am more concerned with how we can think of international institutions in terms of the policy process and actions of governments.

I shall argue that we need a *policy* theory of international institutions. International institutions matter because they have something to say about foreign policy in virtually all areas, be it trade, finance, war, the environment, and so forth. To paraphrase cooperation theorists: international institutions are about policy.

International institutions then matter because they can enter into the policy or decision making process. Part I of this volume deals directly with this issue: how do norms function in individual decision making? Here we have a question which has not been addressed in the institution literature. Those who stress the importance of international norms—often the social constructivists—have no real individual or state-level decision-making model (Checkel 1998). These scholars tend to see norms as located *outside* governmental decision making, usually at the international level. Those who draw on economic or game theoretic models also

---

[1] For example, Chayes and Chayes who approach international norms from a legal perspective define norms in terms of behavior: "We use 'norms' in a generic sense to include a broad class of generalized prescriptive statements—principles, standards, rules, and so on—both procedural and substantive . . . they [principles, standards, rules, and so on] are *prescriptions for action in situations of choice*, carrying a sense of obligation, a sense that they *ought* to be followed" (1995, 113, emphasis in the original).

see norms as existing outside the individual either as constraints or equilibrium-choosing mechanisms in coordination settings.[2] My approach examines the logical structure of a norm to find that therein lies a decision-making procedure. I show that "norm," "rule," and "policy" have the same logical structure (hence I will treat them all as synonyms). Since the formal structure of a norm is that of a policy—and vice versa—I call decision making directly with norms "policy decision making." This is but another name for rule-based approaches such as those found in artificial intelligence, expert systems, and the like.

Roughly then I present two decision making models, one which takes norms and policies directly and calculates a decision based on them—i.e., policy decision making—and a second decision-making procedure used in economics and game theory that I shall refer to as expected utility choice. In the first model norms form the core and are directly used in making decisions while in the second there is no consensus on how to deal with them. I shall argue based on formal criteria that most of the expected utility literature mistranslates the concept of a norm. This becomes possible once one has a clear, rigorous concept of a norm and an alternative decision-making model based on norms and policies.

I propose that policy decision making makes more sense as a way of thinking of government decision making and international institutions than is the case with expected utility choice. Specifically I borrow fuzzy logic decision-making methodology as a concrete expression of policy choice. It is no accident that I refer to policy decision making and fuzzy logic in the same breath, both deal with logic since the logical form of a norm or policy is a syllogism. Since fuzzy logic deals with norms and rules in a decision-making context it is a natural choice. In addition it was developed as a model of actual human decision making. Like expected utility models it has mathematical formulation, unlike most economic models it has powerful practical applications since televisions, trains, elevators, and factories now run using fuzzy logic systems.

Among the many advantages of using fuzzy logic to think about decision making with norms lies in its ability to deal with a standard problem: what does one do when norms and policies provide conflicting advice? The tendency in international relations is to treat this "problem" in a legalistic fashion, via priority rules and interpretation. For fuzzy logic conflict rules are normal and usually good! Instead of thinking of such conflicts as always negative—which they certainly can be—one can think of different norms as reflecting different facets of a problem that should be attended to. One thus needs to come to a final choice taking into account the recommendation that each policy provides.

This ability of fuzzy logic to combine the recommendations of different norms and policies proves absolutely crucial in many contexts in this volume. Conflicting policies arise in many different ways. Within individual choice I discuss two

---

[2]For example, Baily in a recent and typical way says: "The resolution of the paradox of individual responsibilities is achieved by elaborating an account of institutions as equilibria in complex games" (1997, viii).

generic categories, instrumental norms and moral norms, in chapters 4 and 5. However, since both kinds of norms are norms there is no a priori problem in combining them to arrive at a final decision. In fact, I argue in chapter 6 that in the normal state of affairs both kinds of norms enter into the decision-making process. In part II I discuss conflicting policies in terms of the level of analysis. In the organizational formulation it is the conflict between organizational policy and principals or between principals and agents; in the international formulation it becomes international norms and government policies. Here too we need to understand choice when conflicting policies apply, the fuzzy logic decision-making methodology can be applied to situations where the conflicting policies come from different actors, organizations, or institutions.

Part I presents a decision-making model that takes norms and policies as the core of the decision-making process and a way to combine them to arrive at a final choice. One can choose policies based on all kinds of considerations ranging from self-interest maximization to human rights to preserving the environment to increasing wealth. I quoted F. A. Hayek at the beginning of this chapter for a very good reason: he states that human beings are rule-following "as much as" purpose-seeking; fuzzy logic and policy decision making propose that it is not "as much as" but rather "simultaneously." He implies also that such rules come from the outside, but individuals, organizations, and governments can choose—based on consequentialist and moral reasoning—the norms they use in making choices: in short, the rules are chosen purposefully.

ह।

The punctuated equilibrium model makes the case for a *policy* approach to international norms and institutions. Part II in particular makes this argument in recognizing that organizations are the key players in the field of international institutions. What we need then must be a model of *organizational* decision making and policy. An organizational model must be at the same time one of policy creation and evolution, taking what we know about domestic policy and organizational decision making and applying it to foreign policy. The punctuated equilibrium model I present is thus a model of (1) policy decision making, (2) policy creation, and (3) policy evolution.

The biological theory of punctuated equilibrium provides metaphorical inspiration for punctuated equilibrium theory of policy (e.g., Baumgartner and Jones 1993; Diehl and Goertz 2000). The policy and organizational version of the punctuated equilibrium model underlies all three sections of this volume. Important in individual, organizational, and international policy is the distinction between choosing a policy or norm and then making decisions—often over years and decades—with that policy.

In part II I focus specifically on the punctuated equilibrium model of policy and organizational decision making. This perspective reflects, at the organizational level, a number of key factors underlying the policy decision-making model at the individual level outlined in part I. One such factor is the distinction between (1) choosing norms and policies, and (2) using norms and policies in making individual decisions. This distinction is quite clear in fuzzy logic expert systems. The goal of a systems engineer is to come up with a structure of rules which is then programmed into the machine, the machine then interacts with its environment; each situation invokes some of the rules which then get combined to produce one final choice, hopefully the optimal one. Governments often have this same basic structure: legislatures determine norms and policies which are then implemented in concrete circumstances by the administration.

The punctuated equilibrium model not only refers to this structure of policy choice–implementation but also to the evolution of policy itself. During periods of (major) reform new policies are established which then remain in effect—often for decades—until the next reform period. The basic pattern is thus major change followed by incremental periods. One cannot understand governmental decision making without keeping in mind this pattern of rapid change followed by stasis. The history of U.S. foreign policy provides many examples of this, starting with George Washington's recommendation to avoid alliances.

This basic model of policy was developed in the course of work on this volume, and at the same time in the context of research on enduring rivalries (Diehl and Goertz 2000). The empirical facts are that most militarized conflict and warfare occurs within long-standing rivalries. In spite of the flexibility promoted by classic balance of power realists the historical record shows many long-term, well-entrenched militarized conflicts. Our analysis of enduring rivalries supported many key features of the punctuated equilibrium model, such as quick lock-in of conflict levels and the importance of political shocks in the process, both at the beginning and the end. What is true for military conflict I think is all the more the case when one turns to trade, finance, the environment, and human rights. What was lacking in that study on enduring rivalries was a development of the organizational decision-making bases of the model. Here I fill that gap by sketching out an organizational decision-making model.

An organizational decision-making model must take into account that organizations exist in one sense independently of individuals, yet at the same time it is various individuals within them who make and carry out policy. This aspect of organizational choice can be expressed in terms of the level of analysis or agent–structure problematique. I distinguish three levels in organizations: (1) the organization as a structure of norms and policies, (2) leadership, and (3) bureaucrats. Final organizational action results from the interaction of these three levels. An organizational decision-making model must then take input from these three levels to produce a decision or action.

Within organizations, as between governments and international institutions, there can be policy conflicts. These can be differences between the policies of a new leadership and existing organizational norms just like there can be divergence between government policy and international institutions. My "solution" to the level of analysis problem in both these two variants is to reformulate the problem in terms of conflicting norms. Chapter 6 deals exactly with this issue in the context of conflicting norms—say, instrumental and moral—within a single individual. Fuzzy logic provides a decision-making methodology for producing decisions when multiple policies apply. Hence I have procedures for dealing in general with the problem of conflicting norms.[3] Nothing prevents me from using this methodology in order to combine norms that come from different sources but apply to the same decision. In the case of the organization the conflict can be between leadership norms and existing organizational ones or between leadership and bureaucrats' views on policy. In the international version, it can be combining government policies with international institution ones.

Within an individual person the various norms are weighted in part by the importance of that dimension for the person involved. In the level of analysis context policies are weighted by the power of the individual, organization, or international institution that holds them. As within an individual the end result is a compromise reflecting the weights attached to each applicable norm in the decision.

In summary, part II presents the punctuated equilibrium model of government policy. This approach takes seriously that governments qua organizations are the key actors in the creation and implementation of international institutions. The model proposes a standard pattern for the evolution of policy involving rapid change followed by incrementalism. Since it is an organizational model it takes explicitly into account that governments are organizations that are composed of different individuals and bureaucracies each with different policy preferences. Decisions arise from the interaction of these different policy norms. These chapters address many of the issues that Paul Diehl and I left in suspense when we first proposed the punctuated equilibrium model in the context of enduring militarized rivalries (Diehl and Goertz 2000). Virtually all the issues that I address in this volume apply in that context as well. Security policy is a policy just like trade, the environment, human rights, and social welfare issues.

---

[3] When I was an undergraduate student in mathematics there was a famous principle in the department which was called the "tea kettle on the table by the stove" principle. The story went that there was a mathematician who got up each morning and took the tea kettle from the table and put it on the stove to heat water for tea. One morning he found the kettle on the floor. The question then (to prospective math majors) was: how does he solve the problem of getting the tea kettle to the stove? A good candidate for a physics major would say: "He picks up the tea kettle and puts it on the stove." A mathematician would say: "He puts the tea kettle on the table since he knows how to solve the problem of getting the tea kettle from the table to the stove."

ぉ

Part III consists of an analysis of international institutions per se. Chapter 2 makes it clear that most definitions of an institution have missed the key issue: what is a rule, norm, or principle? Chapter 3 makes it clear that the core concepts of the institution definition—principles, rules, norms, and decision-making procedures—all have the same logical structure (a syllogism). The use of formal analysis also reveals that the idea of policy belongs to this same family. In short, one restatement of my definition of an institution consists of replacing "norms" by "policies." This becomes important when one realizes that most institution norms are carried out as national policies. While this is explicit in virtually all case studies of institutions, there is nothing in institution theory that stresses the links between institutions as policies and the incorporation (or not) of these policies by individual governments.

My analysis of international institutions can thus begin with a clear conception of government decision making in terms of the organizational, punctuated equilibrium model. I use much of this policy model at the international level. For example, the punctuated equilibrium model makes a clear distinction between policy adoption and implementation. In terms of international institutions this becomes a clear differentiation between institution creation and institution functioning.

Chapter 9 presents my theory of institution creation. Here we see one major and concrete advantage of my conceptualization of an institution which clearly removes all behavioral components (i.e., behavior following or not institution norms). In the typical case, an institution comes into being when a treaty is signed. My approach to institutions has no problem in saying that an institution exists starting at this moment. From a functional point of view of course nothing guarantees (1) that governments will adopt institution policies and (2) that even if they do, that these actions will improve or solve the problems the treaty addresses.

My theory of institution creation is a functional, policy-oriented one. I use as my starting point John Kingdon's (1984) agenda-setting framework. Many of his ideas can be found in parts of the institution literature. For example, the idea that shocks and crises can open windows-of-opportunity for action. He also stresses the importance of political entrepreneurs which translated into international relations–speak becomes epistemic communities as well as Young's (1991) emphasis on the importance of leadership.

The model proposes four essential conditions for institution creation: (1) perceived problems, (2) an institution as the solution, (3) a favorable political context, and (4) sufficient power behind one solution. Like Kingdon, I argue that an institution will come into being only at those times when there is a favorable conjunction of *all* factors. The second level of the theory claims that there are many ways in which each of these four slots can be filled. For example, there are various means by which problems can get onto the international agenda such as exogenous shocks, interest group or epistemic community activity, and actions by powerful governments. The model thus has a very functionalist character at one level with core concepts such as problems and solutions. At the same time the second level is quite social constructivist in nature since the content of most of the categories depends on the social construction of the problem and what counts as a good solution.

Once an international institution is formed and underway one naturally asks: how well does it work? This of course poses the question in functionalist terms, to which chapter 10 gives a functionalist answer. One prominent trend in the institution literature talks about international institutions in terms of collective goods and prisoners' dilemma.[4] I borrow from a different part of economics and think of international institutions as *producing* goods and services. International institutions produce free trade, security, reduced pollution, and other desirable things. The question then arises about the means of production: what are the inputs which an international institution uses to produce its output?

In principle an institution works through its policies; ideally, if all the relevant actors follow the rules, norms, and principles, the institution produces the desired goods and services. (Obviously, this makes the nontrivial assumption that the rules are really solutions to the problem, and do not, for example, make it worse.) If we examine the general literature on institutions there appears to be at least two general functions that an institution must perform to be effective. It must be able to monitor the extent of compliance of actors with institution norms. Second, in case of violation it needs to sanction such acts. For example, Ostrom's work (1991) on common pool resource institutions proposes that there are eight essential functions such institutions need to perform for the institution to work correctly, among these monitoring and sanctioning stand out: "Most robust and long-lasting common-pool institutions involve clear mechanisms for monitoring rule conformance and graduated sanctions for enforcing compliance" (Ostrom 1998, 8).

If one examines the content and issues surrounding the negotiation of international institutions one finds a constant concern for the ability to monitor the actions of the relevant actors and the concern (often not translated into rules) for what to do about violations of institution norms. For example, Benedick (1998) notes that once trade sanctions for nonparties were put into the ozone treaty there was a sudden increase in the number of adherents.

The final chapter of this volume deals with the thorny problem of sanctions. The preceeding chapter argued that sanctions were an essential part of a well-functioning institution, yet international relations has kept itself separate from domestic policies as a discipline based mostly on the claim that the lack of an effective international government makes it special, where effectiveness mostly means sanctioning power.

---

[4]One curiosity in the international relations literature is the lack of consensus on how to spell "prisoners' dilemma." I use the plural possessive since the dilemma is one the prisoners have together, not the dilemma of a singular prisoner.

Chayes and Chayes (1995) illustrate the traditional (often legalistic) view of sanctions in terms of the official actions by institutions like the UN. As they discuss, if one takes international institution sanctioning in this sense they are rare. Throughout this volume I have stressed that much of the action takes place at the state level. To understand sanctions one needs to view the issue in terms of government policy and the reactions of key actors to the violations of international norms. The main theme of chapter 11 is thus that international institutions and norms provide justifications and incite individual actors to sanction norm violations.

An international norm matters because without it individual and corporate sanctioning action is much less likely. A realist—anti-norm—position claims that government action is purely based on material self-interests. My claim is that it is founded on interests *and norms*. I argue that two actions, one norm-following and one norm-violating, but with *equal* negative impact on government interests receive different treatment. An actor will respond in a qualitatively and quantitatively different—more severe—fashion when a negative action is norm-violating than when it follows the rules of the game. This makes sense of Martin's (1992) finding that international institutions play a significant role in coercive cooperation. Institutions as sanctioning forums come into play only when a norm of the institution is violated, while such is not the case for norm-complying behavior. Additional examples can be found in the literature on international negotiations where if the weaker party (e.g., Latin American states) can successfully argue that it is following U.S. or international policy norms then it does much better than one would expect based only on a consideration of realist factors.

Here we come full circle back to the importance of an organizational and policy approach to governmental decision making. Governments, starting with the United States, do not like to go against established policy even if there are strong (domestic) interests pushing them to do so. When the United States targets Japan on trade issues it not only makes decisions based on economic interests but also chooses areas where Japan can be argued to be in violation of international trade principles. It is difficult and often undesirable for a government to stray from well-entrenched policies, which is exactly the inertia and stability that the punctuated equilibrium emphasizes.

In summary, part III proposes a functionalist, punctuated equilibrium model of international institutions. The theory of international institutions parallels and draws upon the punctuated equilibrium model of organizational and individual choice. Institution creation is the international equivalent of a new policy at the state level. I suggest that in both cases periods of rapid change are followed by incrementalism and stasis. Both models focus on output—organizational or institutional—in terms of key inputs. In the context of organizations it is the policy input from different levels of the organization, in terms of international institutions the input is monitoring and sanctioning. Both are functionalist in that policies are designed to deal with specific problems, which are their *raison d'être*.

ॐ

This volume fundamentally outlines a functionalist approach to government policy and international norms. The term functionalist has been subjected to much use and abuse in the international relations literature; while Keohane has abandoned the term, social constructivists continue to use it. I use functionalism in two senses; the first comes from the emphasis on international institutions as policy responses to perceived problems, while the second involves the functions an international institution must perform to be effective.

The first point is absolutely essential in the punctuated equilibrium model of policy. Functionalism means that government policy as well as international institutions are responses (not the only possible ones) to a perceived problem. Policies propose solutions to those problems: the function of policy is problem-solving. For example, a very common hypothesis in the institution literature is that a crisis is a necessary condition for institution formation. This hypothesis becomes in my theory of institution creation an important way in which problems are created or how people become aware of them.

Once a solution/policy/institution comes into being to deal with a problem it is unlikely to change much in the short or medium term, unless it fails dramatically early on. This provides the basic explanation for the punctuated equilibrium pattern of rapid change followed by incrementalism. If the solution does not work well at first, most likely it will be fiddled with (incrementalism) rather than being replaced wholesale.

If one examines existing institutions this problem-solving framework fits well the historical record. For example, system-wide security organizations like the Concert of Europe, the League of Nations, and the UN came into being after the massive failure of the previous system, as represented by world wars. Post–World War II trade institutions responded to the perceived failures of the 1930s trade system. These kinds of examples can be multiplied ad infinitum.

This problem-solving language presents a significant shift from the traditional use of "interest" as the motivating factor in international affairs. A problem means that someone's interests are negatively affected but one moves away from too general, unoperationalizable, and vague notions of self, national, or egotistical interests. Not only that, when one analyzes a given institution it is *impossible* to avoid functionalist language and concepts, be it the Red Cross, the World Trade Organization (WTO), or environmental institutions the rules, norms, and principles of the institution address and attempt to redress problems.

This is largely the functionalism that social constructivists criticize. However, the rest of my functionalist framework draws upon the strengths of the social constructivist approach. First, note that I referred to perceived problems; a problem becomes a policy problem when some organization, government, or group manages to get it onto the agenda. Some problems can be called objective, for example, environmental ones, whereas others are clearly debatable, such as nuclear proliferation. In addition, there are plenty of issues that could easily be considered problems that never make it onto the agenda for action. Also, there is no sense in which the solution is optimal or even that it has an impact at all on the problem. Solutions are tied to interests, ideology, culture, and historical period—just like problems.

In summary, my model has a functional structure with social constructivist content. I cited H. Petroski—an engineer—in an epigraph to this chapter. He argues that the evolution of "useful things" occurs because of their "perceived shortcomings." Government policies and international institutions are just as much cultural artifacts as the forks and tin cans that he discusses. Governments are like his inventors in that they respond to perceived problems by creating policies at the national as well as at the international level.

# Chapter 2

# The Ontology of International Institutions and Regimes

> The processes of *telling* someone to do something, and *getting* him to do it, are quite distinct, logically, from each other.
>
> —*R. M. Hare*

What *is* an institution? a regime? a norm? For some these concepts are problematic requiring discussion and analysis, for others a mere citation, or definition suffices before moving to the analysis of their causes and effects. For example, the concept of a regime provoked much discussion during the 1980s (Krasner 1983) and the 1990s (Rittberger 1993). In contrast, in the special of *International Organization* (2001) devoted to the design of international institutions, the concept of an institution is not discussed (it is defined in the introduction but that is all). What is at stake when some groups of scholars prefer the term "institution" while others use the concept of a "norm"? What does it mean when the term "regime" goes out of favor with scholars to be replaced by "institution"? In this chapter I will examine the issues surrounding the ontology of regimes and institutions. This will lead to the question of the ontology of a norm, a topic of the next chapter.

In one of the most cited definitions in political science a regime was defined in the collection edited by Steven Krasner, what I shall refer to as the "Krasner definition" of a regime:

> International regimes are defined as principles, norms, rules, and decision-making procedures around which actor expectations converge in a given issue-area. (Krasner 1983, 275)

This definition was widely accepted and even called the "consensus" definition by Hasenclever, Mayer, and Rittberger (1997). Ten years later this definition was modified to read:

> Regimes are social institutions composed of agreed-upon principle, norms, rules, and decision-making procedures that govern the interactions of actors in specific issue areas.[1] (Osherenko and Young 1993, 1)

Little changed in the intervening ten years; "social institutions" has been added, and regimes now "govern interactions" instead of "expectations converging" around them. Substantively, and certainly in practice, the definition remains unchanged. These minor modifications do not really address the underlying problems of the original definition, which is not surprising since the same epistemic community devised them both. In spite of it being a consensus definition it generated quite a bit of discussion.

In contrast, the concept of an institution barely requires analysis or discussion, particularly from expected utility theorists. Nevertheless, there is a sort of family resemblance between conceptualizations of institutions. Since expected utility scholars have preferred the term institution to regime it is useful to see how they have thought about this concept:

> Social institutions are sets of rules that structure social interactions in particular ways. These rules (1) provide information about how people are expected to act in particular situations, (2) can be recognized by those who are members of the relevant group as the rules to which others conform in these situations, and (3) structure the strategic choices of actors in such a way as to produce equilibrium outcomes. (Knight 1990, 54)

> We define international institutions as explicit arrangements, negotiated among international actors, that prescribe, proscribe, and/or authorize behavior. (Koremenos, Lipson, and Snidal 2001, 762)

> Institutions are the rules of the game in a society. (North 1990, 3)

> "Institutions" can be defined as the sets of working rules that are used to determine who is eligible to make decisions in some arena, what actions are allowed or constrained, what aggregation rules will be used, what procedures must be followed, what information must or must not be provided, and what payoffs will be assigned to individuals dependent on their actions. (Ostrom 1991, 51)

> [I]nstitutions are no more than rules and rules are themselves the product of social decisions. (Riker 1980, 444)

> A social institution is a regularity in social behavior that is agreed to by all members of society, specifies behavior in specific recurrent situations, and is either self-policed or policed by some external authority (Schotter 1981, 11). [Langlois approves of the Schotter definition and adds "social institutions are

---

[1] Osherenko and Young (1993, 1) report that this definition was agreed upon at a meeting of fifteen scholars representing four large-scale, multiyear research projects on international regimes at Minary Center, Dartmouth College, 22–24 November 1991. Levy, Young, and Zürn add "programs" to the list of "principles, norms, rules, and decision-making procedures":"Regimes are social institutions composed of agreed-upon principles, norms, rules, and decision-making procedures and programs that govern the interactions of actors in specific issue areas" (1995, 274).

made up of rules of the form "always react in manner $X$ to event $Y$." (1986, 17–18)]

In short, there was relative consensus on the concept of a regime but much discussion. There is a similar relative consensus on the definition of an institution, but room for dissent as well. These concepts of institution and regime have produced widely varying interpretations and practices. I propose that this state of affairs has arisen partially because of the problems with the definitions themselves and partially because of lack of clarity about some of the key concepts contained within them, which permits everyone to act like Humpty Dumpty in *Alice in Wonderland*. The scholarly consensus has been to let a hundred flowers bloom and get on with the important task of studying regimes and institutions. This chapter suggests that without a clear conception of what an institution is the analysis of whatever ends up being a regime will tend to have characteristic problems, a result of the many unexamined assumptions that such a process inevitably produces.

For reasons that will be given throughout this chapter and the next I opt for a minimalist concept of regime and institution:

An institution (or equivalently a regime) is a structure of norms and rules.

For most purposes I will argue that institution = regime and norm = rule. This will have the advantage of bring together the literature on regimes and institutions under one umbrella, bringing together those who tend to use "rule" with those who prefer "norm." This definition has two elements: one is the concept of a "norm." The second element is the concept of a "structure." The title of this volume contains "international norms" which makes it clear that the concept of a norm carries most of the theoretical weight. Different kinds of norms can be put together to build an institutional structure.

Notice that all the definitions given above of regime or institution use as a primitive concept the idea of a norm or a rule. I will end this chapter arguing that we really need to answer the question "what is a norm"? But before addressing that issue I want to explore some of the issues raised by these definitions of regimes and institutions.

## The Core of Institution and Regime Concepts

In working with definitional and conceptual issues what often unites observers and vaguely determines their reactions are the *core examples* of a phenomenon. When we think of phenomena as belonging to types or categories certain examples typify the family, they compose the nuclear family, while other examples are more distantly related, they are second cousins (Lakoff 1987). I suggest that core examples have determined the content of the regime concept much more than the actual content of the Krasner definition. Quite explicitly the group that created

the Krasner definition took the post–World War II economic agreements and institutions, particularly GATT, as the archetype. Security regimes, on the other
hand, are not core, and may not even belong to the extended family according to
some. Likewise, prisoners' dilemma and coordination games are core for thinking
about regimes, frequently extended to n-person collective good approaches. Definitions tend to fit these core cases, and eventually are tested against the marginal
ones. The same is true for those, notably expected utility theorists in international
relations, who take their concept of institution from those who have worked ex-
tensively on institutions in domestic politics. The core examples produce issues
and nonissues that come as unaccompanied baggage. I suggest that this baggage
needs to go through security.

Since core examples are partially personal and partially collective there is
room for ambiguity. To include international law or human rights into the core
results in a different perception as to what regimes are about than the focus on
economic agreements. This procedure tends to force all regimes into the framework of the core examples. I shall argue throughout this volume that there are
potentially many different types of regimes, and hence one should consider multiple core examples.

᠎᠎᠎

The use of core examples leads the Krasner definition to require that regimes are
for a *given issue area*. Is this really a necessary restriction? Could there not be
norms or regimes that apply to multiple issue areas? The "sovereignty regime"
might be a part of many different normative structures. Kegley and Raymond
(1990) argue that the distinction between specific versus universal is important
in understanding different types of norms. Within domestic politics the regime
for dealing with minors intersects with many different parts of law; in international affairs there are special rules for poor countries that cut across issue areas.
The "issue specific" requirement comes, I believe, from the tendency to think of
"regime" in terms of trade regimes, environmental regimes, security regimes, etc.
While most regimes do deal with specific issue areas, nothing prevents a regime
from cutting across issue areas, e.g., economics and the environment, and certainly
some of the norms of the regime can be found in multiple regimes. In summary,
nothing in the concept of regime would seem to require that norms, principles,
and rules be limited to specific issue areas, or conversely that they be universal:
the definition should remain silent on this point.

In contrast the definitions of institutions do not specify an issue because they
are drawn from domestic politics. To be sure there are many "issue-area" laws
but many of the constitutional and procedural rules cut across substantive areas.
However, international institutions are much more compartmentalized, most of
the time international institutions really do work by issue area.

⁊⩗

A second and more important issue is the extent to which regimes must have "behavioral conformity" in order to "exist." The Krasner definition requires that regimes "*guide* actors' expectations" (emphasis added). Thus regimes must indirectly influence behavior since expectations determine in part actions. Notice that the authors carefully avoided formulations like "principles and norms that states *should* follow." This would be too close to the much maligned idealist position.

In the revised definition this issue is not resolved but moves in the behavioral direction, since now regimes "govern the interactions" instead of "guide expectations." For example, Keohane appears to be uncertain on this topic:

> Defining regimes simply in terms of explicit rules and procedures risks slipping into the formalism characteristic of some traditions in international law: that is, purely nominal agreements could be considered to be regimes, even though they had no behavioral implications. The futile and empty Kellogg-Briand Pact of 1927, to "outlaw war," could on a formalistic definition be considered an international regime. (1993, 27)

> It therefore seems sensible to define *agreements* in purely formal terms (explicit rules agreed to by more than one state) and to consider *regimes* as arising when states recognize these agreements as having continuing validity. This definition has "thin" substantive content: a set of rules need not be "effective" to qualify as a regime, but it must recognized as continuing to exist. Using this definition, regimes can be identified by the existence of explicit rules that are referred to in an affirmative manner by governments, even if they are not necessarily scrupulously observed. (1993, 28)

Rittberger has explicitly stated:

> [E]ven explicit norms and rules if they remain largely inoperative fail to indicate the existence of an institution, and therefore do not form part of an international regime. (1993, 9)

My conceptualization of a regime states that they are structures of rules and norms[2]: the Kellogg-Briand Pact does represent a new set of international norms since states signed it. It remains an open question the extent to which these rules are followed, guide expectations, or govern actual behavior. Explicitly, and with emphasis, the ontology of institutions is *not* related to whether behavior conforms or not to its norms. According to this conception institutions may exist, but have little impact on behavior. It is a theory of institutions that will determine the links—or the absence thereof—between institutions and behavior. To use a statistical metaphor the ontology of institutions is about the conceptualization of the $X$ variable, a theory of institutions connects $X$ with behavior $Y$.

When regime by definition includes behavior the risk of tautology and circular argument increases dramatically. A crucial question in the regime literature

---

[2]Hasenclever, Mayer, and Rittberger (1997) refer to this as a "lean" or "formal" definition.

revolves around the impact of a regime on behavior. If regime as an independent variable includes behavior, and that has impact on the (same?) behavior as a dependent variable the question arises about the logical coherence of such a theory. For example, if the WTO regime includes by definition the behavior of following free trade norms, how can we say that WTO has an impact on free trade behavior? Zacher (1996) illustrates this general problem. He claims that mutual interests explain regimes: $X$ (mutual interests) $\rightarrow$ $Y$ (regime). He then goes on to say the existence of a regime implies there are mutual interests: $Y$ (regime) $\rightarrow$ $X$ (mutual interests).

Not requiring behavioral effectiveness also permits the existence of competing sets of norms. The New International Economic Order (NIEO) was an attempt to put into place a new set of international economic norms. Collective security under the League of Nations was recognized by treaty but it did not have much impact on state behavior. According to Rittberger neither "existed" but one can say that the League rules "governed interactions." Surely there is an important distinction here. In the case of the League we can say that a regime existed, but in the case of the NIEO we would describe it as an attempt to create a regime that failed. But both cases fail the behavioral control test. For a more banal example, one might agree that the speed limit is 55 mph, but realize that one would not know this by observing traffic. Neither the Krasner definition nor the revised version captures or allows this possibility.

This core issue of behavioral effectiveness illustrates how borrowing and core examples generate issues and nonissues. The contributors to the special issue of *International Organization* (2001) do not find the concept of an institution problematic. As with domestic politics it is *obvious* that domestic governments and international organizations like the WTO have an impact on behavior. Historical context matters as well. The regime idea was born during the Cold War, a period when the influence and relevance of international institutions was not taken for granted. By the year 2001 we can have special issues of *International Organization* dealing with the legalization of world politics (2001) and special issues that assume the relevance of international institutions. But the Kellogg-Briand treaty is not the sort of international institution the contributors have in mind. This procedure raises important questions of selection bias and poses important questions for theory. For example, how does one rationally create an international institution that is completely ignored by the states that created it?

The definition of an institution should remain mute about the relation between institution norms and relevant behavior: let the ontology of institutions be determined solely by the existence of rules and norms.

*ॐ*

At the core of the regime concept lies "principles, norms, rules, and decision-making procedures." In his gloss on the definition Krasner states that principles and norms are really the heart of a regime: "principles and norms provide the basic defining characteristics of a regime" (3). Principles and norms provide the constitution of a regime while rules and decision-making procedures are laws made within a constitutional framework. Regimes change when the constitutional principles change but not when lower-level rules change: *"changes in rules and decision-making procedures are changes within regimes"* (3, emphasis in the original). A new republic in French history occurs when there is a change in the basic form of government.

Similarly, the definitions of institutions given above use the concept of a rule as a means to define what an institution is. For example, Ostrom says "Institutions can be defined as sets of working rules." While some definitions include other elements, all take rules as core of what an institution is. Notably, these definitions do *not* use the terms "norm" or "principle" so there are some potential differences to be explored.

I suggest that institutions and regimes both use the same core. My definition of an institution takes this core notion of norms and rules and strips the Krasner definition and the institutional ones of all their other parts. In fact, I suggest that for many purposes, norms, principles, decision-making procedures, and rules can be considered as synonymous, and will make this argument in the next chapter. All these concepts are variants of the basic concept of a norm. In an analogous way one can speak of a system of law. There may be many different kinds of laws but they all have the characteristic of being a law. Similarly, I propose that regimes are structures of norms. There are different types of norms that can be put together to form institutions, but what justifies the predicate "institution" is that it is a structure of norms.

The Krasner definition provides a loose typology of norms (which I shall use as a generic term covering all principles, norms, rules, and decision-making procedures). The idea that there are different types of norms will be crucial to the analysis of institutions, but Krasner does little beyond defining these four terms where: (1) "Principles are beliefs of fact, causation and rectitude," (2) "Norms are standards of behavior defined in terms of rights and obligations," (3) "Rules are specific prescriptions or proscriptions for action," and (4) "Decision-making procedures are prevailing practices for making and implementing collective choice" (1983, 2). The second part of my definition of institutions which specifies that they are "structures" implicitly suggests that they may have different forms and may be constructed with a variety of norms. We shall see in the next chapter that when we take a formal, mathematical look at norms that there is a typology of norms, but one quite different from the Krasner list.

Krasner's typology is not very useful because it is so vague and ambiguous; for example, the lower-level category of rules is defined as "specific prescriptions or proscriptions for action." Many ethical and moral rules are prescriptions or proscriptions, for example, the Ten Commandments. These certainly do not fit the description of lower level rules for action.[3]

There is an implicit typology of rules in some concepts of institutions. For example, once Ostrom has said that institutions are rules. she provides a list of different kinds of rules that "determine who is eligible to make decisions in some arena, what actions are allowed or constrained, what aggregation rules will be used, what procedures must be followed, what information must or must not be provided, and what payoffs will be assigned to individuals dependent on their actions" (Ostrom 1991, 51; see also Ostrom and Walker 1997, 43–44 for a typology including operational rules, collective choice rules, and constitutional choice rules). In the next chapter, once we have clarified the nature of a norm, we shall see that there is a typology of norms based on the mathematical logic of norms.

In the final analysis both the regime and institution schools of thought say that regimes and institutions consist of different types of norms and rules, and that some of those rules and norms are more important than others. As I shall argue in the rest of this chapter and in the next one, the additions made often hinder more than they help.

**Ontological versus Empirical Issues**

Much of the confusion surrounding regimes and institutions can be traced to the confounding of empirical issues with ontological ones. Beyond the strict definition of a regime, Krasner and others have made a number of claims about what should and should not be considered as a regime. Likewise, for example, Knight says that institutions are equilibria; it is not at all clear that this is the case empirically. Most of these additions fall into what I have termed empirical questions. Since most of these claims are not in any sense *entailed* by the definition of a regime their status remains unclear. The approach I take draws a strict line between the two and puts many characteristics often thought of as part of the concept of a regime into the "to be determined empirically on a case by case" category. Since many of the a priori claims about regimes are empirical issues, confusion arises when the a priori claim does not hold in fact. The question then arises with force whether the phenomenon in question is "really" an institution or not.

Krasner states that regimes are not short-lived: "regimes must be understood as something more than temporary agreements that change with every shift in power or interests" (1983, 2). It is not clear whether this is a theoretical or empirical claim. Certainly laws can be short-lived. Also, the definition of regimes in no way entails this claim. How long a regime lasts would seem to be an empirical question. My definition of institution allows them to exist without behavioral

---

[3] Perhaps the adjective "specific" is the key, where specific means of limited range of application, the "species" definition of specific, as opposed to the "precise, definite, explicit" definition, according to the *Oxford English Dictionary*. One can say that some of the Ten Commandments are specific in the second sense.

impact, so it is not surprising that the definition also allows for short-lived institutions. This possibility is particularly useful in the case of security regimes which have a tendency to be short-lived (as well as ineffective). That states agree to rules that they then shortly proceed to ignore should not imply that an institution did not exist.

Krasner also claimed that regimes have the purpose of promoting cooperation. This is a common view of regimes, and beyond that of society in general. For example, Rawls regards society as a "cooperative venture for mutual advantage" (1971, 4; see also Hume 1739, 484–88). Keohane says: "The concept of international regimes originated not from social scientists' urge to invent new terms for their own sake, but as a way to understand international cooperation, defined as coordinated mutual adjustment of states' policies yielding benefits to participants" (1993, 23). Again, the definition of regime does not entail this. Clearly those that focus on prisoners' dilemma as the paradigmatic situation combine efficiency and cooperation functions since by "cooperating" actors reach a Pareto superior outcome. This sort of claim illustrates what happens when one takes core examples and extrapolates to all regimes. If the core example were human rights then one would not likely make such claims.

To say that the purpose of regimes is to promote cooperation implicitly suggests a functional perspective on them. But it would be incorrect—and once again an empirical question—to suggest that the function which regimes serve is always cooperation. In fact, I think that regimes can also serve the function of oppression (Snidal 1985). Segregation in the United States or apartheid in South Africa were regimes that powerful groups used to remain in power. A common view of post–World War II economic regimes sees them as a provision of public goods by the United States, but it was also an imposition of a set rules that may have been to the detriment of some. Strange (1983) argued that many a regime theorist implicitly or explicitly thinks that the production of order is the purpose of a regime. Rules may promote efficiency, justice, injustice, or the maintenance of groups in power, the concept of a regime should leave these options open.

In a related vein Jervis claimed that the concept of regimes implies "not only norms and expectations that facilitate cooperation, but a form of cooperation that is more than the following of short-run self-interest" (1983, 173). Krasner concurs that "regime-governed behavior must not be in short term calculation of interest" (3). Rational, egoistic, short-term, self-interest maximizers might agree to drive on the left-hand side of the road. Does this norm not count? There may be many reasons why states follow rules, to say that when they follow them for reasons of short-term self-interest should not count seems to be completely arbitrary. *Why* actors follow norms requires a theory of institutions: the explanation of $Y$ (institution) is different from explaining what $Y$ is.

## Summary

The natural temptation in studying institutions is to get on with the important questions about their creation, effect, and maintenance. Krasner's chapter on regimes (1983) illustrates this proclivity, three pages are devoted to "defining" regimes while fifteen pages are spent on why regimes "matter." To use a statistical analogy, defining $X$ takes little space while explaining how $X$ influences $Y$ uses the vast majority. In contrast, this volume devotes this chapter and the next to exploring the characteristics of my $X$ variable.

The previous pages have been almost literally ground-clearing ones. My main purpose has been to remove the numerous accretions that have grown around the regime and institution core of norms and rules. Almost always I have claimed that the ontology of institution or regime should remain silent on the point. The procedure of using central examples to generate concepts has proved harmful in the case of regimes; it proves much more fruitful to conduct the conceptual dialogue with a wide range of examples. The key is to keep the definition of institution (or regime) strictly limited to a structure of rules and norms. This helps avoid mistaking secondary issues from core ones. By keeping in mind many examples I conclude that an institution:

1. may serve numerous different functions, such as justice, efficiency, order, etc.

2. is not necessarily about cooperation.

3. can be used to oppress.

4. can be short-lived.

5. can be based on short-term, self-interest calculation.

6. has nothing necessarily to do with expectations.

7. may have no impact on behavior.

8. may contain norms that cut across issue areas.

Institutions are merely structures of rules and norms. There are probably many different kinds of regime structures that exist. They may serve quite particular functions or they may be quite general. Some may be transient, others may live to be quite old. Some may be created by hegemons, others may arise "spontaneously." These are all important issues but ones which do not concern what a institution *is*.

# Some Implications

In the various discussions of regimes (see notably the chapters in Krasner 1983 and Rittberger 1993) one sees a variety of claims made about the nature of international regimes. In this section I briefly discuss the most important of them.

### Behavioral Regularities Are Not Necessarily Regimes

Puchala and Hopkins claimed that "[w]herever there is regularity in behavior some kind of principles, norms or rules must exist to account for it" (1983, 63). This is the converse of the claim that if rules determine behavior then there is behavioral regularity. Behavioral regularities can exist without being explained by principles, norms, or rules. The laws of supply and demand imply behavioral regularity, but that is not what Puchala and Hopkins had in mind. Neuroses are patterned behavior, but it does not seem useful to call them norm-guided behavior.

Patterned or regular behavior is not sufficient to infer the existence of a regime. Such an approach is the exact opposite of the ontology of institutions proposed here which says *nothing* about behavior and focuses initially only on rules and norms, independent of their eventual impact on behavior or sanctions for their violation.

### Security Regimes Pose No Conceptual Problems

Jervis posed the question: "Can the concept of regimes be fruitfully applied to issues of national security?" (1983, 173). Since security centers on conflict while the concept of a regime for most implies "norms and expectations that facilitate cooperation" (Jervis 1983, 173) a tension arises by definition between regimes and security. As I stressed above there is nothing in the definition of a regime that demands that they be about cooperation. The emphasis on cooperation arises from the conceptual dependence on the prisoners' dilemma game: "The primacy of security, its competitive nature, the unforgiving nature of the arena, and the uncertainty of how much security the state needs and has, all compound the prisoners' dilemma and make it sharper than the problems that arise in most other areas" (Jervis 1983, 175).

This perspective translates into a claim that regimes are irrelevant in zero-sum situations (Ullman-Margalit 1977). But when I play poker—a zero-sum game—I follow many rules, about placing bets, order of play, etc. Almost all zero-sum *games* involve a great deal of rule-following; in fact the game is defined by its rules (i.e., constitutive rules). My point is not that social games are an appropriate framework for thinking about security issues, but rather it is not the zero-sum characteristic of international conflict which implies the irrelevance of norms.

If zero-sum parlor games seems too remote an analogy, then one can look at the example of feuding in societies without central government. To describe a feuding system is in large part to describe the rules by which feuds are conducted. These can be quite precise, explicit, and almost always followed (see Boehm [1984] for a wonderful, detailed description of the rules of feuding in traditional Montenegro). While one might be hard-pressed to call this a zero-sum game, it certainly seems much more like the situation of long-term militarized rivalry between the United States and the USSR than does the story of the prisoners' dilemma.

As with all regimes, security regimes consist in rules and norms. The regime is effective if states conform to those rules, which may include very specific ones about troop movements (e.g., Egypt and Israel) or weapons acquisitions (SALT I and SALT II). Stronger security regimes include rules that cover a wider range of behavior and allow less room for escalatory moves. The purpose of the regime is normally to reduce the likelihood of war. To assimilate that to "cooperation" is a step that I believe confuses the issue.

The rule-based conception of institutions differentiates sharply questions of effectiveness from questions of existence. It may be that security regimes are often ineffective, short-lived, or both. Some of the confusion surrounding the concept of a security institution comes from the feeling that there are few successful cases of security regimes. How can the regime concept be useful if there are so few successful cases? But from a methodological point of view having unsuccessful institutions to study is essential in understanding them. It is only by comparing cases of success and failure that the critical elements of successful institutions can be uncovered.

Jervis asked whether the regime concept was appropriate to the study of issues of war and peace: "Can the concept of regime be fruitfully applied to issues of national security? ... it is anomalous to have a concept that explains phenomena in some parts of the field [of international relations] but lacks utility in others" (1983, 173). My analysis indicates that security institutions are in no way anomalous. They may be simpler, shorter-lived structures, but that of course is an empirical question. Fundamental conflict between parties undoubtedly gives security regimes a distinctive flavor, but I have already made explicit the possibility of multiple types of institutions. Hence, the norm-based concept of institutions resolves the conceptual status of security regimes.

## Case Selection

Rittberger edited a volume on regimes in 1993, which in many respects can be considered the second edition of the 1983 Krasner-edited collection. By the 1990s it had become clear that the behavioral effectiveness requirement was a crucial issue left in abeyance by the Krasner definition (both Rittberger and Keohane address this issue in their contributions, see also the excellent survey in Hasenclever, Mayer, and Rittberger 1997). By the mid-1990s the problem of selecting on the dependent variable is much more in the consciousness of comparative case study scholars (e.g., the deterrence debate in *World Politics* 1989). If the existence of a regime itself means behavior conforms to the norms of the regime then one is basically selecting on the dependent variable. If the deterrence literature selects on deterrence failure then regime and institution theorists tend to select on regime success. While most are now aware of the problem one finds little evidence of this in practice.

Curiously enough, it is only when the group decides to systematically gather data about regimes that the issue really gets attention:

> We agreed to begin with a universe of cases including all arrangements that meet the explicit rules test. This would be followed by an effort to iden-tify that subset of the initial universe meeting the explicit rules test and also achieving prescriptive status in the sense that actors refer regularly to the rules both in characterizing their own behavior and in commenting on the behavior of others. Beyond this, analysts should seek to pinpoint a small subset of arrangements that meet the first two tests and that give a measure of rule-consistent behavior as well. According to the new consensus, no ar-rangement should be call an international regime unless it passes the first two tests. (Rittberger 1993, 10–11)

It is interesting to note that this is the *operational* definition to be used in creating a data set on regimes. Once one begins to think about systematic data collection the weaknesses of the original Krasner definition become clear. Not surprisingly the end result (as in all good committee decision making) is also a compromise between the two positions, one requiring behavioral effectiveness and the other not. Of course, my definition basically is that of the explicit rules test.

In many ways this problem is somewhat surprising. Given that realists think that international norms are basically irrelevant in determining state behavior, it should be possible to find many regimes that do not work. If such is actually the case then the literature—perhaps like the deterrence literature—shows extreme selection bias in only looking at cases where the institution appears to function, at least at some level.[4]

## Conclusion

The reader might remark that with my definition of regimes I have painted myself into a corner. If regimes do not consist of behavior how can they influence actors? Am I inching my way to some sort of idealist position? After all, institutions on my account have no material existence: how can they matter in a world of realpolitik? This objection gains more force when one examines international law. When defined it consists of (1) custom and behavior, and (2) treaties:

> We believe that two criteria should be used to determine if a putative norm is genuinely "law":"authority" and "control." First, any rule of international

---

[4] Another selection bias is to look at regimes that seem about cooperation instead of regimes that are about coercion.

law must be seen as *authoritative*. States must regard the norm as legitimate; they must perceive it to be "law." . . . Second, the prospective legal norm must be *controlling* of state behavior. Through their practice, states must actually comply with the requirements of the rule. (Arend and Beck 1993, 9, emphasis in the original)

Recently Byer has explicitly connected basic concepts of international law with the concept of a regime: "The customary process and other fundamental rules, principles, and processes of international law are, in terms used by Keohane, 'persistent and connected sets of rules . . . that prescribe behavioral roles, constrain activity, and shape expectations' " (1999, 4).

Curiously enough, the concept of international law contains the two main components of the Krasner definition of regimes, accepted norms and rule-consistent behavior. One can legitimately pose the question: has the regime concept really added anything? How is it different from international law and idealism that Morgenthau discarded forty years ago? If international law remained unimportant for most students of world politics, why should regimes be any different?

At the head of this chapter I quoted R. M. Hare who explained that telling someone what to do differs logically from getting that person to do it. An institution tells actors what to do (or not to do) in certain conditions. "Getting them to do it" implies a theory of international behavior which may include institutions as a factor. The Krasner definition hinted at one possible mechanism by which regimes can explain behavior, through their influence on expectations. But as Hare reminds us "telling" is fundamentally separate from "getting to do." The ontology of regimes is telling, not getting, to do.

The reader will have noticed that I have danced around the core issue: what is a norm (or rule or principle or decision-making procedure)? This question has never been posed—as far as I am aware—in the regime literature, particularly in the sense of the logical structure of norms and how they fit into a given choice procedure. For example, Kratochwil (1989) gave a philosophical account of (international) norms, but not a behavioral account. In addition, he consistently considers regimes as system-level phenomena. I submit that one advantage of my approach to the study of international institutions lies in its focus on the ontology of norms. This chapter has just pushed back the ontological problem one step. Just like Tristam Shandy's birth, it takes a while to get to the topic of norms. The first half of the next chapter describes the mathematical and logical structure of a norm. Principles, norms, rules, and decision-making procedures all have this common logical structure, which justifies my treating them as synonyms. The literature on international regimes and institutions has not bothered to examine what a norm is; for example, one would never know that there is a mathematical theory of norms by reading treatises like Kratochwil's or the special issue of *International Organization* on institutional design. The trick is to separate the logical form from the substance of norms. For example, many people when they hear the word "norm" think of moral norms. As we shall see game theorists think of quite different things when they hear the word. I suggest that underneath all this lies a common logic. Hence, the next chapter has two purposes: (1) to describe the logical structure of a norm, and (2) to describe a choice procedure which takes norm as the core concept.

# Part I

# Individual Decision Making with Norms and Policies

# Chapter 3

# Decision Making with Norms

What is it?

—*Sixth Zen Patriarch Hui-neng*

The last chapter concluded that rules and norms constitute the heart and soul of the concept of an institution. I pushed back the analytic problems from the ontology of institutions to the ontology of norms and rules. I continue my exploration of ontology issues in the next section by looking at some common views on what a norm is. While expected utility theorists have studiously avoided using the term "norm" and prefer "rule" (with some notable exceptions such as O'Neill 2000), social constructivists have embraced norms as a core theoretical concept. Along different lines sociologists have long used the idea of a norm. However, for them it has traditionally been associated with the application of sanctions.

My approach takes two quite distinctive tacks in dealing with these issues. First, I want to know the *logical* structure of a norm. Few know that there is a mathematical theory of norms, deontological logic. Second, I want to explore how norms can be used by *individuals* in the decision-making process. For many norms by definition have a social character. I do not deny the obvious, social and international norms do exist, but rather I want to know how an individual can use those norms (or other norms that do not carry societal approval) in her decision making.

## Social Norms and Institutions

Without a doubt it has been social constructivists who have embraced the idea of international norms and have brought a new set of insights and agenda items to the study of international politics. Quite regularly a social constructivist analysis will include a section that discuss the ontology of norms. Hence it is useful to see how they see the concept of a norm:

I would like to thank David Welsh for many helpful comments on an earlier version of this chapter.

> [Norms are] shared expectations about appropriate behavior held by a collec-
> tivity of actors. (Checkel 1999, 83)

> There is a general agreement on the definition of a norm as a standard of
> appropriate behavior for actors with a given identity. (Finnemore and Sikkink
> 1998, 891)

> We should first mention that the chapters [in Katzenstein 1996] employ the
> concept "norms" in a sociologically standard way. Norms are collective ex-
> pectations about proper behavior for a given identity. (Jepperson et al. 1996,
> 54)

> By *norm* I mean a shared expectations about behavior, a standard of right or
> wrong. Norms are prescriptions or proscriptions for behavior. (Tannenwald
> 1999, 436)

Among other things the collective, shared nature of norms stands out in the
social constructivist views. However, this does not help in an effort to see how
social or international norms play into individual decision making. What all these
authors agree on is that norms set "standards for appropriate behavior." In this they
agree with the institutionalists cited in the previous chapter who also stressed how
the rules of institutions should inform behavior. For example, Schotter says that a
rule "specifies behavior in specific recurrent situations" (1986, 17). Much of this
chapter is devoted to fleshing out what this means in terms of the logical structure
of norms and rules, and how they can enter into individual decision making. However, social constructivist conceptualizations of norms do little to inform us about
norms beyond the two characteristics of (1) accepted standards and (2) standards
that apply to behavior.

Sociologists have for decades, but particularly in the 1950s and 1960s, seen
norms as a core part of social systems. In particular, they have seen norms as
mechanisms of social control. To get a feeling for the sanctioning ontology here
are some definitions of (social) norms, most by well-known social theorists:

> They [norms] specify what actions are regarded by a set of persons as proper
> or correct, or improper and incorrect. . . . Norms are ordinarily enforced by
> sanctions. . . . Those subscribing to a norm . . . claim a right to apply sanc-
> tions and recognize the right of others holding the norm to do so . . . I will
> say that a norm concerning a specific action exists when the socially defined
> right to control the action is held not by the actor but by others. (Coleman
> 1990, 242–43)

> The violation of a rule generally brings unpleasant consequences to the agent.
> But we may distinguish two different types of consequences: (i) The first re-
> sults mechanically from the act of violation. If I violate a rule of hygiene
> that orders me to stay away from infection, the result of this act will auto-
> matically be disease. The act, once it has been performed, sets in motion the
> consequences, and by analysis of the act we can know in advance what the
> result will be. (ii) When, however, I violate the rule that forbids me to kill, an

analysis of my act will tell me nothing. I shall not find inherent in it the subsequent blame or punishment. There is complete heterogeneity between the act and its consequence. It is impossible to discover *analytically* in the act of murder the slightest notion of blame. The link between act and consequence is here a synthetic one. Such consequences attached to acts by synthetic links I shall call sanctions ... [It] is the consequence of an act that does not result from the content of the act, but from violation by that act of a pre-established rule. (Durkheim 1953, 42)

A norm ... is the propensity to feel shame and to anticipate sanctions by others at the thought of behaving in a certain way. (Elster 1989, 105)

Sanctions are not defined here in terms of norms ... Norms and values will in turn be defined in terms of sanctions ... *a norm is a name for a pattern of sanctions.* (Scott 1971, 65)

The term convention will be employed to designate that part of the custom followed within a given social group which is recognized as binding and protected against violation by sanctions of disapproval. (Weber cited in Gilbert 1989, 350)

When Axelrod defines a norm, "A *norm* exists in a given social setting to the extent that individuals usually act in a certain way and are often punished when seen not to be acting in this way," (1986, 1097) he is responding to and taking up a long tradition in sociology. He implies that if there are no sanctions then behavior does not fall under a norm. Scott is explicit: "a norm is a name for a pattern of sanctions." He provides this definition in a Skinnerian analysis of the internalization of norms, where sanctions play the standard role in behavior modification. Weber gives a classic definition including both the social dimension as well as the sanctioning component.

Not surprisingly most well-known discussions of the nature of law include sanctions as characterizing it as well:

(i) Rules are conceived and spoken of as imposing obligations when the general demand for conformity is insistent and the social pressure brought to bear upon those who deviate or threaten to deviate is great ... (ii) The rules supported by serious pressure are thought important because they are believed to be necessary to the maintenance of social life or some highly prized feature of it. (Hart 1961, 84–85)

A social order that attempts to bring about the desired conduct of individuals by sanctions we call a coercive order. It stands in sharpest contrast to all other social orders, which rest on voluntary obedience ... Thus the antagonism of freedom and coercion fundamental to social life supplies the decisive criterion. It is the criterion of law, for law is a coercive order. It provides for socially organized sanctions and thus can be clearly distinguished form religious and moral order. (Kelsen 1966, 31)

In both the legal and sociological perspective norms have system-level nature. This is all the more clear since someone *outside* the individual decision maker is applying the sanctions. Here we see an important contrast with expected utility views on institutions. As we shall see in some detail in chapter 4, expected utility theorists define institutions in terms of equilibria, an equilibrium by definition means that no one has an incentive to individually change her strategy, yet norms as sanctions implies that there *are* individuals who have reasons to violate norms. Nevertheless, both the expected utility and sociological approaches to norms and institutions see them as system-level phenomena. Again, this does not help me much in this chapter in trying to understand how norms fit into individual decision-making.

It is usually unquestioned that "norm" means *social* norm: "the central notion in conventional conceptions of a norm [is that] norms have a collective quality . . . no one questions the idea that a norm is a property of a social unit and not of an isolated individual" (Gibbs 1981, 12). This is just as true for game theorists as for sociologists. Basically all current game theory approaches to norms take them, one way or another, as social concepts.[1] As in the last chapter I arrive at negative results: neither the social nor the sanction definition help us with an conceptualization of norms, one which we can use to investigate norms and decision making at the individual level. We need to start with something like a decision theory.

## What Is a Norm?

Beliefs, in short, are really rules for action; and the whole function of thinking is but one step in the production of habits of action.

*—William James*

The basic logical form of a norm, rule, principle, decision-making procedure is a syllogism. Here, finally, is the answer to the ontology question. The reason I can treat principles, norms, rules, and decision-making procedures as the same is because they all have this basic logical form. The literature on deontological logic defines norms in syllogistic terms:

The character, the content, and the condition of application constitute what I propose to call the *norm-kernel*. The norm-kernel is a logical structure which prescriptions have in common with other types of norm. . . . The *character* of a norm depends upon whether the norm is to the effect that something ought to or may or must not be or be done. . . . By the *content* of a norm we mean, roughly speaking, *that which* ought to or may or must not be done. . . . The condition which must be satisfied if there is to be an opportunity for doing the thing which is the content of a given norm will be called a *condition of application* of the norm. (von Wright 1963, 70, 71, and 73)

Deontological logic deals directly with what interests me, the links between norms, decisions, and behavior.

---

[1] We shall see later that norms can be taken as preferences, but this is rarely done.

From Aristotle onward the classic syllogism contains three parts, the major premise, the minor premise, and the conclusion. Here is perhaps the most well-known syllogism in philosophy:

All men are mortal (Major Premise)

Socrates is a man (Minor Premise)

*therefore*

Socrates is mortal (Conclusion)

The major premise is the core of the construction. In examples like the Socrates one, it makes the important claim that "all men are mortal." This is a substantive proposition about the class of animals "man." In scientific syllogisms—covering laws—this becomes the law of nature.

The minor premise usually invokes a specific factual, localized claim: Socrates is a man. While the major premise typically makes a general proposition, the minor premise usually refers to a concrete case. In the above example, the major premise refers to all men while the minor premise only mentions the particular individual Socrates.[2]

The link between the two premises comes from the fact that they both utilize the same term "man"; without such a link one does not really have a usable syllogism. This then leads to the conclusion that "Socrates is a mortal," a specific fact about Socrates which depends on the truth of both premises. *If* the major *and* the minor premise hold then the rules of classic logic tell us that the morality of Socrates is also true.

Classic logic—which still forms a core subject for philosophers—developed and analyzed the validity of different types of syllogisms. For example, the Socrates one is called modus ponens and has the general form:

All $A$ are $B$ (Major Premise)

$X$ is an $A$ (Minor Premise)

*therefore*

$X$ is $B$. (Conclusion)

Most often this kind of structure is seen as a way to make valid inferences about the world, a way to express true beliefs about nature. Hempel (1965) gave the modern version of this in his famous argument about covering laws. He basically argued that all scientific theories had this syllogistic form. The major premise was the scientific law, e.g., the law of gravity; the minor premise was the specific case, such as an experiment; the conclusion was the supposed outcome of the experiment according to the covering law. To see this in an international institution context, take the hypothesis by Keohane that "As applied to the last century

---

[2] We shall see below that more typically the minor premise defines a class of situations where the major premise applies. A specific event that satisfies the minor premise then "triggers" the norm.

and a half, this theory—which will be referred to as the 'hegemonic stability' theory—does well at identifying the apparently necessary conditions for strong international economic regimes, but poorly at establishing sufficient conditions" (1980, 137). In covering law form we have:

> All regimes have hegemonic power at their origin. (Major Premise)
>
> GATT is a regime. (Minor Premise)
>
> *therefore*
>
> GATT had hegemonic power at its origin. (Conclusion)[3]

Since this kind of theoretical reason describes our beliefs about the world I will call it a "scientific syllogism." It is a tool for making decisions about the character of the natural and social environment. Of course, whether people or scientists actually use this mode of reasoning is another story all together. At issue here is its—I hesitate to say—normative status as a rational, valid way of thinking and deciding about beliefs.

ᴁ

In Shandyesque fashion I have not yet arrived at the crucial issue of *behavioral* norms. Scientific syllogisms perhaps are a way to decide about beliefs—assuming that this is not a behavior!—but it remains unclear how they apply to action decisions. For example, in philosophy one often distinguishes between theoretical reason, knowledge about the world, and practical reason—what one should do. It proves easiest to approach decision making about action in the context of norms through the familiar route of morality.

A common reaction to the word "norm," in my experience, often links it to moral principles of various sorts. It is quite natural to think of religion as a set of laws and rules about behavior (as well as beliefs). Often this seems to be things one should not do, e.g., the Ten Commandments, but this must also be considered a valid part of an action decision. The "moral" syllogism is a decision-making one. Moral norms often include "ought" in them, but I will take the position that once a person has adopted a moral norm as her own then the "ought" disappears. I include the "ought" in brackets below for comparison purposes. If this were a standard moral norm with an "ought" then one would need to add an additional premise that "the prisoner of war will not do that which he ought not to do."[4]

> Every act which is a lie is an act that will [ought] not to be performed.
> (Major Premise)

---

[3] Keohane was right the first time when he called his ideas a functional theory, for more see chapter 10 which gives Hempel's formalization of functionalism in covering law terms that matches Keohane's version of hegemonic stability theory given here.

[4] I thank David Welsh for clearing this point up for me.

The prisoner of war has an option of saying [falsely] at 4 P.M. "My regiment went north." (Minor Premise)

*therefore*

The prisoner of war does [ought] not say at 4 P.M. "My regiment went north." (Conclusion)[5]

The major premise in the scientific syllogism expresses a general principle about the natural or social world. The major premise in the moral syllogism expresses a principle of behavior. In this example, the norm says one should not tell lies. As with the scientific syllogism the major premise is the core of the norm, and most of the attention rests on the desirability of the principle of behavior.

The minor premise says that there is a specific occasion where lying is one of the choice options. The prisoner of war has the option (one is tempted to say the dilemma) whether to lie or tell the truth. Hence it is a situation where the norm applies. Recall that in the scientific syllogism the same term needed to appear in both premises, in that case it was the term "man," in this case it is the behavior "lying."

The conclusion of the moral syllogism is then that the prisoner does not lie. If there are only two options, lying and telling the truth, then she decides to tell the truth, since the norm excludes lying. The prisoner has used a norm and syllogistic logic to make a decision.

Finally, we see what a decision-making procedure with norms looks like. The fundamental component of this procedure is the norm "do not lie." The choice procedure is the syllogism. The result is a decision what to do, or in this case what not to do.

Notice that this is an individual level choice procedure, there is no reference to sanctions or system-level factors. Its says nothing about whether other people have this norm, if it is a law of the society, or if there will be sanctions for violations. The prisoner has the "not lying" norm as part of her person, just like a person can have beliefs and preferences. Conceptually this does not depend on any system level factors. Just like preferences are exogenous in expected utility decision making, so one can take norms as exogenous. For the moment we just assume that the decision maker has norms and rules. The issue at hand is how norms are used, not where they come from.

While I have introduced decision making with norms with moral norms, there is no reason to consider the norm about lying as necessarily invoking morality: how can one make such an inference from the words "do not lie"? Nothing in the norm itself makes reference to morality. "Morality" is an attribute that one attaches to certain norms. As we shall see, if a norm does possesses this attribute then there are important behavioral consequences, but from the logical point of view, this attribute does not change the character of a norm. Also, to label a norm

---

[5] Taken with modifications from White (1981, 36).

as "moral" hints at its origin. One way to choose norms is to take them from a religious or moral system. To emphasize, like preferences we can for some purposes consider norms as exogenous. It may well be the case that the prisoner chose the not-lying norm for instrumental not moral reasons (the subject of the next chapter). However, unlike expected utility theory, which rarely endogenizes preferences, I consider that the choice of norms to be of central importance, and it will be an important topic in the chapters to come. But to endogenize norm choice is a topic which exceeds the confines of this chapter.

If this seems remote from the world of international relations then take the central principle of WTO, the Most Favored Nation (MFN) norm:

> If State $A$ signs a reduced tariff with MFN $B$, then it must extend that tariff to all other MFNs.

The realm of application—minor premise—of the MFN norm is the universe of tariff relations with other MFN nations. The norm does not apply, for example, in tariff negotiations with the third world. If one examines the principle norms of WTO (Dam 1979; Jackson 1997) one can see that they all have this fundamental logical structure.

The MFN example illustrates the equivalent "if–then" form of the syllogism. The "if" part of the norm says when the norm applies—i.e., the minor premise. The "then" part provides the behavior, which in this case is prescribed and obligatory. Since this form of the syllogism is shorter I will tend to use it to express the content of rules, norms, principles, and decision-making procedures.

All this seems so obvious that it is perhaps not worth all the ink I have spilled. Nevertheless, I stress that this is individual decision making with norms and this is the structure of a norm. In Morrow's game theory textbook (1994) he spends the first chapters describing the components and procedures of expected utility choice. Once the structure and components of decision making with norms have been made clear then we can move to issues involving governments, institutions, and international norms.

## Types of Norms

The Krasner definition of regimes included a typology of norms: (1) principles, (2) norms, (3) rules, and (4) decision-making procedures. The various definitions of institutions also include various implict typologies. The logical structure of these four types is identical and expressed by the syllogism or the if–then system described above. Hence from a formal point of view they do not constitute different types of norms. For example, decision-making rules concern a different *substantive* type of norm, since they do not directly result in an action but define procedure. Obviously one can have norms for different issue areas. We will see in chapter 6 that decision-making norms are special because they are "second order" rules, norms about norms, but nevertheless they use the logical structure of other rules, norms, and principles.

Within deontological logic—a mathematical logic of norms—there are three basic types of norms: (1) permissions, (2) prohibitions, and (3) prescriptions, what I call the three Ps. Permissions state that an option is allowed, neither prescribed nor proscribed. Prohibitions exclude the choice option. Prescriptions choose an option.[6] All complex norms are some function of these three fundamental types.[7]

For example, the nonproliferation treaty has six articles (Bailey 1993):

Article 1 prohibits nuclear states from transferring nuclear weapons.

Article 2 prohibits nonnuclear states from obtaining nuclear weapons.

Article 3 establishes requirements for reporting (creation of IAEA) and the transfer of materials and technology.

Article 4 assures the right of access to peaceful nuclear technology.

Article 5 is right to peaceful exploitation under appropriate procedures.

Article 6 obliges nuclear states to work for arms control and disarmament.

It is quite obvious that Articles 1 and 2 are proscriptions that tell governments what they cannot do. Articles 3 and 6 are obligations, things governments are supposed to do. Finally, Articles 4 and 5 are rights, permissions to do something, for example, governments *may* pursue peaceful uses of nuclear energy.[8]

Occasionally, scholars have chosen one of the three Ps to characterize all (international) norms or law. Most often this seems to be law as a proscription:[9]

[A]uthoritative practices [norms] are more properly regarded as limiting or constraining that pursuit [of particular ends] (Nardin 1983, 8).

This fits nicely with an approach which says all that is not prohibited is permitted. In empirical fact, normative systems may vary widely, one should not make the conceptual error of focusing on only one of the three types. This also characterizes many economic approaches to norms which describe them as "constraints" on expected utility maximization (e.g., Koford and Miller 1991; see the Coleman quote p. 3 above).

---

[6] Ostrom is one of the few working in political science that recognizes these issues, see Crawford and Ostrom (1995).

[7] One does not strictly need all three as primitive types, two of the three can be defined using the third one as a primitive. This issue is a central one in the philosophical and jurisprudential theory of norms. Alchourrón and Bulygin (1971, 38) show how one can take the primitive operation $P$ for permission and then define the other common normative operators with that and the logical operators "and" and "¬" (i.e., negation or not). If $Pq$ means that $q$ is permitted then one can define: forbidden ($F$) as $Fq = \neg Pq$ and obligatory ($O$) as $Oq = \neg P\neg q$.

[8] Müller (1989, 282–90; 1993, 135–43) finds there are four principles of the NPT regime and nine norms.

[9] This they have in common with children who see parental systems as basically a list of things one cannot do.

It is important to include permission as a distinct type. We saw above that some principles are permissions and often the language is of rights. Some systems may have default rules of the sort "if it is not forbidden it is permitted," but not all systems work that way. For example, no parent would use such a normative structure, though most children think it would be a good idea. Here, the default appears to be proscription: what is not permitted is forbidden.

## Identities and Norms

In philosophy a well-known distinction is often made between "regulative" and "constitutive" rules (Rawls 1955). Regulative rules consist of advice—in the form of rules—of how to achieve a given end. Constitutive rules define the identity of something. This implies a distinction between "identity" norms and "behavioral" ones. I suggest that this classic distinction does not help us understand decision making with norms and by implication how norms interact with behavior.

Take the canonical example of games and constitutive rules. For example, in chess a pawn is *constituted* or *defined* by the moves it can, cannot, and must make. In exactly the same fashion, I argued in the previous chapter that an institution *is* its norms and rules. We shall see that many have constituted institutions and organizations in the same fashion. Identities are in part defined by behavioral rules.

Constitutive norms define identities in terms of behavior, at least partially, and at the same time provide indications about future behavior. A pawn is defined in terms of the moves it makes; conversely, if one knows that a piece is a pawn one knows something about how that piece will behave in certain circumstances. These identity norms have the same basic syllogistic structure as behavioral or scientific norms. For example, *if* a piece is a pawn and it is at its beginning square *then* it can move one or two squares ahead; this is a permission norm. Because identity is defined using norms we can predict behavior. Recall that in the Krasner definition of a regime it "guided expectations"; if a piece is a pawn that guides our expectations about its future behavior.

There are nonbehavioral rules that also define identities, what I would call "ontological" norms. These norms have the same formal structure as behavioral norms but their content differs in that the major premise defines an identity, usually using the ontological verb "to be." The generic form is thus: If ... then ... is ... For example, if someone has a Jewish mother then he is Jewish. A famous example from the literature on speech acts (e.g., Searle 1969) involves the identity characteristic "married": if one performs a certain series of actions then one *is* married.

I choose the label "identity norms" so that it resonates with discussions of contructivism and identity politics. Not all norms which constitute an identity involve behavior but many core identity norms do have behavioral premises. Generically, the shorthand works via the minor premise: if the situation is $A$ and the individual has $Z$ identity then she will do $P$. It is often forgotten that to know identity norms permits one to understand and predict behavior. When a foreigner understands a new culture this means she knows the appropriate behavior in a wide range of situations. If one knows what an orthodox Jew is, one also knows about his behavior. For example, if $Z$ is an orthodox Jew and it is the sabbath then he will not work. This is after all what stereotypes are all about. Faced with a beautiful woman, we expect the typical Frenchman to behave differently from the typical Englishman. It may be that the prisoner of war discussed above (p. 36) acquired the not-lying norm as part of the identity package "Catholic." This is what Finnemore and Sikkink are getting at when they say: "There is a general agreement on the definition of a norm as a standard of appropriate behavior for actors with a given identity" (1998, 891).

These kinds of norms will become quite important when we get to the discussion of organizational and role norms, since a role is fundamentally a set of identity norms. If someone fulfills well the role of teacher or doctor we know and can predict something about the actions of that person.

## What Is a (Foreign) "Policy"?

In using WTO and NPT examples I cheated on my claim to remain at the individual level. WTO norms are obviously for the society of states. At the state level we can use this conceptual framework to answer a question (an ontological one once again) almost never posed: what is a foreign policy? Tens, if not hundreds, of textbooks on foreign policy can be found in publishers' catalogues. It is a standard course offered by most political science departments, yet it is hard to find a discussion of the concept of a foreign *policy*. I suggest that a (foreign) policy has the logical structure of the syllogism. The policy contains all the essential parts of a norm: (1) when the policy applies, the minor premise, and (2) the action permitted, proscribed, or prescribed, the major premise.

Since I have a certain fondness for ontological questions we can ask how some influential scholars have defined policy:

> As commonly used, the term policy is usually considered to apply to something "bigger" than particular decisions, but "smaller" than general social movements. Thus, policy, in terms of level of analysis is a concept placed roughly in the middle range. A second and essential element in most writers' use of the term is purposiveness of some kind. (Heclo 1972, 84).

> [A policy is] a hypothesis containing initial conditions and predicted consequences. If $X$ is done at time $t_1$, then $Y$ will result at time $t_2$. (Pressman and Wildavsky 1973, xiii)

> We can think of a *policy* as a program that serves as a guide to behavior intended to realize the goals an organization has set for itself. (Russett, Starr, and Kinsella 2000, 117)

These three definitions illustrate key aspects of what a policy is. Heclo makes clear that a policy is more than an individual decision; instead of "bigger" what he wants to say is that policy has an impact on multiple individual decisions. This is exactly what lies implicit in the minor premise: the possibility that many situations arise where the major premise applies. Heclo and Pressman and Wildavsky stress the instrumental nature of policy. Usually the "predicted consequences" are positive and what the policymakers and implementors are trying to achieve. This is what I refer to as the functional aspect of policy, the problems that international institutions and national policies are designed to solve. Take for example the various "doctrines" in the history of American foreign policy, the Monroe, Truman, Carter, etc. They state that the United States government obligates itself to take certain sorts of actions, often militarized, if other powers intrude into certain areas. These doctrines clearly have a purpose in terms of American foreign policy goals.

The Monroe Doctrine also illustrates the issues discussed in the previous chapter about the existence of institutions, but this time at the individual level. In terms of behavior the Monroe Doctrine had no effect on U.S. foreign policy in the first decades after its promulgation. To use the logic of many, one would be forced to say that the Monroe Doctrine "did not exist." It would only exist after the Civil War when the U.S. government actually began to behave in conformity with the doctrine (Corrales and Feinberg 1999; Atkins 1995). Of course, my position is that the doctrine existed the whole time.

Courses in foreign policy obviously discuss policies, but in reality they are much more courses in foreign *actions*. They focus on the acts of governments, particularly during crises and wars. To put the spotlight on norms brings out the fundamental ambiguity in the use of the word "policy." In practice, for the average observer or academic it means both policy in the proper sense as well as a particular action. The question "what is U.S. policy in the Balkans?" usually means "what is the United States going to do?" It usually refers to the next action, but it implies that there is a norm/policy that can be used to predict U.S. behavior in *multiple* future occasions.

For example, Hybell (1990, 30), when modeling U.S. foreign policy in Latin America, expresses it in syllogistic form:

> If (host government) does (expropriation),
> then (host government) is (host government procommunist).
> If (host government) is (host government procommunist)
> then the likelihood of (presence of Soviet control) increases.
> To avert (presence of Soviet control)
> then (overthrow),
> If (overthrow) then (covert paramilitary invasion).

This example illustrates nicely how beliefs about the world combine with strategies of action, all within the syllogistic format.

We can now see that policy has the same structure as SOP. As its name indicates, a SOP is a standardized (operating) procedure that one applies in a given situation. The literature on organizations, SOPs, and foreign policy has examined this phenomenon at the bureaucratic level, e.g., how to carry out a naval blockade. But there is nothing in the formal structure of norm, or conversely of an SOP, that makes one inherently specific and the other inherently general: a foreign policy is just a higher level SOP. For example, Walker's analysis of Kissenger's decision-making (1977) argued that Kissinger basically had a SOP for dealing with Cold War issues.

Finally, consider alliances, a core phenomenon in the study of international war. There too we find policies formulated as commitments to act in certain ways under certain conditions. Usually the minor premise consists of an attack on an ally, and the prescribed action is military action in support of the ally. Alliances also form part of foreign policy in the proper sense. I suggest that governments continually make decisions guided by norms, institutions, and policies, all of which have the same formal structure, that of a syllogism. Here too we see the basic problem with standard regime ontology; it is well-known that not all states fulfill their alliance commitments: does this mean that the alliance never existed?

**Policy Decision Making**

A key issue for this volume is then that a policy and norm have the same logical structure, in fact they are synonyms. One central goal of this volume is to develop a policy model of decision-making that works expresses and works within the punctuated equilibrium framework. I often refer to "individuals"; in general the individual I am most concerned with is government. Hence the basic decision-making framework I call "policy decision-making" or "decision-making with policies." More as a matter of style than anything else, I will tend to use the term "norm" in Part I and "policy" in Parts II and III, but nothing important hinges on this. It just seems to feel more natural to talk about norms with the generic— and often implicit single—individual and to speak of policies when refering to governments and organizations. My examples in Part I remind us that the core focus is on governments and international policies.

Much of the work of this chapter and the following revolves around the task of understanding what policies and norms really are in terms of a decision-making logic. Much of the next chapter analyses how "norms" can be instrumental, here the language of policy would be more natural. In chapter 5 on morality it would be more natural to speak of norms than policies.

# Methodological Principles and Implications

Twice saying "pardon" doth not pardon twain, But makes one pardon strong.

—The Duchess of York seeking mercy for her son from Henry

Shakespeare's *Richard II* (Act IV, scene iii)

The case study dominates the regime and institution literature as the research design of choice. I approach methodological problems from the perspective of statistical modeling. The statistical methods choice suggests that one should be able to gather systematic data concerning norms and institutions. I do not claim that measuring norms is either easy or without its pitfalls, but it is not clear that they are more severe than for concepts such as power, foreign policy attitudes, preferences and the like. In fact, in some ways the character of norms facilitates the data-gathering project. But this is certainly not the dominant attitude in the international regime literature, where many think that somehow statistical approaches are not appropriate or impossible:

> Yet there remains a fundamental difficulty in assessing the impact of regimes: causal inference is difficult where experimental or statistical research designs are infeasible. (Keohane 1993, 31)

Such opinions are based on aversions to statistical methods, not something inherent in international institutions.

Common to any study of international institutions are the norms that constitute the institution. Be the concern with norms as independent, dependent variables or both, one must come to grips with the identification and eventual measurement of these norms. For present purposes—like with the origin of norms—I am not concerned with the causes or effects of norms. In statistical terminology we are interested in a *measurement* model of norms, not a causal one. Regardless of the theory these issues must be addressed. This section is thus devoted to the analysis of the methodological issues surrounding norm identification and measurement.

The vast majority of the literature on norms, regimes, institutions, etc., focuses on the problem of the identification of a *social* norm, in the regime literature this is the identification of *international* institutions. My approach has been to start at the individual level, so for the moment these issues are not relevant. Whatever social norms end up being, they will certainly depend on the activities of individual states. This is all the more true in the international realm where we have no real legislatures and police forces that we can reliably use as a means of identification.

But at the same time, however, many of the methodological principles apply both at the social and individual level. We shall see that in a number of instances the methodology is the same regardless of the level of analysis.

I argued in chapter 2 that an international institution consisted only in norms and rules: one could say that regimes are only words. This is a distinctly non-behavioral definition. The first part of this chapter suggested how these words get linked to deeds. All decision-making models make this kind of linkage, in the expected utility mode one links preferences with actual choice. The methodology of norms must include the two realms: words and deeds. Realists often claim that there is no real link between words—particularly words in the form of norms—and foreign policy choice; the evaluation of the claim of (no) impact requires examining the links between norm and action.

## Words: The Structural Analysis of Policies

By focusing on rules rather than behavior as characteristic of the ontology of an institution the researcher's task is facilitated in one sense: to identify a institution is to ascertain its rules and norms. The same is true of decision making with norms at the individual level. Hence, I will conduct much of this discussion in terms of international institutions, but the principles are identical for a single actor.

Because of the behavioral focus of most institution analysis there is little clarity about what any given institution actually is. One consequence of a norm-based approach is to require that any analysis of an institution *must begin with a description of the rules and norms that compose the institution.* In spite of the general consensus around definitions of regime and institution, rare is an analysis of an international institution that states clearly that (1) the norms and principles are a, b, c, and (2) the decision-making procedures and rules are x, y, and z that guide actors' expectations in specific issue areas. The German literature on regimes (e.g., Rittberger 1990) presents the major exception to this. They have shown a concern for providing a description on the principles, norms, rules, and decision-making procedures. The American literature, in contrast, has on the whole taken these issues quite for granted. One positive methodological and research design consequence of my approach is to require a clear, explicit statement of the norms and rules of any institution.

One of the frustrating aspects of the literature on international norms and institutions is the frequency with which authors talk about the rules and norms of international society without ever specifying what those rules actually are. For example, analyses of the security institutions à la Jervis almost never give an explicit list of the norms of the putative institution (e.g., Jervis 1985; George 1986). Except for the German school, on the rare occasions where the author actually does provide a list (Hoffman 1987; Mann 1988; Cohen 1980) one never gets a detailed analysis of the norms, much less how these norms form institutions; never is a norm discussed for more than one page.

Once one understands the logical structure of a norm then its description becomes the dissection of the norm into the major and minor premises. One needs to know the criteria for invoking the norm, what are the empirical situations described in the minor premise. The second part of the dissection involves the kind of behavior the norm permits, proscribes, or prescribes. Thus the norm description always includes two parts, the "if" part which describes the range of application, when, where, and to whom the norm applies, and the "then" part which describes the behavior in terms of the three Ps.

We see now the dramatic methodological implications of a clear understanding of what an institution and a norm are. If one uses this result of my analysis alone, most studies of international institutions already have serious problems. We see related implications for the study of foreign *policies* or other norm structures at the individual level. We need to have a clear analysis of the logical structure of the policy, both in terms of its range of application as well as the behavior it requires. Just as expected utility analysis must describe preferences before getting on to strategic considerations so must one describe norms before understanding how they get used in decision making.

## Deeds: Behavioral Conformity to Norms

The methodology of the study of norms has not received the attention that it deserves, at least from students of international politics. One can be concerned with the purely formal properties of structures of norms (e.g., deontic logic); for example, much of legal philosophy was traditionally quite uninfluenced by the actual operation of legal systems. Within law the reaction to this tendency was legal realism (!); it stressed that one needed to examine how legal systems functioned in fact, not just in theory. The parallel in international relations is the contrast between idealism which focused on the rules (law) that govern interstate relations and realism which emphasized how states actually behave. In the yin and yang of intellectual history the emphasis on words (norms) passed to focus on deeds (behavior). I have defended the concept of a norm as a means of making decisions about action. Undergirding my project is the desire to understand how norms function in international affairs. A successful theory of norms must link word with deed. It may well be the case that norms are not relevant to behavior, but this can only be ascertained once a methodology has been determined for linking norms with behavior.

One can assume that students of institutions and international law are interested in the relation between institution and state behavior. But what *kind* of empirical methodology to be employed remains a controversial question. Chayes and Chayes (1993) illustrate the confusion that can easily arise:

> the general level of compliance with international agreements cannot be empirically verified. . . . According to Louis Henkins (1989, 69) *"almost all nations observe almost all principles of international law and almost all of their obligations almost all of the time."* The observation is frequently repeated without anyone, so far as we know, supplying any empirical evidence to support it. A moment's reflection shows that it would not be easy to devise a

statistical protocol that would generate such evidence. . . . No calculus, however, will supply a rigorous, nontautological answer to the question whether a state observed a particular treaty obligation, much less treaty obligations in general, only when it was in its interest to do so. Anecdotal evidence abounds for both the normative and the realist propositions, but neither of them, in their general form, is subject to statistical or empirical proof. The difference between the two schools is not one of fact but of the background assumptions that informs their approach to the subject. (176–77)

These remarks by Chayes and Chayes illustrate a number of confusions regarding the methodology of norms. One confusion is that part of their claim revolves around explaining *why* states comply with international norms. They suggest that there is no easy way to determine if norm-following is driven by self-interest and when it is not.[10] In this I believe that they are correct, but this is a problem of *explanation* not of description. Here I am asking not *why* states follow norms, but *if* they follow norms. One can often describe phenomena without being able to explain them. I assume that we need to know whether a state is complying with a norm before we can begin to understand why it did so.

Chayes and Chayes entitle their article "On compliance," which points at a crucial issue, the links between the norm and the behavior permitted, forbidden, or required by the norm. While they have problems with determining overall compliance, systematic data on compliance with specific norms seems possible: "Four years after the Montreal Protocol was signed, only about half the member states had complied fully with the requirement of the treaty that they report annual chlorofluorocarbon (CFC) consumption" (194); thus there appears to be no particular a priori reason why systematic data on behavior could not be gathered about important norms of any given institution. In fact, Chayes and Chayes frequently refer to the lists of putative Soviet treaty violations generated by the U.S. government: why cannot this be done for other institutions? This is not a simple matter since some governments do not have the will or the means to collect these data, but of course this does not prevent researchers from doing so. In addition, it may not be clear whether a certain act is in violation or not. Depending on the norm, problems of interpretation may be severe: for example, do voluntary export quotas violate WTO norms? But questions of interpretation must be determined on a case by case basis, not based on an a priori position.

In contrast, Mitchell quite clearly states that compliance is defined in terms of international institution rules: " I define compliance, the dependent variable, as an actor's behavior that conforms with an explicit treaty provision" (1994, 429). The Weiss and Jacobson volume (1999) illustrates this nicely. When possible they give data about how often states follow the various parts of international environmental treaties.

Norms provide guidance for behavior, hence one actually speaks frequently about compliance with norms. Henkins remarked (see above) that most states

---

[10]Goertz and Diehl (1992) as well as Gelpi (1997) controlled in a statistical sense for self-interest in order to evaluate the impact of international norms.

comply most of the time with most norms; the same thing can be said of people. I suggest that really the key issue is norm *violation*. One focuses explicitly on violations. This is not a particularly novel claim; in the United States the FBI regularly publishes statistics on crime, not law obedience. Obviously such statistics do not cover unreported or undiscovered crime, and some reported crime never occurred, but people do use such data. Human rights organizations attempt to do the same thing in their reports (e.g., the annual reports of Amnesty International). The U.S. government followed the same policy with regard to the USSR, they published lists of violations not compliance.

However, one cannot just focus on violations, absolutely essential to this procedure is the denominator: on how many occasions does the norm apply? We have the empirical situation where violations are much more visible than compliance. For example, violations of WTO principles attract more attention than does increasing trade within WTO principles. It is easy to point out violations of any norm—as realists are wont to do—but this is quite meaningless without a standard of comparison. Likewise, when Henkins says most states follow international law most of the time, that is not much use either.

Depending on the type of norm—prescription, proscription, or permission—the determination of what counts as one *occasion* may not be an easy matter, but this can vary from case to case. Take the supposedly difficult case of the security regime between the United States and the USSR represented by the SALT treaties. Clearly, each major weapons acquisition decision is an occasion when the United States can or cannot behave according to SALT norms. Chayes and Chayes, in the above example, implicitly define "number of occasions" as the number of treaty signatories.

WTO provides an interesting possibility—and shows why one must include the dominator. Assume that the amount of WTO-violations in terms of trade lost is increasing. Is this in itself cause for alarm? First of all, it may also be the case that the amount of WTO-conforming trade is also increasing. These two facts may be the simple consequence of increasing *total* trade. It may well also be the case that the amount of WTO-violations in terms of trade lost as a percentage of total trade is going down! To make valid comparisons across time or space one almost always has to standardize the raw data (this can involve quite sophisticated considerations, see Goertz 1994 for a discussion of contextual indicators). To choose an analogy close to home, certainly the amount of crime in New York City has risen since the nineteenth century, but until we take into account the increase in population we really know nothing at all.

If we talk about U.S. foreign policy in the proper sense of policy, we can ask to what extent a particular act by some president conforms with U.S. policy. Take the example of security regimes between the United States and the USSR which contain norms of the three P sorts. Both sides spent a great deal of effort to ascertain whether the other side was acting in accord with its foreign policy, virtually always policies that were officially and publically announced. Both sides were gathering norm data (fortunately they had not consulted regime theorists to find out this was infeasible). It is somewhat ironic that Chayes and Chayes take the position they do since one of them was intimately involved in this sort of activity during the Kennedy administration.

The major point with regard to the theory of international institutions is that there is nothing that prevents the gathering, and hence by implication, the statistical analysis of numeric data. In principle, for each norm we can gather data about behavioral conformity or violation when the norm is applicable. Some regime scholars do invest in systematic data gathering. For example, Mitchell (1994) provides excellent time-series data regarding behavior vis-à-vis oil tanker pollution norms; Weiss and Jacobson (1999) have systematically gathered data on behavioral conformity to environmental treaties; Kegley and Raymond (1990) have gathered extensive data on alliance norms.

## Dynamic Aspects

It may appear a bit odd to talk about the evolution of norms since in their "if $p$ then $q$" form they seem to be quite discrete entities, but time-series data are critical for any description and analysis of an international institution. Many crucial questions can only be answered with time-series data, for example, Keohane asks about "after hegemony?" which implies a longitudinal analysis (Keohane 1989). It is a matter of empirical fact that some norms come into effect only gradually, often official treaties only mark an important but not final stage in their evolution.

The evolutionary dynamics of norms are key at both the state and international level, and part of the reason why time-series data are needed is to disentangle the interactions between global and state level patterns. If international norms are *both* cause and effect then this requires some sort of dynamic analysis.

Change takes place at both the words and deeds level. Usually, norms give the image of stability, related as they are to notions of custom, tradition, religion, and culture, in which forms they can remain quite fixed over long periods of time. In contrast, deeds for many seem to vary widely over time and space. Central to the international institutions puzzle lies the connection between the two. Both at the individual and society level I used examples of norms—foreign policies and institutions—that have exhibited remarkable staying power.

In my conceptualization, institution change occurs when the norm—words— change. The more important the norm in the overall structure the more important the change. From this perspective it makes no real sense to talk about changes "within" and "between" regimes (Krasner 1983). We can use this kind of talk informally to distinguish between "major" and "minor" differences, but that is about all.

Another more frequent dynamic description of institutions is that they are getting "weaker." This usually refers to deeds, the extent to which actors' behavior conforms to institutional norms. However, there is a structural sense to weak and strong, independent of behavior. This will be key to the analysis of institutions as structures of norms, but to get a feel for this one can say that an institution is weak if there are many exceptions to its major principles.

A central question in the literature on hegemonic regimes is their eventual course in the absence or decline of the hegemon. Not surprisingly, with no explicit formulation of the norms and their structures, it is hard to determine—at the level of logical structure—how or if the institution is changing. At the level of words one can chart the changes in an institution. For example, much of the GATT rounds were attempts to extend the rules of GATT to new areas such as agriculture and services. Formally, the "if $p$ then $q$" norm becomes "if $p$ or $n$ then $q$." From a structural point of view we can say WTO is getting stronger because its basic principles are being extended to cover new occasions, for example, the extension of WTO principles to trade in services. This says nothing about whether behavior will now conform in these new occasions, but only that the institution now indicates new action for those situations.

Norms also change when their major premise changes, the cases covered can remain the same but the required course of actions varies, i.e., the norm "if $p$ then $q$" becomes "if $p$ then $r$." Depending on the role that norm plays in the institution these changes can also be fundamental or minor.

In any case, the principle is simple, change in an institution is change in its rules—be it in the major or minor premise. In addition change occurs in the form of new rules or new relations between rules. Methodologically, this requires a description of the new content of the norms, i.e., the new major or minor premises.

When scholars speak of an institution weakening it is usually in the sense of behavioral trends within an institution. To understand claims about institution dynamics in this sense of weakness requires time-series data about compliance and violation. These data will be the only rigorous means of evaluating intuitive impressions.

Unlike norm change, which most of the time involves discrete leaps, it is clear that behavior can vary continuously from 100 percent compliance to 100 percent violation. Not only is the deed measure continuous between zero and one, it tends to vary more. Empirically, norms rarely change. In contrast, many think deeds change rapidly and frequently. It is this belief that provides one of the central puzzles of the theory of institutions, to which I will devote a good portion of chapter 7.

One can see why I stress the ontology of institutions as consisting of norms and rules. They are methodologically and theoretically prior to behavior. In the context of this chapter the key methodological point is that the dynamics of deeds lies within a formal structure of norms. Deeds change within a fixed norm, but at the same time norms themselves change. It is easy to confound the two, with theoretical confusion as the likely result.

# Punctuated Equilibrium Decision Making

Punctuated equilibrium notions have been most closely associated with policy and institutions. The stasis that this framework stresses arises because of the inertia characteristics of large organizations—like governments—and institutions which are also the creation of large numbers of people or states in the case of international institutions.

Above I have just argued that norm, rule, and policy are synonyms, they have the same basic logical structure and are used in the same basic way in decision making. I propose that decision making with norms produces as a natural consequence the punctuated equilibrium pattern of behavior:

> Much of the punctuated equilibrium behavioral pattern shown by organization, governments, and institutions arises because of decision making with norms and policies.

I will argue in part II that organizations *are* (that ontological question again) a set of policies and roles. Since organizations make decisions in this mode they produce as a matter of course the punctuated equilibrium behavior path.

The punctuated equilibrium pattern has two core stages. The first includes periods of rapid change, the second is a, usually long, period of stasis until the next point of rapid change. Decision making with norms has two stages as well. The first is the one when one chooses a norm or policy, the second, usually long, is when the norm is used in many individual decisions. Choosing a norm often means a major shift in goals and means. It is a time of change and large-scale experimentation. Once institutionalized, the norm becomes a SOP and fades into the background and relatively obscurity until something provokes a reevaluation of the policy. Hence, the title of this volume which links "norms," "punctuated equilibrium," and "decision making."

The next two chapters deal with the first stage of the punctuated equilibrium process, choosing norms. There are two basic reasons why individuals and governments choose norms, instrumental and moral. There are almost always various means to a particular end, some of which cost more than others. Hence we choose policies on instrumental considerations. Economists teach us that trade increases wealth; hence, we have international norms that permit trade. We also choose norms that incorporate basic values that we cherish. Most people think that torture is bad and hence there are international norms that proscribe that behavior. In democracies we find that civil liberties are a good thing and hence we have international norms about human rights that prescribe tolerance.

# Chapter 4

# The Instrumentality of Norms

> Behavior is ultimately a social matter . . . and thinking in terms of what "we" should do, or what should be "our" strategy, may reflect a sense of identity involving the recognition of other people's goals and the mutual interdependencies involved. Even though other people's goal may not be incorporated in one's own goals, the recognition of interdependence may suggest following certain rules of behavior, which are not necessarily of intrinsic value, but which are of great *instrumental* importance in the enhancement of the respective goals of the members of that group.
>
> —*Amartya Sen*

Decision making with norms as outlined in the previous chapter appears to be quite different from the expected utility decision making of economics and game theory. Here we have an interesting tension worth exploring. The previous chapter provided the broad outlines of a decision making procedure that takes norms as its core element. In the first part of this chapter we shall enter into the world of expected utility decision making to investigate what role norms have played there. In the second part of the chapter I explore what instrumental decision making with norms looks like.

In the last chapter I constantly dodged the question of the origin of norms. This chapter discusses one core reason to choose a norm, namely, instrumental concerns. One picks a norm because its seems the best way to achieve a goal, what I call "instrumental norms."

It is important to realize that instrumental norms are still norms. They have the same logical structure of any norm. The *content* and *why* they are chosen may differ, but their fundamental nature does not. This must be emphasized since often norms are taken in opposition to the rationality of the expected utility calculus:

> Rational action is concerned with outcomes. Rationality says: If you want $Y$ do $X$. I define norms by the feature that they are not outcome oriented. (Elster 1990, 863)

In a similar spirit, norm-following is often contrasted with self-interest:

What is distinctively *moral* about a system of rules is the possibility that the rules might require people to act in ways that do not promote their self-interest. (Beitz 1979, 23)

There is no reason why norms cannot be good and good for you.

This kind of fundamental mistake leads to confusion in regime theory as well. For example, some would claim that regimes do not exist if states follow them for self-interested reasons. Jervis claimed that regimes imply "a form of cooperation that is more than the following of short-run self-interest" (1983, 173). Krasner also contrasted institutions with self-interest since "institution-governed behavior must not be in [the] short-term calculation of interest (1983, 3).[1] This issue arose in chapter 2 in the context of distinguishing the explanation of an institution from its ontology. Here I am suggesting that self-interest can be a reason to choose a norm.

Such claims arise when people look at the content of norms or their origins in social systems. A norm is just a logical structure, the ontology of norms says nothing about the content of norms. I see no reason why norms cannot serve self-interest. Remarks like those cited above often appear when discussing morality, the topic of the next chapter. But it must be an odd conception of morality that requires one to act—frequently?—against self-interest.

Hidden behind the false opposition of norms versus self-interest lies the feeling that norms, particularly moral systems, are social while interests are individual. Part I of this book assumes that actors choose their norms. Specifically, in this chapter, they choose them for instrumental reasons. Instrumental norms may involve both decision making against nature, e.g., how to produce the most crops, as well as decision making against man. The actor picks the norm because it is good for her, it helps her achieve her goals. We are not yet concerned with the contrast—if it is one—between social norms and individual norms.

As is customary in game theory and economic models, in this chapter I take preferences, goals, and interests as exogenous. The character of preferences and interests remains outside the purview of instrumental rationality, particularly in its expected utility and game theory formulations. A fundamental question in this chapter revolves around the role of rules and norms within this perspective.

As it turns out, there is no agreement among game theorists about what a norm *is*. That nasty ontological question sticks with us still. This chapter investigates what I think is quite clearly the dominate interpretation, at least within game theory, but others will arise as we go along through this volume.

---

[1] These two quotes suggest a crucial distinction between "long-term" and "short-term" self-interest. This is not a distinction that economic models make since the whole future is subject to a single discounting function. Too much emphasis on the short term can lead to preference reversals and other inconsistent behavior, see Ainslie (1992).

# Norms as Equilibria

Before entering into how norms are portrayed within game theory, it is important to understand that the concept of a norm is not native to expected utility decision making in general and game theory in particular. Hence it is necessary to express the notion of a norm in game theoretic terms. This I refer to as the "translation problem." As with translation between natural languages it is often not clear what is the best rendering, there may be several plausible alternatives, depending on the reading of the concept in the source language and the conceptual resources in the target language.

The nonnative character of the norm concept reveals itself in the examination of game theory textbooks. For example, Morrow's textbook (1994) does not have an index entry for "norms." If we consider the synonym "rule," it only appears in the context of "legislative rules" (note the system-level concept used here). It is not that Morrow is not aware of the literature on norms and rules in game theory, he does not consider it central enough to be included in an introductory textbook, except in the legislative area. Morrow has done work on international institutions (1994), but this lies too far from the concerns of a general, all-purpose political science textbook to merit inclusion.

It is quite evident that the most prominent, and probably historically first, use of norm appears in the framework of coordination games and conventions.

A study of conventions in game theory often starts like this:

> In Britain, drivers almost always keep to the left-hand side of the road. Why? It is tempting to answer: "Because that is the law in Britain." Certainly someone who drove on the right would be in danger of prosecution for dangerous driving. But British drivers don't keep slavishly to *all* the laws governing the use of the roads. It is a criminal offense for a driver not to wear a seat belt, to drive a vehicle whose windscreen wipers are not in working order, or to sound a horn at night in a built-up area; but these laws are often broken. Even people who cheerfully break the law against drunk driving—a very serious offense, carrying heavy penalties—usually keep left.
>
> The answer to the original question, surely, is: "Because everyone else drives on the left." To drive on the right in a country in which people normally drive on the left is to choose a quick route to the hospital or the cemetery. The rule that we should drive on the left is self-enforcing.
>
> So we do not always need the machinery of the law to maintain order in social affairs; such order as we observe is not always the creation of governments and police forces. Anarchy in the literal sense ("absence of government") cannot be equated with anarchy in the pejorative sense ("disorder; political or social confusion"). The notion of spontaneous order—to use Friedrich Hayek's phrase—or orderly anarchy—to use James Buchanan's—is not a contradiction in terms. Perhaps driving on the left is a rare example of spontaneous order, and in most cases the absence of government does lead to disorder and confusion; but this is not a self-evident truth. The possibilities of spontaneous order deserve to be looked into. (Sugden 1986, 1)

TABLE 4.1: Battle of the Sexes: Multiple Equilibria and Norms

Woman

|        |        | Ballet | Boxing |
|--------|--------|--------|--------|
| Man    | Ballet | 1, 2   | −1,−1  |
|        | Boxing | −1,−1  | 2, 1   |

This long passage sums up most of the themes of the large literature on "conventions" and the "spontaneous creation of order." There may be situations where norms "naturally" evolve.

The question "which side of the road should I drive on?" is of course a specific decision-making problem. In this case there are two obvious possibilities: always drive on the left or always on the right (there are less obvious ones like drive on the left on even days and on the right on odd ones). The principal characteristic of this choice problem is that there are at least two best choices.

Within a game theoretic framework what distinguishes this situation is the existence of *multiple equilibria*: driving on the left or right are *both* equally good solutions. Since both are equally good, how shall we decide upon one rather than the other? Norms provide a way for choosing between equilibria: "[norms] are possible solutions to problems posed by certain social interaction situations" (Ullman-Margalit 1977, vii).

Early in the history of game theory Schelling (1960) suggested that choice in games with multiple equilibria might be guided by reference to social norms and conventions. A famous example from Schelling concerns the coordination problem of two people lost in New York City who need to figure out a place to meet but cannot contact each other. The most widely chosen strategy was noon at the information counter at Grand Central Station. David Lewis's book *Convention* made the topic a serious one for research by philosophers; that work spawned a large and significant literature in philosophy on this type of problem.

Perhaps the archetypal multiple equilibria game is Battle of the Sexes, shown in table 4.1 (as presented by Luce and Raiffa 1957). As reflected in the payoffs, the couple would rather be together than apart, but the man would prefer to be together at the boxing match and the woman prefers togetherness at the theater. The usual assumption is that they choose independently with no communication. Without communication (or with it for that matter) the two need to *coordinate* their choices, just like drivers need to coordinate which side of the road to drive on. Lewis (1969) sees conventions as solutions to coordination problems of this sort.

Some prominent games, such as prisoners' dilemma, if played only once do not have multiple equilibria, but if one allows repeated play then the problem of multiple equilibria expands dramatically. Since many social interactions recur this is a reasonable extension of the problem. For example, the one-off prisoners' dilemma has only one equilibrium, DD, but the repeated prisoners' dilemma has several (Axelrod 1984; Sugden 1986), the most famous of which is of course tit-for-tat; but DD is also an equilibrium in repeated play. Both strategies are equilibria since they are the "best responses to themselves": if the group norm is tit-for-tat then your best play is also that strategy, if it is always defect then that is the best choice.

Thus from the game theoretic perspective a traditionally sociological phenomenon, norms, has been explained without recourse to sociological concepts, but rather as a result of self-interested behavior. A norm or convention becomes in game terminology a stable equilibrium:

> I shall define a convention as: any stable equilibrium in a game that has two more stable equilibria ... To say that some strategy I is a stable equilibrium in some such [repeated] game is to say the following: it is in each individual's interest to follow strategy I provided that everyone else, or almost everyone else, does the same. Thus a stable equilibrium may be understood as a self-enforcing rule. (Sugden 1986, 32)

From all this we can see one response to the translation problem—or the ontological question—in game theory:

norms are equilibria.[2]

I am not aware that any game theorist has explored the implications of this definition, but there is no question that this translation dominates the game theoretic literature on norms, particular when dealing with issues of institutions and institutions. For example, Morrow illustrates this in his discussion of international institutions:

> If the players believe they are playing battle of the sexes, coordination on one of the two moves is in both players' interest. The pure coordination equilibrium does this by creating mutual expectations about the move to be played ... The equilibria also produce norms of behavior. ... The expectations about one another's moves are analogous to norms within a institution. ... Like norms, the players' cognizance of one another's equilibrium strategies allows them to determine when another player has deviated from suggested behavior. Norms then are generated by an equilibrium of the model. ... Different institutions produce norms of varying strength just as the equilibria in the model do. (1994, 408, 409)

---

[2] In chapter 2 I suggested that not all "patterned behavior" was necessarily norm-driven. This claim lies implicitly in the games which contain *multiple* equilibria. In the one-off prisoners' dilemma game the DD equilibrium is not normally termed a norm, they enter only in repeated plays of the game when multiple equilibria appear. From a game theoretic perspective one-equilibrium situations do not involve norms. Since norms are used to choose between equilibria they serve no purpose in the unique equilibrium case.

Now the converse does not appear to be the case:

    not all equilibria are norms.

For example, Sugden also requires norms to be *stable* equilibria. Also, other types of equilibria, particularly situations with a unique equilibrium, do not count either. Equilibria resting on randomized strategies seem equally to be a gray area.

Historically, the use of norms arose within the coordination game setting, but the norm-as-equilibrium position also characterizes the game theoretic literature on regimes and institutions. However, norms can also serve other functions in determining equilibria. For example, Shepsle's concept of "structure-induced equilibrium" (Shepsle and Weingast 1981) uses institutional rules for related purposes. Why did he need this concept? He was responding to game theoretic models of institutions with *no* equilibria: "there is no equilibrium in pure strategies under majority voting when there are two or more issues" (Morrow 1994). Hence, there is no way to predict legislative action from actors preferences. However, if we introduce considerations of legislative procedure—rules—then an equilibrium can emerge. With structure-induced equilibrium the rules *create* an equilibrium, in coordination games norms *choose between* equilibria. In both cases they are needed to arrive at a final unique equilibrium.

This implies an empirical hypothesis: the norms we observe in society are equilibria. There exists a universe of equilibria—rules of the road—permitting different societies to have different customs and mores. The English drive on the left and the Americans on the right: each society has chosen one of the possible equilibria. A question immediately leaps to mind given this perspective: do there exist norms which are *not* equilibria? Sugden suggested (above 55) that not all laws of the road are self-enforcing, e.g., drunk driving. This question seems to me to be a key one, and one which does not get posed until one begins to discuss more thoroughly the concept of a norm in game theory. One possible answer in the institutional context is that these norms exist but elicit no behavioral conformity.

The essential point in the present context is that we have a clear answer to the ontological question from some game theorists: norms are equilibria. The question then becomes how well does this jive with the definition of norm given in the previous chapter.

## Norms as Strategies

One method for understanding norms in the game theory world revolves around examining the practice of game theorists, which was the methodology of the previous section. Another approach takes the concept of a norm as defined in the last chapter and searches through game theory for a concept that comes close to being an accurate translation of the norm idea, which is the approach I take in this section.

A norm or rule in policy decision making consists essentially of two parts. The minor premise says when the norm applies, and the major premise gives the

TABLE 4.2: Translation Table: Policy Decision Theory and Game Theory

| Decision Aspect | Game Theory | Policy Decision |
|---|---|---|
| Terminology | Strategy | Norm/Rule |
| Occasion for decision | Node | Minor premise |
| Choice | Move | Major premise |

behavior prescribed, proscribed, or permitted. If we search through game theory we discover that this fits quite closely the definition of a *strategy*. Going to Morrow for a textbook formulation:

> A strategy is a complete plan for playing a game for a particular player. It specifies what moves that player would make in any situation. Imagine that the players are scheduled to play the game at a set time. However, one player has a pressing commitment at the time they are to play. The referee asks that player for a comprehensive plan to play his or her position. That plan must specify a move for all possible moves that the player could make, even those that the player thinks will not occur. (1994, 66)

Formally this is almost identical to the definition of a norm, a strategy consists of a series of if–then statements about what an actor will do in a given situation.

In game theory a strategy is normally a *complete* plan of action in all conceivable (as defined by the game) situations. For clarity I will call this a "complete strategy," because it gives a decision in all possible circumstances. The simple norms I have discussed are not complete strategies, since they only provide some guidance in some subset of all situations. But obviously we can add norms to the structure until we have a complete strategy. Hence a strategy can be defined as a complete and consistent structure of norms. In the other direction, we can define a norm as part of a complete strategy.

Table 4.2 provides the translation between norm and strategy. Clearly, the minor premise describes one or more choice points. In extensive form these are the nodes of the decision tree where a player must make a move. The major premise is basically the move the player would make at that node. Here the strategy says what to do, in norm terms it is a prescription. However, we have seen that norms can also say that a choice option will not be taken (proscriptions). So unless there are only two options this sort of norm does not give enough guidance to provide a complete strategy. Permissions barely fit within the scope of strategy, they are used in defining the choice options or game itself. A correct definition of the game includes all permitted or possible choices.

With a little work one can translate policy decision making into strategies and vice versa. For example, take the well-known tit-for-tat strategy:

> Do what the other player did in the previous move. (Major Premise, Strategy)

The other player played D last round. (Minor Premise, Decision Node)

*therefore*

Play D on the current move. (Conclusion, Move)

This norm does not constitute a complete strategy since it does not say what to do on the first move. We would have to add another norm for this situation to get a complete strategy.

On the issue of complete strategies, game theorists always provide complete and consistent strategies, but it is not clearly that in real-life situations this is always the case. The issue of structural completeness of both expected utility and norm decision-making modes will be the topic of chapter 6. The point here is that in practical terms complete strategies are rare, actors usually do not have contingency plans for all possible situations. A complete strategy is something that can sometimes be achieved in the simpler world of game theory but not in the real world. The difference lies in the theoretical discourse where in game theory strategies are assumed to be complete, while normative systems are usually presumed to be incomplete. This will be a key issue in the analysis of institutions. Are they complete in the sense that they have rules for all plausible situations? There may be important issues not covered, hence because of incompleteness the institution may be less effective.

Another major difference between norms and strategies is that norms are usually general and apply to relatively large classes of action, for example, the prisoner of war's not-lying norm applies to a wide variety of strategic interactions. While some norms in a institution may be quite specific (e.g., weapons acquisitions in security institutions) the archetypal norm applies in a variety of situations, or some like the categorical imperative apply universally. Strategies are more tied to specific situations (games). Strategies normally change when payoffs, information, etc. change, while typical norms are much less sensitive to changing situations.

The key result is that in game theoretic terms a norm or rule is a strategy or part of a strategy. Within game theory strategies are the result of preferences, game structure, etc. Likewise, norms and rules can be chosen to achieve goals and ends. Both strategies and norms are instrumental means. Where decision making with norms diverges from game theory is in assuming that norms chose between or impose equilibria. In addition, it is not obvious that international institutions are the best solution to problems (see chapter 9) or are equilibria at all.

## Instrumental Norms as Intervening Variables

One common interpretation of institutions since the early 1980s sees them as intervening variables. Krasner (1983) explicitly states that this is one potential way institutions matter: Power/Interests → Institution → Behavior. However, it is not clear exactly what "intervening" really means. If one writes out the equations that correspond to $A$ causes $B$ causes $C$ and does a little algebra the institution variable $B$ disappears. The cause of $C$ is $A$, the $B$ variable has no impact at all. If one omits this variable from the analysis it has *no* effect on the other parameter estimates (Blalock 1969). Hence they could be left out of the analysis without distorting the results. For example, if this is an appropriate representation of hegemonic institution theory then omitting the institution variable does not really change things, power and interests explain everything.

The intervening variable concept sees institutions as a middle link in a causal chain: normally the first link in such a chain is the *cause*, everything else flows from this initial push. It may be objected that this is an overly simplistic view of intervening variables—and it is: but that is what Krasner's figure means. Krasner himself may mean something else by "intervening variable" but his figure does not express that. The point is that the concept of intervening variable in terms of causation is not the intuitively clear concept that its usage in the regime literature might imply.

When Krasner makes claims about institutions as intervening variables he implicitly is arguing that they are causal variables of some sort. One central concern of this book is to examine carefully what it means to say that institutions matter: in statistical terms, how the institution functions as an independent variable. In the simplest version of institutions as intervening variables they have no causal impact, they do not really matter.

The concept of norms as strategies fits quite naturally with the interpretation of institutions as intervening variables. Preferences, power, game structure are all prior to strategies; strategies are the *result* of expected utility decision making using these inputs. A strategy "intervenes" between these basic factors and the achievement of desired ends. The decision maker can choose among strategies/institutions, and may well choose strategies/institutions that maximize her self-interest in the most realist sense of the term. Strategies matter since a bad strategy does not produce a good outcome (usually at least), but the choice of a strategy is determined by payoff structure, preferences, and information. This seems to be exactly what Keohane means when he says: "I explore . . . how we can account for fluctuations in time in the number, extent and strength of international institutions, on the basis of rational calculations under varying circumstances" (1983, 142). Depending on the circumstances it may be quite rational to choose an institution as an expected utility maximizing strategy.

The use of game theoretic frameworks in the institution literature illustrates well the logic of considering norms as strategies. Be it coordination, prisoners' dilemma, chicken, the structure of the situation and preferences are given, the question is to find a strategy—e.g., tit-for-tat—that can move actors to better payoffs, e.g., the Pareto frontier.

## Nash Equilibria and Expectations

In chapter 2 I required an individual level concept of norms, the principle is to investigate norms at the actor level before moving to the social or system level. As Sugden illustrates (see above page 55), game theorists, like sociologists, identify norms as society level phenomena. In its choose-the-equilibrium application one arrives at a common choice because the players have common culture, which provides "common conjectures" (Morrow 1994) or focal points. The basic project of some game theorists is to explain a distinctively sociological concept—norm—in terms of expected utility rationality.

While it is virtually never discussed in the institution literature, it is useful to examine the equilibrium concept which is the game theoretic translation of the norm idea: the Nash equilibrium. Though different equilibrium concepts exist, without question the Nash equilibrium provides the fundamental position, most further developments like subgame perfect and perfect Bayesian are refinements on the Nash equilibrium. As Morrow says, "these equilibrium concepts reduce the number of Nash equilibria by imposing additional rationality conditions" (1994, 121). Faced with the common situation of multiple equilibria the game theorist has two general options. The first is equilibrium selection from the outside, where institutional rules or cultural norms can determine the final equilibrium. The other option moves to the inside and makes more stringent rationality requirements of or assumptions about the players: for example, one can use the subgame perfect equilibrium concept instead of the Nash equilibrium.

The Nash equilibrium relies crucially on the criteria that a best strategy provides the highest payoff *given the strategy of the other player.* Of course we assume that all players will be looking for their best strategy.[3] A Nash equilibrium is a stable situation where each player is playing the best strategy given the strategy of the other. It is an equilibrium since no player individually has an incentive to deviate because it is after all her best strategy given her expectations.[4] This equilibrium concept is so widely used that when one reads "equilibrium" (with no adjective like "subgame perfect") the writer almost certainly means a Nash equilibrium.

The Nash equilibrium concept relies crucially on there being some self-evident way to play that can guide one's expectations about the other's strategy. If such is not the case the Nash equilibrium concept begins to crumble:

> Unless a game has a self-evident way to play, self-evident to the participants, the notion of Nash equilibrium has no particular claim upon our attention. Hence when economic analysts invoke the notion of a Nash equilibrium they are asserting at least implicitly that the situation in question has (or will have)

---

[3]This is where more stringent rationality assumptions come into play. For example, a Nash equilibrium player can make incredible threats, but if subgame perfect players are assumed then incredible threats do not occur.

[4]There are situations were joint changes in strategy can provide both players with better payoffs and which are also equilibria. This can easily arise in coordination situations.

a self-evident way to play. When, as so often happens, they don't say why it is that there is a self-evident way to play, then it is left to the reader either to supply the reason or to be suspicious of the results. (Kreps 1990, 31–32)

Crucial to the Nash equilibrium concept is the *expectation* of the strategy of the other player. A best strategy is one given the expectation that the other will play in a certain fashion. Even if the other player is rational, in multiple equilibria situations he has a number (greater than one) of reasonable expectations regarding the possible play of the other. In unique equilibrium cases the expectation is clear (though perhaps only to a game theorist). Norms, cultural and social, can save the day when there are multiple reasonable expectations regarding the strategy of the other actor. Since a social norm is a strategy it may be quite reasonable to expect that the other will use society's strategy. So game theorists are right to associate Nash equilibria with norms. Cultural norms provide a self-evident, or at least plausible, expectation about the strategy of the other.

We can see a plausible game theoretic interpretation of the "normative" explanation of the democratic peace. It is a reasonable expectation that a democracy follows the norms of a democracy, and analogously for nondemocracies. Hence the Nash equilibrium for two democracies may be quite different from the equilibrium when two nondemocratic states interact. This becomes clear once we understand that norms translated in game theory language are just strategies. Kreps (1990) used as his example how norms of behavior in the Korean academic subculture might produce different Nash equilibria from those produced by the American academic subculture. With the understanding of norms as strategies we can begin to link the "normative/cultural" and game theories of the democratic peace.

This brief example also shows the importance of classical realist assumptions. Realists assume all states have the same character, i.e., a realist one. The normative explanation of the democratic peace suggests that even within the expected utility maximization world, the nature or identity of the state matters because it determines expectations.[5]

Recall that the Krasner definition of institutions included a clause about institutions "guiding expectations" in issue areas. The expectations about what other players will do determines in part the Nash equilibrium and hence the best strategy. Many definitions of norms include common expectations or common knowledge as a feature that characterizes a norm. I expect you to drive on the right and you expect that I have such expectations, and I expect that you expect that I expect, and so forth (Lewis 1969).

A more sociological definition of a norm or convention take these common expectations as the defining characteristic of a social norm. No longer is it necessary to have a set of multiple equilibria to choose from. A social norm is simply

---

[5] I shall return to the democratic peace in the next chapter when I discuss the interpretation of norms as preferences and Bueno de Mesquita and Lalman's explanation of the democratic peace.

what a group of people decide to accept as the norm: "The conventions of a group are, I say, principles the members jointly accept. They are, in this case, principles with the simple form of a fiat. . . . No questions asked, no reasons given" (Gilbert 1989, 402). Conventions are when groups decide to use a common rule or set of norm for guiding their decisions. It is also more sociological in that there is no mention of self-interest maximization or optimality.

Equilibria are of course strategies, but of a special sort. Both Sugden and Gilbert suggest that some norms are not equilibria. I came to the same conclusion by looking at the formal structure of a norm, the conclusion was that a norm was part of complete strategy, but nothing more. Once this is clear, many issues of institution theory and practice become intelligible. It may be that an institution that exists (according to my definition) is not a Nash equilibrium. If that institution elicits little behavioral conformity then we have an obvious explanation. If it is not obviously an equilibrium and governments conform to the institution anyway then we have an interesting puzzle.

The possibility of nonequilibrium norms (to give them a name) raises the issue of nonequilibrium behavior. In these situations it is not very clear what to expect of the other player. Going back to the democratic peace, what does one do with a democracy run by a realist? As Morrow says: "Nash equilibria assume that the players share a common conjecture about what strategies they each will play. Otherwise, the players cannot know that their strategies are best replies to each other" (1994, 97). What expectations should one use when the institution is not an equilibrium? Realists assume that states do not follow international institutions but are guided by self-interest alone. But there seem to be many situations where it is not clear what to expect. Should Japan expect the United States to follow WTO norms in its trade policy or not?

## Instrumental Norm Choice

One aspect of rationality is process. Rationality also has a substantive dimension: we expect rational decision-making procedures to produce good outcomes (Herek et al. 1987). We can ask are there multiple decision-making procedures that can efficiently achieve our ends? Not surprisingly the answer is yes. This chapter argues that one chooses norms and institutions as a way to achieve goals. In the second part of this chapter I would like to briefly explore how decision making with rules can be seen as one optimal—in the substantive sense—way to choose.

Decision making with norms and policies as described in the previous chapter does not seem particularly suited for practical decisions. The examples that most often come to mind are abstract moral principles. In this chapter it will seem more natural to speak of rules, practical, "of thumb," or production. Recall that "rule" has the same logical structure as a norm, so there is no sleight-of-hand involved as terminology shifts: the formal, logical structure does not change.

It may come as a surprise that there exists a large body of literature on practical decision making that uses rule-based theories. The international relations literature tends to look to economics as the only source of decision-making models, but if we take off our blinders and look around rule-based decision-making models are widely used in order to efficiently achieve goals.

## Expert Systems

Economics is not the only discipline that occupies itself with optimal choice in the instrumental sense. Students of world politics have taken—either for or against—the "rational actor model" as defined by economics and game theory as *the* rational actor model. Other disciplines are centrally involved with producing theories and actual (in the sense of to be used in real-life situations) methods for optimal choosing.

One approach arises within the field of artificial intelligence and is concerned with expert systems. What after all is an expert system? It is a computer program, which given information and a well-defined goal, tries to make the best choice. A doctor expert system takes data about the patient and generates what it thinks is the best treatment.

Virtually all expert systems implement the goal of instrumental, substantive rationality. Like expected utility rationality goals are exogenous to the system, the artificial intelligence program does not decide on what counts as success or failure in the final analysis. Like utilities and preferences in expected utility choice the goals of the system are given by definition. In the case of the doctor program, health may be elusive but this differs not greatly from the even more elusive utilities. The purpose of the computer program is to produce a decision that achieves best the exogenously set goal.

When we look into many—if not almost all—expert systems what do we discover? Fundamentally they are rule-based decision-making procedures: the core element of expert systems is, in my terms, policy decision making. These programs consist of a complex set of if–then rules. In the language of artificial intelligence what I called the minor premise—when the rule applies—is referred to as the rule "firing." Firing is the occurrence of the situation described by the minor premise. Of course, in a given situation many rules may fire, i.e., several norms may apply.

The design of an expert system thus implies choosing rules that best achieve the goals of the system. This is instrumental choice with norms. Each norm or rule is chosen for its role in optimizing the final decision, each is an instrumental norm. Here we have then what I might call a class of instrumental norm decision-making procedures.

We can also see why the best translation of norm into game theory language is strategy. An expert system is a complicated strategy which for each situation provides a choice (hopefully the optimal one).

Economists recognize that such rule-based systems differ from their expected utility ones. This can be clearly seen in the literature on the optimality of rules-of-thumb (e.g. Baumol and Quandt 1964; Bell et al. 1988; Bray 1990; Day et al. 1974), which compares the results of production rules (i.e., rules-of-thumb) with expected utility calculations. The key point here is that these rules-of-thumb are recognized as different decision-making procedures, the point of the study is to evaluate their relative advantages:

Of course these rules-of-thumb become foreign policies in the realm of world politics. I suggested in the previous chapter that governments can adopt policies—foreign policy production rules—which maximize power, wealth, and security. With the more useful concept of production rules, we can see that any given situation can—and probably does—fire several foreign policies.

The artificial intelligence international relations literature (Sylvan and Chan 1984; Hudson 1991) has focused on modeling foreign policy choice, particularly that of the United States. All these models use a complex combination of if–then rules in the style of expert systems. For example, a typical rule from UNCLESAM, one such model, states: "IF U.S. posture to the Dominican Republic Government = 4 and stability level > 5, and stability level change > 0, THEN increment (+1) U.S. use of force level." (Job and Johnson 1991, 236; see also the Hybell example above page 42).

These rules often get described as heuristic (Kanwisher 1989; Lenat 1982; Simon 1977). It is often much easier to describe decision making in terms of heuristic rules. For example, Ellsberg suggests that the decision-making heuristics in Vietnam were (based on the Pentagon Papers):

> Rule 1: Do not lose South Vietnam to communist control before the next election.
>
> Rule 2: Do none of the following unless it is essential to satisfy rule 1 (in order of acceptability): (a) bomb South Vietnam or Laos, (b) bomb North Vietnam, (c) commit U.S. troops to Vietnam, (d) commit U.S. troops to Laos or Cambodia, (e) setup wartime domestic controls, (for) destroy the Hanoi/Haiphong dikes or harbor, (g) mobilize reserves, (h) assume full civil control of South Vietnam, (i) invade North Vietnam, (j) use nuclear weapons. (1972, 132–33)

Walker describes Henry Kissinger's basic foreign policy strategy in terms of the rules: "negotiate throughout the conflict; use threats only to counter threats or the use of force initiated by the opponent; if necessary, use force to counter the use of force initiated by the opponent; use enough force combined with generous peace terms so that the opponent is faced with an attractive peace settlement versus the unattractive alternatives of military defeat or the necessity to escalate" (1977, 142). These kinds of examples, which could be multiplied easily, indicate that instrumental decision making can be, and often is, described in terms of sets of rules.

The artificial intelligence–international relations work has evolved outside debates on decision making in general, and the literature on international norms and institutions in particular. Most international relations scholars who use expert systems see this as a good methodology and way to model foreign policy choice. In contrast, I use these ideas as a fundamental tool for thinking about individual, organizational, and institutional choice.

An expert system model of government policies could provide an analysis of the interrelationships between these different policies and how that produces a final choice. At the individual level the relation between rules, or in the institution context the *structure* of the institution, is the topic of chapter 6. Also foreign policy involves individual decision makers as well as official government policy, norms at different levels of analysis (in this case the individual decision maker is one level and the government is another). Here I just want to introduce the concept of instrumental decision making with policies. The topic of this chapter is choosing norms in order to achieve exogenously determined goals. The norms of WTO illustrated different kinds of norms in the previous chapter; we can now more clearly see that these can be chosen on purely self-interest and efficiency grounds.

**Fuzzy Logic and Decision Making**

Within the field of artificial intelligence there exists a variety of approaches and problems. The problems can range from theorem-solving to machine control. I propose that expert systems originally developed for machine control provide the best way to think about decision making with norms.

Since the 1970s a new approach to the machine control problem has rapidly accelerated in influence which starts from different premises; it goes under the name of fuzzy logic. This approach has a clear creator in the person of Lofti Zadeh and the article which launched the field was published in 1965, entitled "Fuzzy sets."[6]

Part of Zadeh's insight was that in spite of much progress, in many situations human control proved still much superior to machine or computer control systems designed by systems engineers. A brilliant insight was to flip the traditional procedure on its head: instead of a model of the system, use a model of an expert operator! If we can get a good model of how an expert manipulates her machine—how she makes decisions—then one does not need a model of the physical process itself. Of course, implicit in the expert actions lies ideas about how the physical process works but these are usually intuitive and certainly never formulated mathematically.[7]

---

[6] See Cioffi-Revilla (1981) for a nice introduction to fuzzy logic ideas in the context of international relations. See Sanjian's work (e.g., 1988; 1991) for various applications of fuzzy logic to international politics.

[7] Yager and Filev describe this in their textbook: "The seminal work by L. Zadeh on fuzzy algorithms introduced the idea of formulating the control algorithm by logical rules. . . . The main differences between these [other earlier] approaches was not in the type of logic (Boolean or fuzzy) but in

One can parallel Zadeh's approach, which focuses on the human expert vis-à-vis the traditional strategy of developing a model of the physical system itself, with game theoretic approaches to human behavior. Game theory works with a definition of the situation and then works to deduce strategies. This is like the traditional systems engineer who develops a model of the physical process then based on that creates a computer program or machine to manipulate the modeled process. My approach, like Zadeh's, focuses on the rules that individuals use to achieve their goals. Like artificial intelligence–international relations scholars, I assume that individuals are goal-oriented and choose rules that they think best get them to those goals.

It begins to become clear why a fuzzy logic approach could interest a social scientist. Zadeh was really more interested in human decision making than machine control. Given his background as an electrical engineer he focused on decision making with regard to operating machines, but the methods he developed are quite general ones. While he wanted to model people who are good at their task, we can use these tools to think about foreign policy decision making without believing that those making or implementing foreign policy are particularly good at their job.

The first key characteristic of fuzzy logic is then that it was developed to model human decision making. The second one, especially relevant in the context of this chapter, is that it was developed to model optimal behavior. One chooses to study the person(s) who are the best at performing a task. While this may not be a theoretical maximum, it may be the practical one, which is what engineers are concerned about anyway.

While a hotly debated issue, defenders of fuzzy logic systems claim that they perform better than traditional ones that use a model of the process and not one of an expert operator. Within the more narrowly defined case of machines it is easier to say when one system performs better than another. What is certainly clear is that the Japanese—and more recently the Germans—have embraced fuzzy logic technologies with great enthusiasm. Many Japanese-produced machines incorporate fuzzy logic decision-making procedures. Auto focusing systems on VCRs, cameras, automatic train conductors, one-button washing machines all use decision-making control programs based on fuzzy logic. The interested reader can consult McNeill and Freiberger (1994) and Kosko (1993, this work also contains a large dose of philosophy) for nontechnical histories and discussions of fuzzy logic and its technological applications. What is much more relevant here is the use of these ideas for thinking about decision making with rules.

---

the inspiration. The former attempted to increase the efficiency of conventional control algorithms; the latter were based on the implementation of human understanding and human thinking in control algorithms. Real life supplies many examples confirming the effectiveness of human-based control algorithms. Fuzzy set theory offered appropriate tools for handling the heuristics of linguistically described algorithms. It was natural that the first [practical] approach to fuzzy control originated by Mandami and his coworkers, was not from the viewpoint of control theory, but from the viewpoint of artificial intelligence" (1994, 110).

With the label fuzzy *logic* it is not surprising that we find the if–then construction at the core of the methodology. Zadeh suggested that a good way to model expert decision making was with the basic syllogistic logic I outlined in the previous chapter. At the core of fuzzy decision-making systems lies a set of fuzzy if–then rules. As with strategies in game theory, a good system will have rules to cover all possible situations; a good fuzzy logic decision-making model is a complete one.

Here we see clear decision making with norms which is developed and conceived of in purely instrumental terms. For fuzzy logic engineers the goal is a decision-making program which makes the machine perform its task as well as possible. These models provide us with means for thinking about individual decision making with norms and rules. This is more useful than the syllogistic logic I presented in the previous chapter, which did not seem to be of much practical use.

Many scholars when they hear the word "norm" begin to think in terms of philosophy, law, and interpretative approaches (e.g., Kratochwil 1989). Fundamentally this volume argues that it is only when we first understand how actors can use norms as core parts of decision making, in the pursuit of the most mundane and egotistical goals, can we begin to make sense of international norms as system level phenomena. Fuzzy logic provides just such a no-nonsense, pragmatic approach to rules and norms.

Fuzzy logic proves useful not only because it provides a decision-making procedure using rules as a core concept, it is also very relevant to social scientists since it is an attempt to model human decision making. Unlike the image of rigor and clarity associated with Aristotelian logic, fuzzy logic starts from the fuzzy language that we use when thinking and making decisions. A constant criticism of game and decision theory is that people do not actually make choices in that fashion; while useful as normative theories of choice they are not useful as empirical descriptions of human behavior.

Fuzzy logic takes as part of its beginning point ordinary language notions like "high," "a lot," "little" and gives them fuzzy mathematical expression. Fuzzy models use expressions like "if the motor is going a little too fast then brake moderately." This is exactly what one needs to begin to model international norms and institutions whose content is expressed in ordinary language with its concomitant ambiguity.

The goal here is to capture the meaning of the ordinary language expressions including the fact that its meaning is not precise. Since the real world of human decision making is conducted with such fuzzy terms, fuzzy logic is a natural choice for me as a technique for thinking about decision making with norms. Not only is it rule-based but it attempts to capture the meaning of the words people use to describe norms.

Particularly objectionable to the Cartesian mind was the notion of *fuzzy* logic. This specific term struck at the image of logic as crisp and rigorous, with no soft edges. But empirically the great advantage of fuzzy logic lies in the realization that

*Chapter 4*

FIGURE 4.1: Fuzzy Concepts: Full

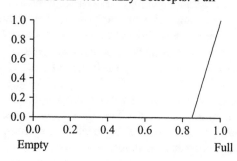

people use fuzzy concepts. Instead of assuming away the fuzzy, Zadeh embraced it, and in fact he argued that it constituted a strength of the fuzzy logic system. In summary, fuzzy logic seems exactly what we need to analyze of decision making with norms and rules. It uses rules as the core decision-making methodology, and it models the ambiguous terms with which people form their (instrumental) norms. We now need to examine how fuzzy logic captures the fuzziness of concepts and then how it combines fuzzy concepts into fuzzy rules.

**Fuzzy Concepts**

Fuzzy concepts start with the idea that some cases are better examples of a concept than others. The idea is to give a number to how applicable a certain case is of the concept, where zero indicates that the concept does not fit at all to 1.00 where the concept applies perfectly. The Y-axis indicates the extent to which the X-value represents well the underlying concept, from 1, maximum, to 0, not at all. This is easy to see with a simple concept. In figure 4.1 the X-axis runs from "empty" ($X = 0$) to "full" ($X = 1$), a one quart container with .99 quarts of liquid we would describe as "full." The ordinary concept of "full" ranges from 1 quart to somewhere just below that, say, .85 quarts. For these values very close to but not equal to 1.00 we say that they represent less well the "full" concept. For $X$ below, say, .85 we describe the container as not full, i.e., $Y = 0$. Thus the X-values in the range [.85, 1.00) count as full but not as completely as $X = 1.00$ cases. As the values approach 1.00 they better typify "full," with 1.00 being the archetypal value for "full." Fuzziness comes in then because "full" expresses a range of X-values, with each X-value being given a Y-value that says how well it fits the concept of "full," ranging from zero to one.

Figure 4.2 illustrates how fuzzy logic formalizes the ambiguity in ordinary language with an example relevant to the topic of norms. The horizontal axis represents various degrees of norm compliance. As we have seen most norms have behavioral implications that we can observe. The discourse of institution theory is repleat with terminology like "flagrant violation," "full compliance," etc. We can

FIGURE 4.2: Fuzzy Concepts: Norm Violation and Compliance

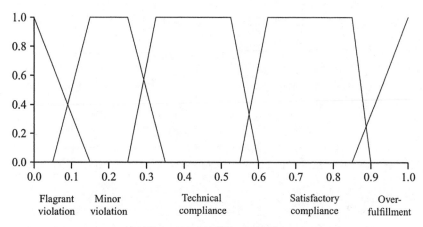

| Flagrant violation | Minor violation | Technical compliance | Satisfactory compliance | Over-fulfillment |

*Minor premise: Norm compliance*

consider this as constituting a spectrum from overt, flagrant violation to actions above and beyond the requisites of the norm, i.e., "overfulfillment." Mathematically, it is convenient to use the 0–1 scale to represent this range (nothing hangs on this, it is just a matter of scaling).

The ordinal ranking of the levels of norm compliance, expressed in words, is rather straight forward, the modeling question arises when translating these terms into fuzzy mathematics. One possibility is to put "satisfactory compliance" in the middle at .5. Figure 4.2 does not do this because our concerns—and those of decision makers—lie more with norm violation than norm compliance. As a result the scale has more gradations for the violation end of the spectrum than for the compliance end. Figure 4.2 has five degrees of the ordinary language categories from norm compliance to norm violation. The extremes of "flagrant violation" and "overfulfillment" have their maxima at the extremes of the compliance-to-violation scale, just as full and empty would have their extremes at the end of their scale.

The steep declining lines indicate values from .85–1.00 and 0–.15 count as "overfulfillment" and "flagrant violation" but to diminishing degrees as $X$ decreases or increases, respectively. We could say that a value of .90 is "moderate" overfulfillment; analogously we might say that .10 is a "pretty" flagrant violation.

"Satisfactory compliance" illustrates another possible linguistic variable which has a number of cases that fit perfectly (i.e., $Y = 1$) the concept. This gives the trapezoidal shape in figure 4.2: X-values of anywhere from .625 to .825 we call without hesitation "compliance." The fuzzy boundaries of the concept are indicated by the sloping lines on either side of the flat top. Again this fits well with

FIGURE 4.3: Fuzzy Concepts: Sanctions

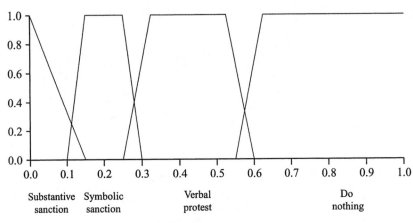

Major premise: Sanctions

our intuitive understanding of the fuzziness of real categories. Even when international institutions contain numerical limits, such as the Montreal Protocol which had precise schedules for phasing out dangerous chemicals, certainly a range of values near those in the protocols would be considered by all parties as satisfactory performance.

A second aspect of fuzziness lies in the gray zone between concepts. The fact that the regions *overlap* indicates that borderline values weakly fit two categories. The proverbial example of this is half-full or half-empty. Some quantities are poor examples of full and simultaneously poor examples of empty. Instead of forcing a demarcation line where none exists fuzzy logic just allows one to say both.[8] A major advantage of fuzzy logic is that it actually encourages one to create categories that overlap. It represents part of the essence of fuzziness, and is at the same time a fact of conceptual life.

These zones are situations where one can use two different descriptions of the same thing; for $X = .11$ we say it is *both* a "flagrant violation" and "minor violation." Fuzzy logic says two things about these gray cases: (1) both concepts apply and (2) neither concept applies very well, (i.e., Y-values are small, near zero). In ordinary language we indicate this with qualifying adjectives, like "very," "not too," "a little," etc. In the example above one might say it is "not a real flagrant violation," indicating how weakly the act fits into the flagrant violation category. In data gathering this means that one coder might say the event fits in one category while another coder puts it into the adjacent one.

---

[8] I shall discuss this issue in more detail in chapter 6 since it often means that two rules apply.

The engineers who have developed fuzzy logic based their system on an intuitive examination of how they and others use language. But the same ideas form an important theme in contemporary linguistics, semantics, and philosophy. Starting famously with Wittgenstein, philosophers have talked about "family resemblance," the idea that it is not possible to establish clear-cut memberships in sets. Some elements are clearly members but others fall into a gray zone. Concepts have core examples, which fuzzy logic gives value 1.00, but also borderline ones. The concept "bird" has core elements like robin, blue jay, etc., (these would all be on the top of a trapezoid in figure 4.2) while other varieties such as ostriches, are not a core member of the concept (see Lakoff 1987 for an extensive discussion of these points).

The advantages of this technique for the modeling of international norms should now be clearer. As I emphasized in chapter 3 the first step in the methodology of institutions is a clear statement of the content of its norms. A statement of the norm involves mostly linguistic variables, and even a "clear" statement of the norm involves fuzzy concepts. Fuzzy logic provides a way to translate this into a formal decision-making model, one that keeps at least some of the ambiguity of the original.

Figure 4.2 gives a fuzzy scale of norm violation–compliance. In this continuing example that represents the "if" part of the fuzzy rule. Before we can construct fuzzy rules, however, we need a major premise to provide the "then" action.

If the norm-related actions of government A are the minor premise then the response of government B constitute the major premise of the syllogism. Figure 4.3 illustrates the spectrum of possible reactions on the part of government B. These range from "do nothing" to "substantive sanctions." Paralleling the compliance–violation scale's emphasis on violation, the reaction scale of the major premise stresses the different kinds of sanctions government B can take in response. One end consists of "do nothing" and lies to the right of center. To the left one finds differing degrees of protest and sanction. Clearly one could break the major premise variable into more or fewer categories with different kinds of fuzzy shapes.

With the two fuzzy variables, one indicating norm-related behavior by government A on a violation-to-compliance scale, and the second providing a gamut of possible responses by government B from serious sanctions to nonresponse, it is now possible to construct fuzzy rules or policies. This subsection focused on the *fuzzy* part of fuzzy logic, now we need to direction our attention to the *logic* part of the system.

## Fuzzy Rules

A "complete policy" for government B consists of rules for every possible action taken by government A. Of course this is exactly what game theorists mean by a strategy: what one does at every possible decision node. The parallel is perfect: a complete fuzzy decision-making system has a rule—and usually more than one—for every possible event. In my example, I have assumed that every norm-related action can be put on the violation–compliance scale, hence this defines the universe of possible actions by government A.

Using the kinds of actions that government A can take—minor premise—along with the kinds of responses by government B—major premise—we can define a fuzzy strategy for government B. For it to be a complete rule system we need a response from B for all possible moves of A:

1. If government A does *flagrant violation* then *do substantive sanction.*

2. If government A does *minor violation* then *do symbolic sanction.*

3. If government A does *technical compliance* then *do symbolic sanction.*

4. If government A does *satisfactory compliance* then *do nothing.*

5. If government A does *overfulfillment* then *do nothing.*

Government B has thus a strategy for each possible action by government A. These are expressed in terms of fuzzy syllogisms.

Whether this is a good decision-making system is of course another question. Remember the idea is to model the decision-making process of governments. The main point here is that the actor chose these norms in order to best achieve its ends. These can be instrumental norms in the service of realpolitik.

The core of the decision-making system is thus a set of five rules. We can get a visual presentation of the rule set by plotting the minor premise on the X-axis and the major premise on the Y-axis. If we have chosen our rules well—in the sense of a good model of behavior—then all the actions of government B in response to the actions of government A should appear in the various boxes of the graph. Each box represents one rule, a combination of the actions of government A (X-axis) with B's responses (Y-axis). Each "+" in the figure represents one action by government B in response to actions by government A which matches the rule set. The asterisks (*) represent actions which do not fit the rule set.

More needs to be said about the *structure* of the rule system. An analogous issue arose in my definition of an institution as a structure of norms. I leave this topic to chapter 6. This section is just an introduction to fuzzy logic as instrumental decision making with rules and norms.

## Nothing New Under the Sun

Surprisingly enough there is one reference in the international relations literature which pops up regularly in discussions of fuzzy systems, it is the Axelrod-edited volume (1976) on cognitive mapping.[9] If one goes back to this work it shows

---

[9] Some work exists in international relations that uses fuzzy logic methods, for example, the work of Sanjian (1988; 1991; 1998), see Cioffi-Revilla (1981) for a survey of possible uses.

## FIGURE 4.4: Fuzzy Rules

*Major premise:*
*Sanctions*

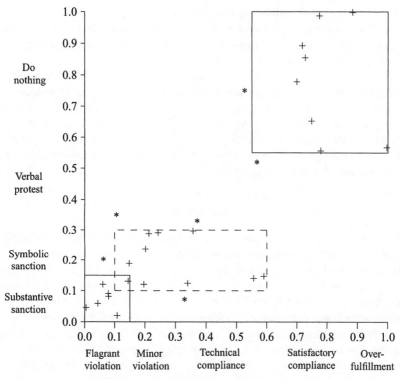

*Minor premise: Norm compliance*

characteristics that mark an affinity for the fuzzy logic approach. Fundamentally, the idea behind fuzzy logic was to develop a cognitive map of an expert, how that person reacts and makes decisions. The cognitive mapping approach typified by the Axelrod volume tried to do the same thing for political elites.

Fuzzy logic applications are much more narrowly defined, while the studies collected by Axelrod aimed at a much wider spectrum of belief and behavior. Published in 1976 it did not have the advantage of artificial intelligence and fuzzy modeling techniques, which were either not yet invented (fuzzy logic was first applied to a real problem in the early 1970s) or still in their beginning stages (artificial intelligence). Nevertheless, the same spirit animated the two perspectives. Bart Kosko, a prominent promoter of the fuzzy logic approach, has himself constructed a cognitive map of Henry Kissinger (1986).

The normative dimension of the debate about fuzzy logic makes a significant contribution here. Not only do defenders of fuzzy logic claim that it can model expert choice but also that fuzzy logic is a better decision-making procedure, particularly in dealing with complex systems. From an engineering point of view if one has a simple physical system, i.e., one with a well-understood physical theory, then traditional systems approach works well, but when the character of the system is complex then mathematical models of it will not be very useful in practice. The fuzziness of the fuzzy logic helps effectively deal with complex systems producing better decisions than tradition methods.

Axelrod's prisoners' dilemma tournament (1984) may be a good metaphor for this. Game theory can tell us a little but not much about the best strategy in a prisoners' dilemma tournament. Recall that the Nash equilibrium is the best strategy given the other player's strategy, what does this mean when one confronts a large number of different players? The winning tit-for-tat strategy has the character of a simple rule. Complicated strategies did less well in a relatively complex environment than did a simple rule-of-thumb.

## Conclusion

The most egotistical, power-maximizing leader can choose to follow norms as part of her strategy for achieving her ends. Game theoretic examples such as the repeated prisoners' dilemma and battle of the sexes illustrate how following norms can maximize self-interest. Imposing an institution on the world may be the best strategy for a hegemon. One does not need to see a benevolent, benign state providing collective goods; rather, an egotistical, realist one suffices.

However, the game theoretic tendency to define a norm as an equilibrium strategy misses the point. A norm is a strategy *tout court*. That all international norms are equilibria seems dubious; as we saw Sugden himself said that not all laws can be explained as "spontaneous order." In addition, the existence of international norms that few governments follow hints that self-interest dictates other behavior. The "norm = strategy" formula makes perfect sense when one realizes what instrumental norms are: means to an end. This is what a strategy *is*.

While norms play a secondary role in game theory, decision-making procedures do exist that use rules as the core concept. Expert systems in general and fuzzy logic in particular provide us with examples of rule-based decision-making procedures. It is not an accident that it is called fuzzy *logic*; syllogisms are part of the discipline of logic.

What is especially interesting about fuzzy logic is its dual claim to be a good decision-making procedure and one which embraces the language and ambiguity of human cognitive processes. Also, its history as a pure instrumental decision-making approach makes it all the more suitable in the context of this chapter.

Fuzzy logic decision making will reappear frequently in the pages to come. I think it serves admirably as a concrete and specific theoretical framework within which to discuss norms. It is all the more useful since many discussions of norms in international relations are characterized by lack of theoretical clarity.

This chapter has emphasized that one can choose norms for instrumental reasons, but other motivations for choosing norms exist. Morality, ethics, and religion provide values that are often expressed in norms. We need to understand that a system of norms can include moral ones as well as instrumental ones. This topic deserves as much consideration as instrumental norms, since many international institutions cannot be understood or explained without recourse to moral values.

# Chapter 5

# Moral Norms

> Es gibt gar keine moralischen Phänomene, sondern nur eine moralische Ausdeutung von Phänomene.
>
> —*Friedrich Nietzsche*[1]

> What is right is not derived from the rule but the rule arises from our knowledge of what is right.
>
> —*Julius Paulus* (Roman jurist, 3rd century A.D.)

> On pourrait . . . ajouter à l'acquis de l'état civil la liberté morale, qui rend l'homme vraiment maître de lui; car l'implusion du seul appetit est esclavage, et l'obéissance à la loi qu'on s'est prescrite est liberté.
>
> —*Jean-Jacques Rousseau*[2]

The last two chapters provide a distinctive starting point for the consideration of moral norms, they throw the discussion of ethical values and international norms into a different light. First of all, I retain the perspective of the individual decision maker. As we shall see, much of the discussion of morality involves, explicitly or implicitly, system or society level factors. These aspects of morality and international norms will come into play later in this essay, but here it is important to firmly resist the temptation to resort to society level criterion to characterize moral norms or values at the individual level.

Many take the concept "norm" to involve ethics and morality. Clearly, the previous chapter rejected this notion. Another tendency is to separate morality from self-interest. This too obscures the fact that these are often closely related: is *fair* trade an instrumental or moral norm? (Not to mention the value implications of "free" trade within Western ideologies where freedom is a key value.)

---

[1] There are no moral phenomena at all, but only a moral interpretation of phenomena.

[2] Man acquires with civil society moral freedom, which alone makes man the master of himself; for to be governed by appetite alone is slavery, while obedience to a law one prescribes to oneself is freedom.

In this chapter I continue my examination of the translation problem of norms in the expected utility context. I suggest that what are often considered moral values fit most naturally into the preference function of an individual. The previous chapter took goals and preferences as exogenous—both for expected utility and norm decision making—but one way to translate (moral) norms is as a certain sort of preference function.

Taking moral norms as preferences does not distinguish ethical values from other matters of taste: the preference for human rights does not differ from the preference for big cars. If we examine moral norms—both conceptually and empirically—they do have distinctive characteristics. I focus on two of particular relevance for international norms and institutions. One characteristic is that those who favor a moral norm think *others* should follow it: whether it is in their self-interest or not. This differentiates moral norms from matters of taste which almost by definition allow for individual differences.

The second characteristic of moral norms lies in the willingness of individuals and institutions to sanction norm violations. This arises both at the individual and governmental level. Both institutions and people are willing to sanction violations and hence pay the costs of those sanctions. As we have already seen, many *define* norms in terms of willingness to sanction (see also the definitions of morality below). Here the key point is that people are willing to sanction violations that have no direction impact on them.

These issues suggest the need to start with an ontological question—it would be a pity not to have at least one for this chapter: what is morality?

## What Is Morality?

I have characterized norms by their logical structure and role in decision making. However, my experience indicates that the word "norm" often invokes notions of morality. What is it about a decision that makes it moral? Hare states that the primary purpose of moral judgments is "to prescribe, or advise, or instruct" (1952, 159). This fits with my definition of a norm, but seems too general since it includes instrumental norms as well. Below (in alphabetical order by author) are some conceptualizations of morality which permit us to pick out some key issues. I include some that treat specifically morality and international politics, such as Beitz, McElroy, and Welch.

> What is distinctively *moral* about a system of rules is the possibility that the rules might require people to act in ways that do not promote their self-interest. (Beitz 1979, 23)

> In summary, for an individual to have a personal moral code is for him (1) to have intrinsic motivation for or against, his, and to a large extent, others performing certain kinds of actions; (2) to experience guilt-feelings when his action shows a deficiency of such motivation, disapproval when another person's does, and admiration or esteem when another person's actions show

a super-abundance of such motivation; (3) to think the forms of behavior he is motivated to perform or feels guilty about not performing . . . are important; (4) to think his attitudes of all the foregoing types are justified; and (5) to have the linguistic capability to give all this verbal expression. (Brandt 1979, 169–70)

The rational actor seeks to maximize his net (expected) utility. Defining rationality in this way enables us to give a simple and minimal definition of morality: Morality is constrained utility maximization. (Coleman 1988, 311)

Morality . . . is traditionally understood to involve an impartial constraint on the pursuit of individual interest. (Gauthier 1986, 7)

[A] moral principle . . . has got to be universal . . . a man is not to be said to accept a moral principle unless he is making a serious attempt to *use* it in guiding his particular moral judgments and thus his actions. These two requirements are . . . that moral principles have to be universal, and that they have to be prescriptive. The latter of them compels us to look for principles that we can sincerely adhere to; the former insists that these should really be moral principles and not the *ad hoc* decisions of an opportunist. (Hare 1963, 47)

[E]ach individual has two sets of preferences. One consists of his *personal* preferences, defined as his *actual* preferences, which will be typically based mainly on his own personal interests and the interests of his closest associates. The other consists of his *moral* preferences, defined as his *hypothetical* preferences that he *would* entertain if he forced himself to judge the world from a moral, i.e., from an impersonal and impartial, point of view. Mathematically, an individual's personal preferences are represented by his *utility function*, whereas, his moral preferences are represented by his *social welfare function*. (Harsanyi 1976, ix)

Thus the definition of a moral norm that will be utilized throughout this work is: a behavioral prescription that is universal in the claims it makes and that involves a consideration of the effects of the actor's action on others, not from the point of view of the actor's own interests, but from the point of view of the others' interests. (McElroy 1992, 31)

We do not call anything [morally] wrong unless we mean to imply that a person ought to be punished in some way or not for doing it—if not by law, by the opinion of his fellow creatures; if not by opinion, by the reproaches of his own conscience. . . . To recapitulate: the idea of justice supposes two things—a rule of conduct and a sentiment which sanctions the rule. (Mill 1979, 47, 51)

[A] theory of justice is . . . a theory of the moral sentiments setting out the principles governing our moral powers, or more specifically our sense of justice (50–51). Together with the veil of ignorance, these conditions [on the equality of human beings as moral persons] define the principles of justice as those which rational persons concerned to advance their interests would consent to as equals when none are known to be advantaged or disadvantaged by social and natural contingencies. (Rawls 1971, 19)

*The principle of co-operation.* Let $R$ be any strategy that could be chosen
in a game that is played repeatedly in some community. Let this strategy be
such that if any individual follows $R$, it is in his interest that his opponents
should do so too. Then each individual has a moral obligation to follow $R$,
provided that everyone else does the same. (Sugden 1986, 172)

[W]e have been using the phrase "the justice motive" to denote the drive *to
secure legitimate entitlements* or *to discharge the obligations attendant to the
entitlements of others*. Thus a theory of justice is "that part of the theory of
morality that deals with the legitimate structure of institutions," ' where by
"institutions" we mean the principles, rules, norms, practices, and procedures
that define entitlements and specify certain obligations. An entitlement, like
a promise, presupposes the existence of an institutional substructure to give
it meaning and moral authority. (Welch 1993, 197)

Obviously this is neither a random nor representative sample. Given my interest in norms and expected utility choice I have taken some prominent expected
utility theorists, such as Coleman, Gauthier, Harsanyi, and Sugden. Since this
book focuses on international relations I want to examine those who have focused
on moral values and international politics such as Beitz, McElroy, and Welch. Finally, I include some well-known philosophers such as Brandt, Hare, Mill, and
Rawls. I think these give a feel for the ways that morality and hence moral norms
have been conceptualized.

# Norms as Preferences

Analogous to the previous chapter on instrumental norms, in this chapter I pose the
question of how moral norms fit into individual decision making. Once again there
is no consensus among expected utility theorists on this issue. But one obvious
place to put moral rules is into preferences. Some actions, for example, altruistic
ones, are often considered moral because they are not self-interested, at least in a
crude sense of self-interest. More generally, actions which particularly benefit the
group, often at the expense of the individual, are characterized as moral. Morality
is thus a function of the beneficiary of the act. It may appear that I am trying to
sneak system level aspects in by the back door. I am not. From an individual
decision making point of view the difference between a moral and a nonmoral act
lies not at the society level of analysis but in the preferences at the individual level.

I think the interpretation of moral norm as preference fits most of the classic international relations literature on morality and foreign policy. The classic
realists—such as Morgenthau, Kennan, and Hoffman—did not focus on decision-
making models (most disliked expected utility research), it was the *substance* of
certain policies they objected to. This applies as well to those who have explored
morality and foreign policy from a more favorable position. Lumsdaine (1993)
looked at food aid to poor countries, McElroy (1992) examined decolonization,
food aid, and chemical/biological weapons. Human rights foreign policies have

been constantly attacked by realists as the history of the Carter and Reagan administrations illustrate. The list of substantive moral values also contains items such as democracy, abortion, slavery, environmental issues, and so forth.

Equally rational individuals can have different preference functions, since preferences, ends, goals lie outside expected utility choice. However, in international relations practice, most expected utility modelers assume preferences of a realist sort (though see O'Neill 2000). Much of the literature on ethics and foreign policy revolves around whether moral and ethical values actually play a role in government decisions (Welch 1993; Lumsdaine 1993).

Hence, we see one possible solution to the translation question posed in the last chapter. We saw that many game theorists translate "norm" as "equilibrium." Here we examine a less popular alternative whereby "(moral) norm" becomes "preference." This makes the best sense of morality as defined by objective or goal. When we speak of actions that benefit the community as typical or characteristic of moral actions then the obvious place to put such moral norms is into the preference function.

In the classical von Neumann and Morgenstern (1944; see also Savage 1972; for a more accessible discussion see Luce and Raiffa 1957) system of determining utility functions there is nothing that particularly excludes moral issues from consideration. The utility function is determined by the willingness to make trade-offs. What I am willing to pay for a can of tuna may be a function of how much I like tuna relative to swordfish, but it can also include how much I am willing to pay for tuna that is caught without killing dolphins. Or, I might be willing to pay more for batteries that do not contain mercury because of my environmental values. I chose the above examples because in some sense environmental values can be given a cost (usually represented in higher prices). In terms of economic theory this merely means an addition to the list of factors that determine the demand for goods; to the standard list of price, quality, appearance, etc., one adds environmental characteristics. In this sense moral values are similar to aesthetic ones. It seems completely reasonable to pay more for something if it is beautiful; in some cases aesthetic factors determine a large part of the price, e.g., clothing. In this way the moral dimension is not different from taste.

We have seen that preferences that concern the well-being of others are often taken as distinctive of morality. However, this does not appear to exhaust what we can observe, in an anthropological sense, as constituting morality. The above quotes are take from social scientists and philosophers. Once we move to anthropology and religion we see that the content of morality can invoke a bewildering array of objects and practices. A brief survey of Catholic and Protestant ethics shows that a large number of behaviors concerning only the individual or the couple are forbidden, say, suicide, masturbation, and birth control. Some religions have strong moral values about animals, e.g., Hinduism and Buddhism. Hence from an empirical—not normative—perspective, we must conclude with something close to a nominalist position: morality is whatever a group or individual decides it to be (This is Gilbert's position, see page 64 above). This has the practical value of obliging one to actually examine the content of morality and nonmorality. This is not a problem with fuzzy decision-making logic since we are concerned with the content of norms in any case, but it does require a major change in expected utility modeling practice in international relations.

Within an expected utility perspective it is certainly possible to examine the preference function of the actor. Nothing obliges us to accept the realist postulate of constant goals across space and time. It seems much more empirically well-grounded to assume that leaders are the product of their cultures, they cannot shed their skin when they move from domestic to foreign policy.

There is growing evidence that preferences in international affairs are not so isolated from opinions on domestic politics. For example, Hill (1993) has shown a—perhaps not surprising—congruence between opinions about race relations and civil rights of most members of the U.S. Congress with attitudes about policy toward South Africa. Much of U.S. foreign economic policy is based on the export of domestic models (Goldstein 1989). Zürn (1993) found that those countries with corporatist domestic political systems were also more likely to sign on to international institutions. Those that were the strongest supporters of the Cold War were also those who fought hardest against left-wing movements domestically. Even in the realist halcyon days of the nineteenth century one cannot begin to understand international relations without considering positions for and against democracy as a form of government. So instead of boring the reader with a discussion of whether all governments have the same (realist) goals and preferences, I note that this is empirically false. There is nothing in expected utility theory that requires such an assumption and nothing in the history of international relations justifies it either. This is not to say that all states do not value wealth, security, and power, but rather that they value them differently and that they value other things as well. One can safely say that almost all individuals desire wealth and security, but this does not get us very fair in the analysis of domestic politics, and it does not get us very far in international affairs as well.

The literature on the democratic peace provides the most dramatic, current illustration of an argument where domestic culture, politics, and institutions matter in world affairs. This example is particularly interesting here since the two "competing" explanations contrast norms with expected utility choice. The cultural, normative explanation represents the former, and the institutional, constraint position is the label for the latter (see Russett 1993 for a discussion).

Here is a perfect international relations example of the position that morality is expected utility decision making under constraints (Morgan and Campbell 1991; Siverson 1995). The institutional constraints argument takes the main decision maker as independent from the government and the country. She is then maximizing her own preferences, e.g., reelection, under the constraints of democratic institutions. In this sense the institutional theory does not belong in this chapter since it involves two levels of analysis, the individual leader and the institutional context within whose constraints and sanctions she operates, but this fits with a number of expected utility conceptualizations that see morality as constraint on self-interest maximization.

Since Bueno de Mesquita and Lalman (1992) are the most well-known proponents of the institutional explanation it is worth examining how they *translate* "democracy" in their game theoretic model. The last chapter argued that from a formal point of view the concept of a norm should be interpreted as a strategy. If one takes the constraint perspective the obvious place to put norms is into the payoffs. Behind constraint usually lies sanction: the purpose of sanctions is to reduce the payoff of a given action. Hence two decision makers with identical preferences acting within different constraint systems will have different payoffs for the same action. The difference in the payoffs arises from the different constraints. The morality perspective also places the moral value in preferences but directly. Hence we have two possible ways to get to the same set of payoffs: (1) constraints of democratic institutions change a leader's payoffs or (2) democratic leaders have different preferences to start with.

Bueno de Mesquita and Lalman (1992) provide us with an example where the democracy variable is placed exactly in the preference function. Unfortunately they are not very explicit about whether it is the constrained preferences or the different preferences that they use:

> In the context of this enquiry we mean by a norm of cooperation a generally agreed-upon set of values that restricts preferences over the outcomes of the domestic/constrained international interaction game such that negotiation is held to be a more desirable way to settle disputes than are alternative means of resolution. Two particular distinctions implied by this definition warrant further elaboration. First is that norms are not universally adhered to but rather are the commonly accepted values or behaviors in a community. In the Judeo–Christian world, for instance, the ten biblical commandments represent norms of . . . . Norms are of interest if they represent common—usually socially induced—restrictions on actions that otherwise would be unconstrained. They are akin to the notion that certain orderings of preferences are simply unacceptable bases for interactions between leaders of "civilized" states. (1992, 95–96)

Here we see the tension between norms as preferences and norms as constrained preferences. Bueno de Mesquita and Lalman use both the language of constraint and identity. When they say that certain orderings of preferences are "unacceptable bases for interactions of "civilized" countries" this suggests democracy as preferences of the individual, but they also use the language of preference restriction and constraint.

Another preference position says that democracies value each other differently from authoritarian states, full stop. Part of the putative special relationship between the United States and Great Britain involves them both having the same democratic culture. Owen (1994) makes this argument in explaining the democratic peace for the U.S. cases he examines. Of course much of what he examines as culture, such as public opinion, is exactly what the institutional position considers as restrictions or sanctions on the decision maker's preferences.

The point here is that both the cultural and institutional arguments are translating norms as preferences. The difference is that the constraint argument works indirectly via payoffs and is external to the decision maker, while the cultural position says the content of the norms themselves is expressed in preferences of the decision maker herself.

Hence another possible answer to the translation question is that norm is interpreted as preference. Implicit in a systems of norms is a preference function. The *expression* of the preference function is through a set of rules. This is true just as well for instrumental as for moral norms. In theory one could work backward from the norm system to a preference function. Loosely this is the idea behind "revealed preferences," by looking at the choices the rules dictate in given situations we learn what the preferences of the decision maker are.

Easton (1965) famously defined politics as "the allocation of value." From the individual and governmental point of view one can attempt to achieve (efficiently) different sets of goals. In expected utility decision-making preferences and goals remain exogenous. In principle they can contain almost anything, including the moral values discussed above. In practice, expected utility theorists tend to assume values of a realist sort and the same values for all players. Of course, this is an empirical question: the extent to which all governments have the same, and realist, set of preferences. Nothing in expected utility models (except actual practice) prevents one from including moral values in the goals to be achieved. In short, it seems that many moral norms or values fit most naturally as preferences in the expected utility decision-making framework.

The content of values, norms, and preferences appears repeatedly as characteristic of morality. Rawls requires norms to be those of a person behind the veil of ignorance; hence, an individual with a very curious preference structure. Beitz expresses the common view that moral action is distinguished from self-interest. Welch says that governments strive to achieve goals defined in terms of norms of justice. Unlike those who put morality outside the individual this places it directly at the individual decision-making level.

## Characteristics of Moral Norms

One theme that runs through many of the conceptualizations of morality given above is that moral codes apply to everyone. Hare expresses when he says "It is in their universality that value-judgments differ from desires. . . . If I want to do *A* in these circumstances, I am not committed to wanting anyone else placed in exactly or relevantly the same similar circumstances to do likewise. But if I think that

I ought to do *A* in these circumstances, I am committed to thinking that anyone else similarly placed ought to do the same" (Hare 1963, 71). McElroy in his study of morality and foreign policy requires that a moral norm is "a behavioral prescription that is *universal* in the claims it makes" (my emphasis). Sugden from an expected utility perspective states that an action is moral if it is in an individual's interest that others follow the same strategy, hence by extension everyone.[3]

That a moral norm applies to everyone seems a particularly modern and Western notion. In many societies duties, rights, and obligations are a function of class, birth, and sex. Nevertheless, moral norms concern large groups of people and organizations. Of course from an internal point of view universality can be a consideration. I can choose a norm because I think everyone should follow it: I might find Kant's arguments morally attractive.

This will be a central theme when we consider international institutions. An international institution by definition is a set of norms that all nations should and/or do follow. To adapt Rawls: they are norms which all rational, interested states do choose. However morality as norms that everyone should follow would also include a fair number of instrumental norms, just like the cases illustrated by coordination games. What seems more distinctive of moral norms is that according to the individual, institution, church, etc., everyone is supposed to follow them but not everyone wants to (they are not equilibrium strategies unless sanctions change the payoffs).

Sugden and others suggest that a norm applies not only to oneself but to everyone in the society (often independent of self-interest calculations). An individual not only follows the norm herself but thinks everyone should do likewise. Unlike some preferences, which are a matter of taste, moral norms are to be followed by all:

> You sometimes make a moral judgment that you later decide was mistaken. If your moral beliefs were simply feelings, it is not clear how they could be mistaken in this way. At one time you felt one way; now you feel another way. In what sense can you suppose that your first feeling was mistaken? Years ago you used to like sugar in your coffee; now you do not. But you would not say that you were mistaken to have once liked sugar. On the other hand, if you once thought that incest was wrong and now think it is right you do suppose you were mistaken before. How can change in moral belief be simply a change in your feelings? (Harman 1977, 37)

The same logic applies to others: some choices depend on individual taste, by definition outside parties let the individual choose. Such is not the case with acts governed by moral sentiments. The individual has chosen the moral norm for some reasons, *additionally* she thinks it is a norm that others should adopt (as well as herself in the future).

---

[3] Sugden is thinking of coordination and prisoners' dilemma situations when he defines morality as he does. There is a tendency to forget the games where the Nash equilibrium is asymmetric, such as chicken (Hawk-Dove for biologists), which Ullmann-Margalit (1977) finds typical of property norms. It is not clear that this game fits Sugden's "principle of cooperation."

If others should follow a norm then sanctions are appropriate if they do not. Another common feature of many of the definitions above is the notion of sanctions. These sanctions take two forms. J. S. Mill said that "Morality pertains to what is wrong or not wrong, and ... there ought to be a sanction against it." The sanction is an action applied by a third party, it is external to the agent. Brandt suggests that sanctions can come from within the individual: "to experience guilt-feelings when his action shows a deficiency." Guilt is not a concept that appears frequently in expected utility theory. Not only does an individual think everyone should follow the norm, but is willing to *enforce* it, either himself or through the agency of the state, church, or school.

External sanctions are just costs for an expected utility decision maker and cannot be distinguished from other costs of an action. Coleman, like Gauthier, quite explicitly states this: "Morality is constrained utility maximization." However, in the present context sanctions are exogenous to the individual, and thus there is nothing distinctively moral about them to the decision maker herself. These conceptualizations evade the issue of moral choice at the individual level, morality as chosen by people and not imposed from the outside.

That moral norms are to be followed by all which itself justifies sanctions will be a key aspect when we get to the relation between individual norms and system level ones. Behind the creation of international institutions lies the desire on the part of some countries that everyone follow a certain norm. Moving the other way, many governments acquire norms largely because those are the international ones. Often they do not choose these norms as much as the norms are imposed on them. In short, many aspects of morality and international institutions require an analysis of the relation between international- and state-level norms. States exist in an international society and that society influences which policies a government chooses to follow. But governments have policies that they choose relatively autonomously as the result of internal politics. It is these latter in terms of individuals that interest me in this chapter.

In short, two characteristics of moral norms seem important for the analysis of international affairs. The first involves the universal nature of moral norms. These norms are not a matter of taste but should be followed by all relevant others. The second characteristic is the willingness to sanction others who do not follow such norms. Hence, we come back to the fundamental fact that most norms are guides to action, moral norms do not differ in this regard. What distinguishes them is that actors want to impose these norms and think that others should adopt them.

## Identity Norms

Now I am going to tell you about a scorpion. This scorpion wanted to cross a river, so he asked the frog to carry him. "No," said the frog. "No, thank you. If I let you on my back you may sting me, and the sting of the scorpion is death." "Now, where," asked the scorpion, "is the logic of that?" (for scorpions always try to be logical). "If I sting you, you will die and I will drown." So the frog was convinced, and allowed the scorpion on his back. But just in the middle of the river he felt a terrible pain and realized that, after all, the scorpion *had* stung him. "Logic!" cried the dying frog as he started under, bearing the scorpion down with him "There is no logic in this!" "I know," said the scorpion, "but I can't help it—it's my character."

                —Orson Welles, in *Mr. Arkadin*[4]

In terms of identity the expected utility maximizing person is distinguished by two characteristics, the first is the expected utility way of decision making, the second, and much less discussed one, is the values she maximizes.[5] However, given that most expected utility theorists in international relations assume constant preferences over time as well as over space, this means that identity does not really come into play since all individuals are identical.

My analysis of international institutions as structures of norms focused on the concept of behavioral norms. This linked up with the concept of strategy, which is a guide to action. I also distinguished an ontological norm: this type of norm is like behavioral ones in that it has an if–then logical structure; what distinguishes it from behavioral norms is the major premise which contains the identity verb "to be." For example, if you pass a prescribed exam then you *are* a lawyer. This becomes part of the definition of you, which may have many social, political, and economic consequences. Identity from my perspective then is a structure of these two types of norms.

Ellickson's study (1991) of norms of conflict resolution among ranchers in California (generally outside official government structures) illustrates how behavior and conflict management work in terms of norm structures and identity. Ellickson's description of the behavior of ranchers often comes back to the basic norms that govern relations between them, which rest on the identity and values of a rancher. One conflict resolution norm involves the nonuse of courts to deal with problems between ranchers. Ranchers define many of their relations based on the overall norm of good neighborliness. One definition of a good neighbor involves *not* using legal means to resolve disputes: " 'being good neighbors means no lawsuits,' said one rancher; when asked why they did not pursue meritorious legal actions, they would often respond by remarks like 'I'm not that sort of guy' " (Ellickson 1991, 60–61). Like Orson Welles's scorpion they may do harm

---

[4]Peter Bogdanovich: What is the origin of the fable of the scorpion and the frog?
Orson Welles: Who knows? I heard it from an Arab.
Peter Bogdanovich: It relates to a lot of your films besides *Mr. Arkadin*—*Othello*, for example. Do you believe the world is divided between frogs and scorpions?
Orson Welles: No, there's a lot of other animals.

[5]The third characteristic would be her beliefs about the world. Sometimes these are assumed to randomly vary around the "correct value" as in the rational expectations literature, sometimes they gradually adapt to the correct value as in the adaptive expectations literature, or sometimes learning follows Bayes rule. All these have in common that they get quickly to the right value or center on the right value.

to themselves (not chose an optimal legal strategy) because they are not "that sort of guy."[6]

Realists claim that states should follow self-interest. One obvious, and correct, poststructuralist move is to ask: who is the self? what/who defines its interests? I suggest that realism is just one kind of identity politics. What after all is an identity? It is a definition of self and its interests. Here we see a variation on the ontological question: we ask about the constitution of the self and its interests.[7]

According to Bueno de Mesquita and Lalman (1992) a democracy is an expected utility decision-making entity but with a different set of preferences. Of course whether this is a good way to characterize a democracy is an open question. If we take the example of a business firm, we can say that these organizations are defined in terms of profit maximization (at least as a reasonable first approximation); that is what a business *is*. However, it is much more natural to speak of identity in terms of norms, both behavioral and ontological. What is a Quaker? In addition to constitutive rules, being a Quaker also means using a large number of behavioral norms that define what such a person does, or does not do, such as serving in the military.

Implicit in all norm sets are values and preferences. Democracy is not just a decision-making procedure, that procedure implies values like freedom of speech, press, protest, individual choice, etc. Realists like Kennan have tried to deny the character of democracy by saying that foreign policy requires secrecy and authoritarian decision-making procedures. They see democracy being a self-destructive identity, like the scorpion's dealings with the frog. I suggest that all politics are identity politics. Once we examine the nature of the self and its interests this reversal makes much sense.

Individuals and states are often defined in terms of norms and policies. If security is defined as protection of "self," then the propagation of like selves may very well be an important part of security. Certainly Kissinger's hero Metternich understood this quite clearly, and it was a cornerstone of his foreign policy.[8]

Knowing Kissinger is a realist allows us to predict much of his behavior. As Walker illustrated (1977), Kissinger can be modeled as a structure of rules of behavior. Leng (1983) provides another version of the realist identity in the form of rules and belief systems. Realist norms come as part of an identity package. Because we know many of the norms that constitute that identity—both in terms

---

[6]Another very interesting aspect of this study is that ranchers have quite erroneous beliefs about law, for example rules about legal liability for cows, that connect very closely to their value systems.

[7]In the same light as the above footnotes we can ask about realist beliefs about the world, particularly in terms of what would be an effective foreign policy. It is quite clear that realists believe strongly in force as an effective tool of foreign policy, one need but examine those who support nuclear proliferation such as Mearsheimer (1993) to see this. What is not clear is whether this is the best strategy for assuring the physical security of a country.

[8]To use a different self-interest model, states decide based on kin-selection. A democracy feels safer in a world of democracies than in a world of dictatorships. It is rationally self-interested in the biological sense to help those with the same genes survive.

of strategies and preferences—we can predict and model behavior. From an anthropological point of view realism is just another identity construct.

## Moral and Instrumental Norms

I have argued that moral and instrumental norms can coexist within a policy decision-making structure. Norm choice can respond to different interests, more fundamentally they can express the basic identity of the individual or institution. Much of the literature on morality tries to separate moral acts from other kinds. At the individual level one separates self-interest from morality (e.g., Beitz). Another common practice is to move morality outside the individual to the group, as we have seen with constraint and sanction conceptualizations. Elster tries to make norms a different kind of decision-making procedure when he claims normative decision making is not "outcome oriented" (1990, 863). This obviously contradicts the feeling that altruism is a moral action, since altruism is by definition outcome oriented.

I suggest that all individuals and institutions are a combination of instrumental and moral norms. A good empirical decision making theory must take this into account. Much of the next chapter on structures of norms deals with the implications of this for decision making. The previous chapter showed that decision making with norms can promote self-interest, however defined. There I followed traditional practice by keeping goals and preferences as exogenous. However, once we consider moral and identity norms the barrier separating means and ends begins to break down. By treating moral norms as preferences the barrier remains in place, but once one begins to see the "self" in terms of norms it becomes difficult to separate the two.

Kant argued that if the honesty of the shopkeeper resulted from calculations of interest the resulting action was not a moral one. In contrast, equilibria can arise from self-interested motives. For example, Axelrod showed that cooperation in repeated prisoners' dilemma can be self-interest maximizing. Sudgen suggested that equilibria *then* become morality. However, it may be the case that the history of the process is the reverse. A well-known example of this is the relations between capitalism and protestantism. It may be that the shopkeeper is honest for good Calvinist reasons, and a positive, but incidental, side-effect of this is to increase his trade. Given a choice the consumer makes a better choice by going to the Calvinist shopkeeper (Frank [1985, 1988]) has made this argument in economic terms). If the shopkeeper is honest for only instrumental reasons one can expect her to cheat if the chances of detection are small. The Calvinist shopkeeper as part of his identity does not cheat, in public or private. Here the scorpion's identity creates positive reputation effects that an expected utility realist can never achieve.

The WTO norms provide a transitional example. One plausible argument is that free trade corresponds to *both* instrumental and justice concerns. They are efficient and fair. We can call these rules the "good and good for you" norms. Before choosing a norm one can reflect on a variety of issues, morality, wealth, security, etc., the choice may be some compromise between these considerations. This seems to be the case at the level of government policy as well. Policy often is the result of the struggle of different interests. If we look at environmental policy (domestic and international) we can see "self-interest" in terms of economic interests and "moral values" in terms of environmental lobbies. The end result may a hybrid norm. Welch (1993) makes this basic argument with regard to war, security concerns play a role but so does the "justice motive." If we think of morality as involving ultimate values then these may be worth fight'en for.

If we examine the U.S. trade policy of reciprocity (Keohane 1986) it is not clear that it was only adopted because of its effectiveness as a payoff maximizing strategy. It seems there was a concern for equal trade gains. In contrast to the realist who argues that states refuse unequal deals because of concerns with relative gains in a survival sense, I think the actual history of U.S. trade shows a much clearer normative concern for a *fair* distribution of the benefits of trade. Particularly in the pre–World War II period, there was no sense in which the U.S. economy was threatened in any significant way by foreign trade, at least in high technology and advanced industries. One can find this even in account's like Mastunduno's (1991) that try to argue the realist position. The international relations literature on reciprocity has ignored that this strategy has attractive moral characteristics (Becker 1986). This may be a case more like the Calvinist shopkeeper than a Smithian one.

Realists tend to claim that morality is a cloak for other interests. There may be the appearance of several motivations but the realist interests are the "real" ones. For example, one might concede that when Truman announced his Point Four project of aid to the Third World his main motivation was the conduct of the emerging Cold War with the USSR. From a moral point of view, doing the right thing for the wrong reason.

However, the evolution of the institution that started for realist reasons cannot be explained by realist principles. Lumsdaine's account of the evolution of foreign aid shows that many self-interest norms were replaced by moral ones. Here is an exemplary case where identity politics matters, welfare states domestically (e.g., Scandinavia) are also much more likely to be welfare states internationally. Knowing the identity of the government is a pretty good predictor of foreign aid policy. The same principle works in reverse, if one knows the foreign policy norms of a decision maker one has a good idea about how he will attack domestic problems. Internationally realists try to obtain security with military force, not surprisingly they choose the same basic strategy domestically in the form of increased police forces and prison sanctions. Identity politics works both ways.

Realists claim that morality is a cloak for self-interest, but the two may be completely intertwined. Human rights provides another example of something which is typically seen as a nonrealist foreign policy. However, if one examines the history of European human rights conventions after World War II, one reason for their adoption by states was basic security! One conclusion drawn from the experience of World War II was that Nazism and Fascism might have been prevented by protecting human rights (Sikkink 1993). The explanation of the Human Rights Convention can rest on completely realist grounds of national security. In the 1990s this argument resurged in the form of the democratic peace; if it is true that democracies do not fight each other then the encouragement of democracy is a part of security policy.[9]

In short, many norms—and a fortiori most institutions—cannot be classified as pure types; they are hybrids reflecting combinations of values and interests (and beliefs). From an expected utility point of view this means one must begin to consider that individuals and governments have different preferences. From a decision-making with norms point of view it is easier since moral and instrumental rules have the same logical structure.

# Conclusion

If many define rationality in terms of expected utility decision making, then many define morality in terms of rules and norms. Moral norms are for many what norms are. Many people, both culturally and philosophically, conceive of and talk about morality in terms of rules and norms. The trick is to see norms as a *contentless* logical structure. Into this structure we can put content that we describe as moral or instrumental (or both). In this sense it is like preferences in expected utility choice into which can be put whatever one likes.

Within the expected utility literature a prominent tendency is to place morality outside the individual at the social level. This often takes the form of expected utility maximization under constraints, where sanctions may be considered as one form of constraint. The second option is to place morals in preferences, often preferences that concern the well-being of others. This second option is consistent with a methodological individualist position: the first is not. It draws upon the idea that morality concerns ultimate values which determine, at least in part, the utilities to be maximized.

Nothing in general expected utility theory requires a particular content for preferences: preferences are exogenous hence not within the realm of the theory. In international relations it is common to conjoin expected utility decision-making procedure with a realist view of preferences. Often this is more assumed than argued. Even rarer is empirical evaluation.

I have suggested that certain issues are defined by actors as moral ones, while others are not. This is true of realists above all. The normative advice that morality should have no role in foreign policy requires quite baldly that governments

---

[9]I have suggested that beliefs about the world are just as much a part of identity as values. The democratic peace illustrates this perfectly.

should have certain sorts of preferences and not others, and should act according to some rules but not others. Traditionally, issues of national security—and eventually national survival—are thought not to invoke moral claims. Welch (1993) claimed that even in these "extreme" cases the justice motive can play an important role, if the leader has defined the issues in terms of principles of justice. While Welch took on a tough case, there are a variety of other less vital issues—where international institutions are likely to arise—where state behavior cannot be understood without recourse to moral values. In democracies this occurs because voters have not internalized the precepts of realism. As Bismarck said "Public opinion is only too ready to consider political relations [between governments] and events in the light of those of civil law and private persons generally . . . [This] shows a complete lack of understanding of political matters" (cited in Schweller 1992, 248). Voters often think governments should act in order to promote moral values they hold. With elections always around the corner, elected officials must be attentive to such demands.[10]

Implicitly or explicitly much of the literature on ethics assumes a certain content to moral norms. Anthropological evidence forces me to conclude that virtually anything can be considered "moral." In terms of content I think one must take a nominalist position: morality is what a culture defines as moral, the point that Nietzsche made in an epigraph to this chapter.

Using norms as the basic decision-making framework helps makes sense of the notion of identity politics. Behavioral and ontological rules define identity. The identity of a country as a democracy is based on decision-making rules. At the same time those rules imply certain values; democracy as a decision-making system is not independent of culture and values. Hoffmann (1968) complains about "American exceptionalism" and its impact on United States foreign policy, but the United States *was* a big exception in the eighteenth century and early nineteenth century. When the identity of a country is bound up with the contrast between systems of government, and the contrast with other nondemocracies, starting with Great Britain, the United States was unable to slip out of its identity to conduct foreign affairs differently. But, of course, identities have played a central role in European international politics, be it Protestants versus Catholics, monarchy versus democracy, or communist versus capitalist; the character of the state has been at the root of much of international war over the last four hundred years.

Given that morality usually concerns important values—from the internal perspective of the decision maker—we have seen that preferences provide a natural place to put these values in the expected utility model. That this is not an easy fit is shown by the frequency with which expected utility-influenced philosophers

---

[10]Morgenthau writes that preventive war is "abhorrent to democratic public opinion" and states: "It is especially in the refusal to consider seriously the possibility of preventive war, regardless of its expediency in view of the national interest, that the moral condemnation comes, it must come as a natural catastrophe or as the evil deed of another nation, not as a forseen and planned culmination of one's own foreign policy. Only thus might the moral scruples, rising from the violated moral norm that there ought to be no war at all, be stilled, if they can be stilled at all" (cited in Schweller 1992, 246).

and social scientists locate morality *outside* the individual, in the form of constraints or sanctions. This move is all the more curious in that one would expect methodological individualists to start with individual morality before moving to group level analysis.

I suspect that the reluctance to deal with moral values as an endogenous part of expected utility choice lies in the unwillingness to examine the content of preferences. In contrast, looking at moral norms as policies focuses on the content of the norms. Be they instrumental or moral norms a foreign policy decision-making model requires one to express the substance of norms in a series of if–then rules. If asked *why* a particular norm was chosen then the decision maker can give a moral justification for it (or an instrumental one).

This fits naturally with the nominalist position on morality. It is individual decision makers that define what is moral for them. In essence, I suggest that this is a methodological individualist position, because it endogenizes morality at the individual level. It certainly permits norms that benefit others, society, animals or the ecosphere.

I have concluded that in many regards morality—particularly as it is thought about in international relations—involves different preferences and goals. But moral norms also have differences that separate them from preferences or matters of taste. I argued that people generally want to impose moral norms and behavior on others, and as part of that they are willing to impose sanctions on norm violations.

Many philosophers have emphasized that morality invokes universal prescriptions. If one subscribes to a moral norm then one is committed to that behavior for the indefinite future (and regrets past actions which do not conform, see Landman 1993). This characteristic of moral norms holds for institutions as well, since they are policies which many governments should apply and usually do for long periods of time.

Many institutions involve basic values—free/fair trade, human rights, the environment, and democracy —that powerful actors believe all governments, firms, and individuals should follow. I think that we cannot understand international institutions without examining the moral values that underlie them.

ﻪ

A set of (moral) norms always contains implicitly a set of preferences or goals. This poses no real mystery. Take the WTO norms, we can examine who benefits, the goals, and the reasons for choosing such norms. Once the rules described, we can ask to what extent they incorporate what we might call moral values. If we examine the language of WTO and the discussion of its rules, they certainly employ moral concepts, such as "fair" trade, "level playing field," reciprocity, etc. The content of some of these norms as well may express moral values, such as exceptions made for poor countries.

Of course, I call such language and content moral because it expresses Western ethical values, the culture of those countries that created GATT. We can locate these values in a historical-spatial context. By historicizing these norms we also say that they change. An examination of the evolution of WTO rules makes it clear that they change over time. Within fuzzy logic modeling there is no problem with rules changing, new ones being added, or some being eliminated. Modeling individual decision making and, more importantly, international institutions requires techniques that allow for changes in the content of norms.

Another major advantage of fuzzy logic models in dealing with moral norms is that these are often expressed in syllogistic terms. Instead of making an awkward translation of norms into preferences one just can take the syllogistic expression as is. For example, we have seen that some norms are obligations, they prescribe behavior in certain conditions. If we take Coleman's position that morality is expected utility maximization under constraint, one must translate formally the obligation into a constraint. An obligation is equivalent to a constraint forbidding *all* other actions. Expected utility maximization is easy in this case. Obviously the dominant conceptualization of morality for Coleman is a prohibition which still leaves a range of behavior in which to maximize expected utility.

We have seen that norms come in three forms, (1) prescriptions, (2) prohibitions, and (3) permissions. Morality as constraint picks the second option, that morality forbids actions. Not only is it difficult to speak of obligation in expected utility language but the crucial ethical notion of *rights* is difficult to translate as well. Most rights are permissions: they neither oblige nor proscribe. The history of democracy contain many examples of prohibitions which are changed into permissions, including most "freedoms." Going back to WTO, free trade is a permission norm in that it does not require states to trade, it permits them to. We can define permission with the primitive of constraint but it is not an intuitive operation. This is not what Gauthier and Coleman had in mind when they defined morality as constraint.

Herbert Simon emphasizes that goals and constraints are interchangeable and fungible things:

> In the decision-making situations of real life, a course of action, to be acceptable, must satisfy a whole set of requirements, or constraints. Sometimes one of these requirements, or constraints, is singled out and referred to as the goal of the action. But the choice of one constraint from many is to a large extent arbitrary. For many purposes it is more meaningful to refer to the whole set of requirements as the (complex) goal of the action. This conclusion applies both to individual and organizational decision-making. (1997, 155)

This is exactly what I shall argue for in the next chapter when I consider the classic case of the rules of war and the concern for national security. One can see the rules of war as a constraint, but equivalently they can be another goal in the conduct of war.

Cognitively I think the underlying tension arises from the translation problem. As a matter of culture and psychology, it is easy to think of morality in terms of rules, e.g., Golden Rule. If one wants to use expected utility methodology to model choice these norms must be translated into expected utility concepts. One strategy is to locate morality outside the individual, as sanctions, constraints, or group level benefits; but this does not resolve the problem at the individual level. I argued in the previous chapter that one advantage of fuzzy modeling is that it starts much closer to the cognitive operations of people. This is not only true in its modeling of fuzzy concepts in natural language but also for the "logic" of morality, which is much closer to the logic of these models.

The fuzzy logic methodology I introduced in the last chapter thus works just as well for moral norms as for instrumental ones, in fact probably even better given that moral norms are often expressed in syllogistic forms. Moral norms per se pose no problem. There is no need to place moral norms outside of the individual, they coexist with instrumental norms in the total norm structure.

The conclusion of the last two chapters is that one can choose a policy or norm for instrumental and/or moral reasons. Hence, when an individual or a government has multiple policies the question of structure arises. We have a valuable parallel with international institutions, which I defined as structures of norms. Not only does the content of individual norms matter but how they interact with each other influences the final decision. A question that often pops up quickly is what to do when two norms apply and give different recommendations. This is a common problem within legal systems and the tendency is to treat the problem in legalistic terms, but once again I will return to fuzzy decision-making models for a different perspective on the problem.

# Chapter 6

# Structures of Norms

## L'addition

LE CLIENT. Garçon. l'addition!

LE GARÇON. Voila. [*il sort son crayon et note.*] Vouz avez ... deux œufs durs, un veau, un petit pois, une asperge, un fromage avec beurre, une amande verte, un café filtre, un téléphone.

LE CLIENT. .. et puis des cigarettes!

LE GARÇON. [*il commence à composer.*] C'est ça même ... des cigarettes ... Alors ça fait ...

LE CLIENT. N'insistez pas, mon ami, c'est inutile, vous ne réussirez jamais.

LE GARÇON. !!!

LE CLIENT. On ne vous a donc pas appris à l'école que c'est ma-thé-ma-ti-que-ment impossible d'additioner les choses d'espèce différente!

LE GARÇON. !!!

LE CLIENT. Enfin, tout de même, de qui se moque-t-on? ... Il faut réellement être insensé pour oser volumeer de tenter d'additionner un veau avec des cigarettes avec un café filtre, avec une amande verte et des œufs durs avec des petit pois, des petits pois avec un téléphone. Pourquoi pas un petit pois avec un grand officier de la Légion d'Honneur, pendant que vous y êtes! [*il se lève*] Non, mon ami, croyez-moi, n'insistez pas, et vous fatiguer pas, ça ne donnerait rien, vous entendez, rien ... pas même le pourboire.

[*Et il sort en emportant le rond de serviette à titre gracieux*]

—*Jacques Prévert*[1]

---

[1] The check

THE CLIENT. Waiter, the check!
THE WAITER. Here it is. [*He takes out his notepad.*] You had ... two hard-boiled eggs, a pea, one asparagus, cheese with butter, a green almond, a coffee, and a telephone call.
THE CLIENT ... and cigarettes!
THE WAITER. [*He begins to add.*] That's right. That makes ...
THE CLIENT. Do not even try, it is useless, you will never succeed.

"Le client" in Prévert's sketch poses the problem of how one can combine different things, telephone calls, hard-boiled eggs, and the unlike into a final account—"l'addition." The same problem arises with norms and rules: how does one put them all together into a coherent and consistent decision making system? This question comes up immediately since the possibility of conflicting norms seems real. In any plausible situation multiple norms apply, decision making with norms implies a system for dealing with this usual case.

In chapter 2 I defined an institution as a structure of norms. A hierarchy of norms, principles, rules, and decision-making procedures forms the nucleas of the Krasner definition of a regime. These all interlock in some fashion to form an institution. A principle thesis of my treatment of institutions has been that the concept of a norm is core: norms, rules, principles, and decision-making procedures all have the same logical if–then structure. With this basic insight in hand it is now possible to examine structures of norms.

"Structures" is important as opposed to the "sets" of the Krasner definition because it forces one to consider how norms interact with each other, and to try to understand how there can be multiple normative structures just as there can be different architectural ones. "Sets" suggests a nonordered collection; "structure" means relations between elements. Kegley and Raymond make this clear when they define a "normative order" as a "set of linked rules": "An international normative order is not simply a collection of discrete elements. Its rules are patterned and interrelated, although their linkages may vary in strength and they do not evolve monotonically in the same direction" (1990, 14). Hence the question arises about the ways norms can be organized, since in most choice situations there are a number of relevant rules that must be weighed and balanced before reaching a final decision.

In the institution literature one often reads of strong or weak institutions, usually this refers to some notion of behavioral conformity. However, institutions can be strong or weak from a structural point of view as well. A structural analysis of an institution includes how norms and rules interact. For example, an institution can elicit complete behavioral compliance, but at the same time multiple loopholes—which are themselves rules—take out all the bite of the principal

---

THE WAITER. !!!

THE CLIENT. Didn't they teach you in school that it is ma-the-ma-ti-cal-ly impossible to add things of different types!

THE WAITER. !!!

THE CLIENT. Who are you kidding? . . . You have to be crazy to try to add veal with cigarettes with a coffee with a green almond with hard-boiled eggs with a telephone call. Why not an officer of the Légion d'Honneur while you are at it. [*He gets up.*] No, do not insist, you will wear yourself out for nothing, . . . not even a tip.

[*He exits taking with him the napkin ring.*]

*Jacques Prévert*

norms. Institutions can be weak in various ways: because they contain contradictory norms, because they contain exceptions, because they do not cover all relevant situations. Structural analysis can help explain why some institutions have a strong impact while others have little influence.

Methodologically and theoretically we tread on new ground here. Institution analyses rarely—except in international law— include a clear formulation of the norms of the system, consequently it is even rarer to find a structural dissection of an institution. A complete description of an institution includes its norms *and* the links between them. Without understanding that multiple norms apply and what happens in this common case the links between institution and behavior will remain hazy.

A central facet of structural analysis focuses on the consistency and coherency of decision-making procedures. We often demand of governments that they have a coherent foreign policy, that they act noncapriciously and predictably over time and space. These demands come with more force in international relations. It means that a government must coordinate its policies. Each individual decision must be made with an understanding of the larger policy framework that it must exist in.

The structural issues in terms of individual decision making with norms and international institutions are often basically the same. To see this one can take the extreme example of a government that completely integrates an international institution into its policy framework. The requirement of coherence is perhaps even stronger at the state level than the international one, since the impact of incoherent norms can be direct and negative on the government.

Coherence concerns do not distinguish decision making with norms, they arise in all choice procedures. Expected utility decision making requires—and usually assumes—a consistent set of preferences. If Prévert's client had read his von Neumann and Morgenstern (1944) he would have known that one can ma-thé-ma-ti-que-ment combine peas with the Legion of Honor: how many peas would one trade for a Legion of Honor?[2] A consistent utility function results from answering these questions in a fashion that conserves the transitivity of preferences.

The expected utility analogue of conflicting norms is multiple goals and preferences. Most individuals and governments have many things they value. For example, Stafford Crips, the British representative to the International Trade Organization negotiations, argued that the objectives of the ITO—for the British at least—were to "achieve an agreement as to the manner in which the nations can cooperate for the promotion of the highest level of employment and the maintenance of demand and can bring some degree of regulation into world trade and commerce" (cited in Gardner 1969, 271). Likewise, the rules of the nuclear nonproliferation treaty serve to reduce the risk of nuclear war *and* maintain U.S. hegemony. Generally, different rules and norms reflect different goals. Most people

---

[2]More accurately, it is calculated via gambles that make the expected value of the payoff equal for the two goods.

desire security, wealth, freedom, and morality but what varies dramatically are the trade-offs they are willing to make between them.

Chapter 4 established the equivalence between norm and strategy through an analysis of their common logical form. Using this basic insight we can define a complete strategy as a structure of norms. The equation "institution = structure of norms = strategy" sheds an interesting light on the analysis of norm structures. For example, a strategy provides a choice in all possible situations, a structural investigation of an institution poses the completeness question of an institution: are there relevant situations not covered by institution rules? This relates to the coverage of the minor premises of institution norms.[3]

A natural tendency is to address issues of international norms in a legalistic fashion. Given the strong historical ties of international relations to international law this appears quite normal. However, in terms of decision making I think this does not prove useful. That several laws might apply to a given situation is a *problem* in jurisprudence. If we think of this rather in terms of expert systems and decision making then it becomes a *good thing*. The fundamental problem in law is adjudication, while here the fundamental problem is making choices. Instead of deciding who's right or which law applies, we want to make the best possible decision. We do not adjudicate *between* norms but *use* them to make a final choice.

To put the distinction crudely, the legal reflex is to prioritize and choose one norm or the other; fuzzy logic suggests that some sort of averaging is more appropriate. This chapter argues that this is more realistic in terms of empirical decision making, and in fact better in terms of optimal choice strategies. Fuzzy logic decision making provides a means to think about how several norms apply in any given case and how one can combine them to arrive at a decision.

This capacity will prove crucial in chapter 8 where I consider level of analysis issues. The same sort of problem arises between levels of analysis either within organizations—the principle–agent problem—or between government policy and international institutions. What happens when government policy and international norm both apply but give different recommendations? Formally, we have conflicting norms, only the origin of each differs. Once we have the technology to combine norms at the individual level we can extend and modify these techniques to norms which come from different sources, but which apply to a given decision.

With this chapter I complete my outline of decision making with norms at the individual level. It also brings me back full circle to the central topic of chapter 2, where I defined an institution as a structure of norms. We shall be able to begin the rest of the volume with two fundamental components of an institution theory: (1) the logical structure of an international institution, and (2) decision making at the individual level with norms and policies. We have seen that formally and logically norms of international institutions do not differ from individual level norms. On the structural dimension many similarities exist as well. Nevertheless the central

---

[3] In the literature on jurisprudence a classic debate revolves around the completeness of legal systems, see, e.g., Kelsen (1967), Alchourròn and Bulygin (1971).

focus remains on individual decision making, I discuss international institutions whenever it seems appropriate, which serves to emphasize the real similarities between the two.

Crucial to individual decision making as well as a multilevel theory of norms is a model of how norms interact to arrive at a final decision. I continually return to this in different guises throughout this chapter.

## The Fundamental Problem: Conflicting Norms

Much of structural analysis revolves around the problem of conflicting or contradictory norms. With our logical tools we can clearly formulate the problem—the first step toward a solution.

An adequate description of any concrete choice opportunity utilizes multiple dimensions. The "facts" of the case imply the applicability of different rules and norms. A U.S. government decision about food aid involves not only the principles of the food aid institution but also trade norms and principles. What's worse, not only within institutions but also between institutions several norms usually apply.

Generally a description of a choice occasion, $D$, includes multiple dimensions, $D = (d_1, d_2, d_3, \dots)$. The description $D$ of the situation invokes a set of norms, $N$, consisting of all rules with some combination of $d_i$ in the minor premise, e.g., $N_i = $ if $d_1$ and $d_3$ then $Y_i$. There is no reason to assume that all of these norms, $N_i$, suggest the same course of action $Y_1$. In fact, we should assume in general that the $N_i$ propose different actions $Y_i$.

Here we have a clear definition of what it means to have "conflicting norms." A description of the situation invokes a set of applicable norms. If some, at least one, of these norms have a different suggested course of action then we have conflicting norms.

Thus as a general state of affairs we *almost always* have conflicting norms. However, this does not merit the adjective "contradictory" norms. To use the example of chapter 3 $N_1$ might propose "severe sanctions" where $N_2$ suggests only "symbolic sanctions." $N_1$ and $N_2$ do not agree, but they do not go so far as to contradict each other. Part of the problem lies in the fact "contradictory" connotes a dichotomous variable; really it is a continuous one, from no contradiction to complete contradiction. In summary, we can give a satisfactory definition of conflicting norms, while the notion of contradictory norms proves problematic. Fundamentally contradictory means "very conflictual," hence we can use it, understanding this to be its meaning.

Two general techniques exist for resolving this decision problem. The first is to fiddle with the norms $N$ so that all give the same advice $Y_1$. The second lies in somehow combining all the different advice, $Y_i, Y_j, \dots$ in order to give a final decision, $Y_f$.

Most of the time the first option is just not feasible. Many of the norms that apply are general and of long-standing. Tinkering with them for just one decision usually does not make any sense. One must consider the larger ramifications of such fiddling. It might produce a good decision in the current case but provide bad advice in many future ones. Since norms have links between themselves tinkering must consider how these links get affected as well. Finally, such fiddling can be a time-consuming and hence expensive operation. Of course, when considering institution creation or modification norms need to be changed, eliminated, or added. However, most of the time (foreign) policy needs to be carried out efficiently. If one fiddled with norms each time one could not run an organization effectively, not to mention the value placed on a consistent foreign policy.

The first option fiddles with norms, the second possibility accepts the norms as given with their conflicting $Y_i$ values. In fact, instead of seeing this a problem, fuzzy logic decision making takes this as generally positive! The different norms often represent different aspects of the choice, each of which is worth taking into account, either in terms of different valued goals or different aspects of the means of attaining goals. A good final decision considers the advice of each $N_i$ in coming up with a final choice.

Hence, what we need is a method—a function in mathematical terms—that combines the different $Y_i$ to produce a final decision, that is, we need a $f(\mathbf{N}) = Y_f$.

## Fiddling with Norms: Exceptions

One central structural operation with norms consists in making exceptions to general rules. One way to remove conflicts between norms is to say that norm $N$ applies except in situations $\mathbf{E}$. Making exceptions is a form of prioritization, but such a common one that it deserves special discussion.

I entitled this subsection "fiddling with norms" and that is what making exceptions does. It does not weight the norms, in which case the content of the norm does not change, it changes the actual content of the norm itself. Formally an exception is both a rule and a change in the minor premise of other rules. For example, take $N_1 = $ if $d_1$ and $d_3$ then $Y_1$, if we want to make an exception in situation $e_1$ then we change the minor premise of $N_1$ to read: if $d_1$ and $d_3$ and not $e_1$. One then adds the exception rule $E_1 = $ if $d_1$ and $d_3$ and $e_1$ then $Y_e$. It is useful to keep the general category of exception because it reflects common sense of what is central in an institution and what represents modifications from a more pure institution structure.

Institutions and norm structures in general often have several core principles of great generality. However, these principles are so broad that they may not work well in all situations. Or there may exist general subcases which are usually dealt with by exception rules. It is important not to take exception rules always as a negative operation. Often they contribute to strengthening and improving the norm structure. Of course, they can contribute to weakening the structure as well, but a priori neither is true. Exception rules can be used for good or bad. A principle of institution analysis consists in examining closely the exception in order to see if it strengthens or weakens an institution.

Exception rules have a number of characteristics that distinguish them. First, exceptions are class-based. Modern legal systems do not generally allow individual, explicitly named cases as exceptions. This kind of exception strikes the modern Western person, at least, as unfair. Nothing in the logical structure of norms prevents a law from excepting Jane Doe from paying taxes. When this sort of thing does occur it almost always results from power-based exceptions (see below). Most modern legal systems have metaprinciples such as equal treatment under the law which prohibit these kinds of exceptions. For example, the Administrative Procedures Act 1947 "is designed to provide . . . fairness in administrative operation" and to asure . . . the effectuation of the declared policies of Congress" (cited in McCubbins et al. 1987, 256).

A second characteristic is that exceptions often cut *across* institutions or subject areas. Retirees and minors consistently get special treatment in various aspects of domestic law. In international institutions, special classes also exist, notably poor countries. When new institutions are considered one can expect that these exceptions will be carried over into the new institution, with appropriate modifications depending on the function of the institution.

These widespread exception rules illustrate what I call principle-based exceptions. Special treatment of minors is not arbitrary or based on their power as an interest group. We have good instrumental and moral reasons to treat these groups differently. These norms can be seen as strengthening the institution, making it work better than an institution without such principles. We have an acceptable answer to the question "why except old people?" but not a good one to the question "why except Jane Doe?" By definition principle-based exceptions deal with classes since they use a principle to formulate the exception rule.

In contrast to principle-based exceptions we have power-based ones. Here the answer to the "why except" question lies in the power of the group in question. While I focus on international institutions, power-based exceptions are easily found in domestic politics. For example, the state of Florida has something like a value-added tax. If one examines the exceptions to this tax, they easy fall into either the principle-based or power-based categories. Exceptions made for horse feed, barber shops, and the like result from the exercise of power and influence by lobbies. Exceptions made for food and health care rely on the principle of providing the basic necessities of life as cheaply as possible, a principle for which we can provide good reasons.

A final class of exceptions focuses on extreme situations. Most norms are designed to function in average and common cases; over a large range of situations they may work well, but in extreme cases they may break down. Laws forbidding murder cover virtually all situations without any real dispute. However, murder in the defense of one's own life (though perhaps not one's property) often is an exception rule.

Often extreme means at high cost, on rare occasions following a norm entails great pain. This is not generally a good property of a norm, we have seen that norms serve instrumental purposes; usually great pain is not a goal we want to achieve (masochists apart). If such is the case, fiddling with the norm is appropriate, particularly if it is possible to define in some fashion these extreme situations. These exceptions also increase the robustness of the norm structure. This stems from the fact that decision making with norms is outcome oriented. If in some extreme cases the norm produces bad outcomes that provides reason to fiddle with the norms, to improve how well they work in cases.

I call these rules the "hurts too much" exceptions. Unlike expected utility decision making which takes gains and loses symmetrically, this kind of norm fiddling emphasizes the extreme loss category. Notice that we do not make exceptions to the no-murder rule when murder would produce very high gains. In terms of structural analysis one is understandably more concerned with the norms that can produce very bad choices, since the whole structure may collapse, whereas maximization is less important.

Finally, all institution structures contain all types of exceptions. It is this fact that makes structural analysis so important. Power-based exceptions form a particularly crucial class because they tend to increase the incoherency of norm structures, hence increasing their weakness and vulnerability. The power struggle around institutions often focuses on the attempt of opponents to include institution-weakening exceptions and the counterattacks of institution proponents who try to remove power-based rules. Hence structural analysis of exceptions forms a fascinating and core aspect of the dynamics of institution structures.

The GATT charter illustrates well how exceptions typically work. It is also a good example because the Krasner definition of a regime was designed using GATT as the core example. It is one thing to criticize this definition for incoherence on marginal institutions, it is another to show another conceptualization proves superior on the case that the definition was designed to work best on.

Principle 1 of the GATT is the fundamental norm of nondiscrimination in trade: what one gives to one favored trade partner must be given to all favored nations. The next five principles are exceptions to that general rule:

- Principle 2—regional free trade organizations are excepted.

- Principle 3—Commonwealth and such groups are excepted.

- Principle 4—the "if it hurts too much" exception for domestic industry severely threatened by free trade.

- Principle 5—trade preferences for Third World countries.

- Principle 6—exceptions for agriculture, services, etc.

Principle 2 fits the principle-based criterion, it permits exceptions that promote the fundamental free trade norm of GATT. Principle 3 provides a classic example of power-based exceptions. It was the result of the power and particular interests of Great Britain, an influential party in the founding of GATT. Principle 4 is the in extremis clause that often excepts individuals from rules in painful situations. The basic belief at the core of GATT is that free trade is good for nations, but there may be situations where it provokes severe adjustment problems for a government or sector: GATT permits exceptions in these extreme cases. Principle 5 is like exceptions for the poor, charitable organizations, etc. For example, the U.S. government will require some contract work be given to minority firms, which is a violation of the norm of open competition for contracts. Here we have a principle-based exception, one which we have good moral and instrumental reasons for including. Principle 6 reflects the power and interests of special groups in most nations, but particularly the United States. Domestically, free markets in, say, agriculture and banking did not exist. Thus it is not surprising that the United States did not insist on this internationally.

In summary, exceptional rules are part of any institution. They complicate the structure, but at the same time give it more flexibility. General exception rules pose no real theoretical problem. In practice they become more problematic when their range decreases to one or few individuals and when they result from the interests and power of particular groups, which go against the main norms of the institution.

## Prioritizing Norms

The Krasner definition of international regimes provided a hierarchy of norms and rules, with norms and principles being more fundamental than decision-making procedures and rules. From the beginning students of institutions realized that some norms are more crucial than others. It is worth briefly examining this framework to see if it solves the problem of conflicting norms. These four types are defined as:

1. Principles are beliefs of fact, causation, and rectitude.

2. Norms are standards of behavior defined in terms of general rights and obligations.

3. Rules are specific prescriptions and proscriptions regarding behavior.

4. Decision-making procedures are the prevailing practices for making and implementing collective choices.

Krasner argued that principles and norms are more fundamental since a change in them is a change *between* regimes while a change in rules and decision-making procedure is a change *within* a regime. It appears that the criterion is basically the importance of the norm or rule within the institution structure. Notice that this framework does not perceive that these different types might overlap. But it does suggest that in case of conflict the more fundamental norm should prevail.

Unfortunately, this priority order does not stand up under a slight probing. First, the categories themselves do not form a coherent set. This can be seen by the heterogeneous group of concepts listed as principles,"beliefs about fact, causation, and rectitude." The elements "facts, causation, and rectitude" form a diverse lot. Clearly not all beliefs of cause, fact, and rectitude would count as principles, so there must be some other criterion that marks out certain principles as the core of institutions.

Not only are the categories extremely fuzzy—in the negative sense of the word—but the hierarchy itself does not stand up either. This becomes immediately clear by examining decision-making rules. These appear at the bottom of the list, suggesting that they are least important; certainly Krasner explicitly puts them into the bottom category. However, decision-making rules usually are very important in determining choice. For example, how representatives are chosen to a parliament has a huge impact on outcomes. Beyond this we have seen that states are constituted in large part by their decision-making rules. After all, what *is* a democracy?

In short, the Krasner hierarchy of norms and rules must be tossed onto the scrap heap. It is incoherent both within and between categories. In practice, its elimination has little effect since the (American) institution literature has never picked up on it in a significant way.

જ

Just as contradictory norms create difficulties for rule-based decision making, inconsistent preferences wreck havoc in expected utility choice. These are not unrelated phenomena, recall that a norm structure induces a preference function (revealed preferences); implicit in an institution lies a preference structure. Incoherency among the norms may well be directly related to inconsistency among goals.

Within $2 \times 2$ game theory coherence among preferences is achieved by rank ordering them; one prioritizes goals by their importance. Recall that $2 \times 2$ games are *defined* by the preference orderings of the two players. For example, if you change the preference ordering of prisoners' dilemma slightly you get the chicken game. More generally, utilities must be transitive to be coherent. There exist situations, particularly choice over time or those dealing with risk, where preferences appear incoherent (e.g., Loewenstein and Elster 1992; Kahneman et al. 1982).

Another prioritizing system is lexigraphical preferences (Sen 1977). Here one must satisfy goal $A$ before attending to goal $B$. In foreign policy often security is seen as lexigraphically superior to wealth and social issues.[4] Lexigraphical preferences are a different way to structure choice options, one which is more rigidly hierarchical in character. Much of U.S. foreign policy during the Cold War can be seen in this light, when the conflict with the USSR took precedence over economics, human rights, and other nonsecurity issues. Kissinger clearly conducted U.S. foreign policy in terms of its relation to the U.S.–Soviet rivalry. For example, Krasner (1978) argued that U.S. oil policy in the Middle East consistently subordinated economic to security goals in a lexigraphical fashion. Mintz's (1993; Mintz et al. 1994) noncompensatory decision theory explicitly develops a similar idea since it proposes that a possible alternative must achieve a minimum value on key dimensions, high values on other dimensions cannot compensate.

One should note that such preferences do not fit well into the expected utility universe. Recall that the key to von Neumann-Morgenstern utilities was the ability to make trade-offs between $A$ and $B$. Such trades are not possible in lexigraphical systems, or in Mintz's noncompensatory decision theory. Rawls's famous justice principle (1971) requires that the least well off person has lexigraphical priority. Not surprisingly Harsanyi (1976) criticized this from an expected utility perspective. The same sort of criticism can be made of realists who place national security before all other values. This was the sort of principle that as long as national security was at stake human rights should have no impact on foreign policy.

The legal approach to norms resembles lexigraphical preferences. Clear priority is given to some law over others, generally it is an all or nothing affair. But there is no reason why we should adopt the all or nothing approach. I suspect this characteristic of legal thought dominates because there is no clear way to weight norms in terms of their importance or applicability.

Weighting norms becomes plausible once one has seen the possibilities of combining norms to make a final choice. Of course, the legalistic all or nothing represents an extreme option, however, it proves better to think of prioritization in terms of a 0–1 continuum instead of a 0–1 dichotomy.

This seems only strange if approached from a legalistic perspective. If we turn to expert systems and artificial intelligence weighting becomes the norm. For example, Holland (1986) makes rule weighting a central part of his cognitive model. I started my discussion of the syllogism with a discussion of beliefs via the mortality of Socrates. Weighting in this context means assessing the evidence we have for a scientific syllogism; we weight it using the results of experience and experiments.

The parallel with importance in terms of decision making should be clear. Instead of weighting according to empirical experience one weights according to values and goals of the actor. Since many norms are instrumental ones this weighting can change reflecting the learning about how well that rule works in

---

[4]This is expressed by Nye when he says: "Security is like oxygen—you tend not to notice it until you begin to lose it, but once that occurs there is nothing else that you will think about" (1995, 91).

achieving goals. One adds or changes norms in a related way as goals and values change. Virtually all expert systems that incorporate learning do so by changing the weights of norms.[5]

The key point here is that we can prioritize rules by moving from a pure all or nothing hierarchical system to a weighted ordering principle. The need to think in all or nothing terms evaporates once combining enters into the realm of possibility.

## Combining Conflicting Norms

All decision is a matter of compromise.

—*Herbert Simon*

We have seen two general ways to deal with the conflicting norm problem. One involves modifying the norms themselves, in particular the creation of exception rules. The second approach prioritizes norms by giving some norms a larger weight than others. But we have yet to face the crux of the problem: how does one combine the recommendations of two or more norms?

The fuzzy logic philosophy starts with *expert* rules, hence the assumption—at least to start with—that there are good reasons for each rule. Perhaps they each deal with a key dimension of the problem. Fuzzy logic basically suggests:

Take some sort of average of all relevant rules.

The averaging process takes into account all rules—all good reasons for acting in different ways—to arrive at some compromise decision, which is just what Simon says in the epigraph to this section.

The relevance of a norm refers to the "if" part of the rule. Suppose we define norm 1 as $N_1 = $ if $A$ then $Y_1$ and norm 2 as $N_2 = $ if $A$ then $Y_2$. $N_1$ and $N_2$ then are conflicting norms since they both apply when $A$ occurs, but propose different actions $Y_1$ and $Y_2$. When $A$ is fuzzy the possibility of overlap increases since $A$ covers a range rather than single values; here for purposes of exposition and illustration I take "crisp"—i.e., not fuzzy—values for $A$ as well as $Y$. A crisp definition of situation $A$ is a point while a fuzzy one covers a range. Since the topic here is not fuzziness but combining rules I use the simpler crisp values.

To illustrate this situation I take up the rule system used as an example in chapter 3. To say that two norms apply means that a given situation fires two rules, hence we need to look at the minor premise. Situation $A$ in figure 6.1 (taken from chapter 3) illustrates how two norms can be relevant to one situation. Situation $A$ lies in the grey zone between "minor violation" and "flagrant violation"

---

[5]Learning also results in fiddling with norm content or adding/subtracting norms; this can be called more fundamental learning since it normally means structural change as opposed to changes in weights.

FIGURE 6.1: Multiple Relevant Norms

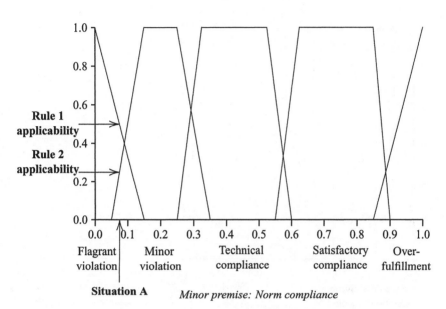

**Situation A**   *Minor premise: Norm compliance*

hence the norms regarding what to do in these two situations apply. Nothing, however, requires this overlap to be equal: generally a situation is likely to be better described by "minor violation" or by "flagrant violation."

In fact this issue has already arise in my earlier discussion of fuzzy rules. It occurred because of the fuzzy character of the terms in the rules. Some situations fall in between categories. If the situation is *A* then neither rule 1 nor rule 2 apply very well, both are marginally relevant. Sections of overlap—what I have called gray zones—between categories means that two rules apply and in this example they propose different actions.

In general one should not assume equal relevance of applicable rules: almost always some rules are more relevant than others. The dichotomous view would say a rule is applicable or not, but again this seems unduly restrictive, undesirable, and empirically implausible. If we stick to the idea that we want to combine rules, then we also want to be able to weight their applicability as well as their importance.

Hence, we have two kinds of weighting that go into combining rules in fuzzy decision making:

1. weights attached to how applicable the rule is.

2. weights attached to the rule itself.

FIGURE 6.2: Combining Rules: Major Premises

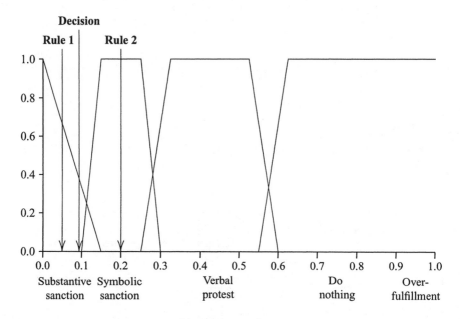

*Major premise: Sanctions*

The first step involves determining how applicable a given norm is to the decision. The empirical situation—the minor premise—determines how applicable the rule is. Another way to think about this is that applicability applies to the "if" part of the if–then rule. In figure 6.1 the Y-axis represents this dimension. Situation *A* is one where two rules apply but neither rule is very applicable. The level of applicability appears on the Y-axis. If a rule is maximally applicable then it has a Y-value of 1.00. In my example (see figure 6.1) rule 1 has applicability of .50, while rule 2 has applicability of .25.

The two rules I used in chapter 3 were:

Rule 1: If government A does *flagrant violation* then *do substantive sanction.*

Rule 2: If government A does *minor violation* then *do symbolic sanction.*

Figure 6.2 provides the possible actions a government can take, the major premise of the norm; what the rule says to do. Rule 1 recommends "substantive sanction," while rule 2 suggests "symbolic sanction." The rule itself gives a fuzzy recommendation, but once again I take crisp values which make it easier to explain how rules are combined. As illustrated in figure 6.2, rule 1 says to do a .05 level sanction—remember that $X = 0$ is a maximal sanction, i.e., $Y = 1$— while rule 2 says to do .20 degree sanction, a maximal verbal protest ($Y = 1$).[6] How do we combine these recommendations to arrive at a final choice? Fuzzy logic recommends to take some sort of average, hence we could take the mean value of .125, i.e., (.05+.20)/2. Of course, this means that one weights the two rules equally. However, assume we have a realist in charge and one needs to be concerned about one's reputation, hence she believes more heavily in sanctioning cases of a flagrant violation. Let's say then that rule 1 is three times more important than rule 2, i.e., rule 1 gets .75 weight and rule 2 gets .25.

If we simply average the recommendation of each rule that means that each is equally applicable, however, rule 1 is more applicable than rule 2. Hence the final choice weights each rule by how applicable (relatively) it is.[7] Recall that rule 1 was .50 applicable and rule 2 was .25 applicable (see figure 6.1), hence rule 1 is twice as applicable as rule 2 thus its weight in the final calculation is .67 and that of rule 2 is .33. If we carry out these calculations we get a final decision of .0935, we apply a weak substantive sanction.[8]

As illustrated in figure 6.2 this decision lies between the recommendations of the two rules. But since rule 1 is both more relevant and more important the final choice lies closer to its recommendation than to rule 2's. What we get is compromise, an attempt to balance conflicting advice or values.

One might object that this is a pretty complex set of operations. However, it but formalizes a very natural way of thinking and deciding. Fuzzy logic started with an understanding of how experts make decisions, one way to actually construct a fuzzy logic expert system is to interview people who are good at the task and ask them to express their knowledge. It comes naturally to express this knowledge in if–then terms. When it comes to conflicts between rules often some compromise is taken reflecting the different dimensions of the problem. The system of rules itself is expressed in natural language categories. This methodology reflects directly the cognitive operations that people use in many circumstances.

While this all may seem complicated, there exist fairly simple software programs requiring little mathematical expertise that allow individuals to set up a fuzzy logic decision-making system (e.g., McNeill and Thro 1994). In terms of complexity one can compare the information processing requirements of fuzzy

---

[6]Formally I take the center of gravity or mean sanctioning level for each rule, which is the center of gravity/mean for the triangle of rule 1 and the trapezoid for rule 2.

[7]If we kept fuzzy values in our rules when we combine them we end up with a "fuzzy recommendation." However in the final analysis we must do *one* thing. Fuzzy decision making then needs a procedure for extracting a specific, nonfuzzy decision out of the fuzzy recommendation. This general process is called defuzzification, logically enough since it means going from a fuzzy recommendation to a crisp, precise one. The general idea then is to take the "average" action in the region defined by the fuzzy recommendation. The most common definition of "average" is the center of gravity of the region defined by the joint recommendation of all relevant rules.

[8]See Cioffi-Revilla (1981) for another example of combining fuzzy logic norms in the international relations context.

logic systems to ones built on expected utility-like decision-making procedures. That is we can compare two expert systems—a fuzzy logic and a expected utility one—with each other. Fuzzy logic systems almost always are simpler and require much less computer power than the expected utility version (see McNeill and Freiberger 1994 for a discussion of this).

Traditional models in engineering rely on a model of the system to be controlled or manipulated. Fuzzy logic attacks the problem from the other side. Instead of modeling the system one models how an expert manipulates the system. Analogously, game theory takes a model of the situation and determines equilibrium strategies. The alternative approach begins with norms and rules that governments and the international community have defined to deal with the situation. It is important to recall a fundamental difference between my approach and game theoretic ones.

> They start from a definition of the situation and then *derive* strategies
> and norms: I *start* with norms and strategies and see how they apply
> to situations.

People often have very good reasons for the policies they chose, what I resist is trying to derive these strategies from the outside via strategic analysis.

A basic problem in thinking about decision making with norms, as well as international institutions, revolves around the existence of conflicting norms. Fuzzy logic decision-making technology provides a realistic way to think about these issues. With fuzzy logic conflicting norms are the usual situation, the "problem" disappears in a general sense. Of course, specific conflicts in specific norm structures may be problematic, but that is because of the specific content or structure of the norms, not because they conflict. Fuzzy logic argues that in general conflicting norms are a good thing: they reflect multiple relevant and important dimensions of a problem. Taking these dimensions into account is a rational thing to do.

**Moral Norms and War**

Commonly scholars have contrasted moral norms with self-interest ones. As we saw in chapter 5 some even define morality in these terms. Nevertheless, there frequently occurs a tension between instrumental norms of winning war or using war as a tool of foreign policy, and international and religious/moral norms about war. In the terms of this chapter we have a classic case of conflicting norms. We can ask as an empirical question: how do people cognitively deal with this situation?

As we shall see in the organizational context in the next chapter, these conflicts involve in a complex way means and ends. Theories about just war involve restrictions on the acceptable means to achieve national goals but these "constraints" also involve differing values attached to in-group versus out-group

TABLE 6.1: Mixed Norm Structures

Just War

|  |  | Moderate | Strict |
|---|---|---|---|
| Realism | Moderate | 73% | 13% |
|  | Strict | 14% | 1% |

*Source:* Brunk et al., p. 146

members. Unlike expected utility frameworks I do not make a radical distinction between means and ends. Recall that formally and mathematically one can transform constraints into goals and vice versa.

I use the Brunk et al. (1996) study to illustrate the way people deal with conflicting values and norms about morality and war. They surveyed a wide range of U.S. elites on their attitudes about when war is appropriate and how it should be waged. They looked at various elite groups, such as retired military officers, retired members of Congress, Catholic priests, diplomats, and journalists. The survey contained items designed to test for various positions that the authors had found in the literature on morality and war, for example, pacifism or just war theory. I want to focus on two belief systems, one which they called "better safe than sorry" which contains, loosely, a conservative, risk-adverse, realist position, the second one holds the basic principles of just war theory.[9]

The "better safe than sorry" position I shall call realism since in its pure form it attaches little weight to moral principles or to international rules about the conduct of war. In its extreme form national interests and security always override moral norms. In contrast, the just war position represents a decision-making structure in which moral principles preempt concerns for war engaging or war winning.

I claimed in chapter 5 that most norm structures contain instrumental and self-interest norms as well as what most people call moral norms. A good empirical— and normative— decision-making theory needs to be able to handle this standard case. In terms of the Brunk et al. survey we can ask to what extend we find pure types among U.S. elites, either in the realist direction or in the just war one. Table 6.1 reproduces their results. I use the term "strict" to designate those who were clear-cut realists or clear-cut just war proponents. The data indicate quite clearly that few elites are either clear-cut realists or just war advocates. The vast majority, 73 percent, fall into what Brunk et al. call the "ambivalent" category, the moderate-moderate cell of the table.

Of course, for me it is not that 73 percent of the respondents were ambivalent but rather that they have multiple values. In any given scenario they try to balance competing concerns. The scholarly literature tends to focus on the polar cases,

---

[9]The results of their survey showed little support for other positions, such as moral crusading (use war to change others beliefs) and pacifism.

TABLE 6.2: Varying Situations and Varying Norm Structures

*Support for a hypothetical war with Nicaragua, by belief system* (in percent)

| Survey Item | Realism | Mixed | Just War |
|---|---|---|---|
| If Nicaragua sets up a communist government | 13 | 4 | 5 |
| If Nicaragua starts a military buildup that overshadows its neighboring states | 21 | 7 | 5 |
| If Nicaragua sends aid (arms, advisers, etc.) to communist revolutionary movements in neighboring countries | 32 | 14 | 11 |
| If Nicaragua invites Soviet military bases to be set up within its borders | 65 | 33 | 27 |
| If Nicaragua invades a neighboring country | 66 | 52 | 36 |
| If there is clear evidence that Nicaragua is going to join an attack on the United States | 95 | 77 | 67 |

*Source*: Brunk et al., p. 148

while most elites appear to fall somewhere in between. This is how I interpret Welch's claim (1993) about the importance of the justice motive in war decisions; it was an important input into the decision, but not the only one.

Two important components of my model of norm combining are (1) the fact that a particular situation fires to different degrees different norms and (2) the fact that different individuals weight the same norms in varying degrees. The first aspect stresses that depending on the situation the combination of norms changes. The second aspect emphasizes that different individuals weight norms differently, hence producing a different decision in the same situation. Brunk et al. provide data that I reproduce in table 6.2 and which illustrate how these two factors enter into decisions.

As you move down the survey questions on the left one increasing gets situations where U.S. national security is threatened. If you move across the columns you get different structures of norms. The categories "realism," "mixed" and "just war" correspond to increasing weights given moral norms about war. Hence, the two dimensions of the table match two key aspects of combining norms in decision making, (1) situations fire norms to different degrees and (2) different individual types give different weights to each norm.

One can see a clear trend on the situation dimension. As the Nicaraguan threat to core national security interests increases the more all types are willing to support a war with Nicaragua. Most of the elites surveyed felt that war was a good policy only if there were pretty clear threats to U.S. security. For the majority a communist government is a threat but a minor one, it fires the war rule but not strongly. Since the moral rules about war also apply one would expect them to have a larger proportional weight in the decision. As the situation becomes a clearer threat to U.S. interests the more relevant the war policy norm becomes, hence its weight increases. Only 13 percent of the realists support war because of a change of government to communism while 95 percent supported it in the case of Nicaragua joining a war coalition against the United States.

This pattern holds for all three norm structures. For the mixed as well as the just war types one sees an increasing willingness to go to war as Nicaragua becomes a clearcut threat to U.S. security. However, because the other norm structures weight the moral norms more highly than the war policy one, they are consistently less likely to end up making the war choice. The pattern shows that quite clearly the mixed type weighs the moral norms higher than the realists but not as high as the just war types.

The study by Brunk et al., which was conducted really for other purposes, illustrates most of the claims made in this chapter and earlier ones: (1) most people have instrumental, self-interest, and moral norms; (2) different people weight those norms differently; and (3) depending on the situation the norms receive different weights.

## Robust Norm Structures

In evaluating a decision-making structure issues of stability and robustness enter into account. In terms of institutional design we desire institutions that work well under a variety of circumstances and that can undergo shocks without collapsing. Any complete institution analysis must include a consideration of these issues. Here I focus on the formal aspects of decision-making structures, but in future chapters I discuss functional aspects of institution stability.

A robust institution means one that is not overly influenced by small changes. It is generally not desirable that small deviations in the situation or the payoffs provoke massive change in behavior. A robust decision-making structure prevents a small aberration on one dimension from making too big an impact on the final decision.

One weakness of game theoretic decision making is that small changes in the structure of the game can mean large strategy revisions. The fact that the Nash equilibrium requires assumptions about the play of other multiplies the instability in these regions. One can see this at work in simple $2 \times 2$ games.

One structural weakness occurs at the boundaries *between* games. If prisoners' dilemma is defined by preferences $T>C>D>S$ and a small change in payoffs makes the ordering $T>C>S>D$ then strategy changes, as illustrated in table 6.3. Here the cell values are cardinal, interpersonal utilities (like Axelrod's prisoners' dilemma tournament). Chicken changes into prisoners' dilemma by flipping the 20 and 25 payoffs. However, relative to the values at stake, 5 units is not that big

TABLE 6.3: Small Differences in Payoffs, Big Differences in Games

Chicken

|     | C        | D        |
|-----|----------|----------|
| C   | 50, 50   | 25, 100  |
| D   | 100, 25  | 20, 20   |

Prisoners' Dilemma

|     | C        | D        |
|-----|----------|----------|
| C   | 50, 50   | 20, 100  |
| D   | 100, 20  | 25, 25   |

a deal. Yet this small change in payoffs means a big change in strategic considerations. A slight change in the payoffs changes the fundamental character of the game and hence the prescribed strategy. The assumption required by the Nash equilibrium concept about the likely strategy of the other player is put into doubt as well, particularly if there is some uncertainty about payoffs.

It is often not clear which game to apply to a given historical institution. Many see international institutions in terms of prisoners' dilemma, but game theorists often use battle of the sexes. For example, Goldstein (1993) argues that GATT is like the battle of the sexes—not prisoners' dilemma—since the emphasis was on distributional issues and each state was pursuing particularistic interests (see also Snidal 1985). Synder (1971) has discussed the distinction between prisoners' dilemma and chicken in the analysis of international conflict. If it is hard to decide ex-post what the game was, it is even harder to reach a firm conclusion ex-ante. As Fearon asks: " 'Which 2×2 game best characterizes the specific empirical case that I am interested in?' [which leads to the question] 'What are the preferences?' understood as how the states in question would rank the four outcomes deemed possible by the theoretical setup. . . . The problem for how to assign preferences often seems so difficult or controversial as to render the exercise pointless" (1998, 272–73; see Hausken, and Plümper 1999 for the same point).

Another weakness can occur *within* the same game. Table 6.4 present two variations on prisoners' dilemma with cardinal utilities. In the first variation, $C$ seems a very reasonable choice. If the other player chooses $C$ then the payoff is high. The temptation payoff does not tempt too much since it is only five points higher than mutual cooperation. But if both play $D$ they both get a very low payoff. In short, playing $D$ risks big losses for little gain. In the second variation $D$ seems the obvious choice: the gains of joint cooperation do not outweigh the

TABLE 6.4: Big Differences in Payoffs, No Difference in Game: Prisoners' Dilemma

First Variation

|   | C | D |
|---|---|---|
| C | 100, 100 | 0, 105 |
| D | 105, 0 | 5, 5 |

Second Variation

|   | C | D |
|---|---|---|
| C | 50, 50 | 0, 100 |
| D | 100, 0 | 45, 45 |

very negative payoffs for being the only one to cooperate. At the same time mutual cooperation does not prove that much better than mutual defection. In short, choosing $C$ risks significant losses for little possible gain.

These two variations are the same game—at least in game theoretic terms: both are prisoners' dilemma. Yet the obvious choice differs, in one $C$ seems the clear choice while in the other it is $D$. Again what is it reasonable to assume about the strategy of one's opponent? (the requirement for a Nash equilibrium). The answer is not clear.[10]

By its very nature fuzzy logic has fewer such critical points. This occurs because of several fundamental characteristics of this decision-making procedure. First, fuzzy categories blur boundary lines, there is no radical jump from zero to one, but rather a gradual fading out of strength. Second, the averaging of rules provides another stabilizing and robustness increasing feature. By taking into account multiple aspects of a decision and using all recommendations it is much less likely that changes in one dimension will result in major modifications in the final choice. Faced with borderline situations which have characteristics of two different games the fuzzy logic philosophy says to take a compromise strategy: the more the situation becomes like chicken the more one should use a chicken-like rule.

Part of the fascination with Axelrod's prisoners' dilemma tournament lies in the robustness test it made of strategies. In the tournaments robustness meant "do well against all sorts of strategies" in a fixed game setup, but Axelrod extended

---

[10]Luce and Raiffa (1957, 109–10) provide other examples where one cell "psychologically dominates" an equilibrium cell. Likewise, the plausibility of the Independence Axiom, the "sure-thing" principle or Allais paradox —which all address the question if one should take a bet of $100 at odds .51 against a sure thing of $50— has provoked much discussion (e.g., Allais and Hagen 1979; Hurley 1989).

that to robustness in the face of changes in the definition of the game situation. For example, he introduced random communication errors into the game setup in order to see if that influenced the usefulness of the tit-for-tat strategy.

Structural analysis thus involves finding situations where the institution or decision-making procedure produces undesirable choices. If these situations appear unlikely then not much reason to worry. If they seem probable then concern about the norms or their structure increases. Going back to $2 \times 2$ games, if it is the case that it is easy to debate about whether prisoners' dilemma or chicken best describes a situation then we have a structural weakness in game theory: in either a descriptive or prescriptive mode it is nonrobust.

Since norms at the individual level are meant to apply over a fairly wide gamut of situations and over significant amounts of time, robustness becomes a key criterion in evaluating norms and norm structures. Since international institutions apply as well to large numbers of states the robustness demands rise again. Traditional institution analyses have focused on power considerations in the maintenance or decline of institutions but structural factors also have their impact.

A robustness and stability analysis of an institution must focus on all exception rules, but particularly on power-based exceptions. These can have tremendous impact on the performance of the norm structure as a whole. For example, over the last couple of decades there has been growing concern over the transport of toxic waste between countries, especially from the industrialized North to poor states in the South. Finally, an institution was formally signed to deal with this. Included was an exception for trade in order to recycle toxic wastes. Soon it became clear that traffickers were using this loophole to continue their dumping under the pretext of recycling, and attempts were made to close this loophole (O'Neill 2000). Another interesting case is the loophole in the Barents Sean institution which led to significant conflict between Norway and Russia (Stokke 2001).

I have focused here on the techniques of formal analysis of institution and decision-making structures. This in no way exhausts the topic of institutional robustness and strength. For example, we have yet to explore the power politics of institution creation and maintenance in any serious way. But structural analysis forms a central part of institution methodology. Here the legal reflex serves well. Lawyers and legal scholars take very seriously the content and relationship between laws. Students of international affairs, after World War II at least, who do so run the risk of being accused of idealism. But having moved norms from the international to the individual level and making them core in decision making means that I take the content of norms seriously as well. We can take this seriousness back to the international level since the coherence issue applies just as much—if not more—at the international level as it does at the state level.

# Coherent Norm Structures

The drive toward coherence in reasoning and decision making is constant both within individuals and governments. For example, a well-known experiment in the 1970s asked about Americans' opinions toward Soviet journalists. In a half-split sample, 37 percent of respondents were willing to allow Communist reporters in the United States. Yet when in the other half-sample respondents were first asked whether U.S. reporters should be allowed in Russia (which most favored), the percentage agreeing to allow Russian reporters into the United States nearly doubled to 73 percent. Schuman and Presser suggest that when

> a norm of reciprocity is immediately made salient a substantial number of respondents feel bound to provide an answer that is consistent with their previous response ... The crux of the matters seems to be that the reporter question has two meanings, one involving an attitude toward an object and another involving an attitude toward a norm. (1981, 28)

This famous experiment shows how incoherence can arise in decisions. The experimenter forces the second group of respondents to think about making choices that are coherent, while in the first group the choice is not put into any policy framework.

Governments sometimes hesitate to make what they think is the right choice in the current situation because they feel that in general such a policy will not produce good decisions. This is not unreasonable since every individual decision implies a policy, just as policy implies a specific action. States hesitate to choose the "best" option in one situation if that strategy generalizes to a norm which rarely works well.

Ronald Dworkin (1986) has forcefully argued that judicial decisions should be guided by a concern for the coherence of law as a whole. He faces a situation where individual judges do not like the direction constitutional law has taken over the last 30 years and often want to reverse that pattern. This same problem will arise in the analysis of norms at multiple levels of analysis. For example, conflict between the individual and the organization or a government policy and international norms has the same fundamental character as judges faced with existing law. Just like Dworkin's judges some governments may not like the trend expressed by international institutions. At the organizational level, newly chosen leaders may not like the policy structure they inherit as they enter office.

However, in part I of this volume I have ignored multilevel issues; the individual chooses norms and naturally desires that they form a consistent and coherent decision-making structure. Hard decisions arise but the individual follows Dworkin's principle of concern for the decision-making system of norms as a whole in making her choices. At the individual level the power-based exceptions, which prove a central issue for institution analysis, are much less important than the positive use of principled and extreme-case exceptions, both of which strength the decision-making structure.

Considering structural issues makes one sensitive to the dynamics of institution change, both for good and bad. Learning is structural change in the positive sense. Though experience certain rules appear to produce good outcomes, these then receive increased weight in decision making; analogously, rules which seem to lead to bad results are downgraded or eliminated.

In addition, Dworkin's principle of structure coherence implies certain sorts of changes. Some exceptions in the GATT charter move in the spirit of GATT, such as regional free trade areas. Other exceptions, such as those for agriculture and services appear quite arbitrary. Pressure by institution proponents constantly pushes to eliminate these structural anomalies. We can see how this works over the long haul in the history of democracy. Once the nation was constituted by its people (not by rules of monarchical acquisition and transmission) in the seventeenth and eighteenth centuries, it is not clear why the "people" should consist of only adult, white, male, property-owning individuals. With the benefit of hindsight, the justifications for excluding women, blacks, and the poor seem completely specious, self-serving arguments based more on power than reason. The lack of structural coherence in voting rules made these exceptions vulnerable to attack. In the 1960s coherency arguments influenced decisions to reduce the voting age in the United States: if one could die for one's country then one should be able to vote. These issues prove essential when moving from the individual to the international or organizational level. Structural weaknesses often result from bargaining between groups and depend dramatically on power relations.

Multilevel and principle–agent problematiques have not appeared much so far. I have argued that before understanding how decision making with norms works between agents and structures we need to know how it works within agents or structures. We have now acquired some key tools for dealing with the level of analysis problems posed by international norms. Fuzzy logic has provided some key theoretical support in giving a way to conceptualize decision making with norms. It gives a formal structure for expressing the if–then nature of norms and also techniques for modeling the language in which they are often formulated. Not only that, this methodology provides a way to deal with the crucial problem of conflicting norms. This problem becomes much more serious when we move to multiple levels of analysis since the opportunities for conflict increase manyfold.

While I have focused here on conflicts *within* an individual or institution nothing in the fuzzy logic methodology prevents us from expanding and modifying these ideas to deal with conflicting norms *across* levels of analysis. I assumed in this chapter that rule 1 and rule 2 both belong to the same decision maker, but with some modifications we can use extend the fuzzy logic framework to deal with conflicting norms when rule 1 belongs to government A and rule 2 belongs to an international institution. At the individual level rule weighting involved instrumental concerns and prioritizing goals. When we move to agent-structure analysis relative power will constitute the crucial weighting factor.

To develop a theory of how individual governments create and maintain policies, and are influenced by international norms is the goal of the remainder of this volume. We can begin to deal these issues with a firm individual level theoretical foundation:

1. We know that an institution is a structure of norms.

2. We know that a norm is an if–then statement.

3. We know that strategy, norm, and policy are synonyms for an if–then rule.

4. We know instrumental and moral concerns generate the choice of norms.

5. We know that norms can be combined to produce a final choice.

The bridge that will allow us to traverse the levels of analysis is the fact that the character and formal properties of a norm do not differ at the individual, organizational, or international level. The same logical structure appears at all levels. Hence the individual level foundation laid in this and preceding chapters will serve us in our voyage through a discussion of institution or policy creation, change, and impact at different levels of analysis.

# Part II

# Organizational Decision Making

# Chapter 7

# The Punctuated Equilibrium Model

> The standard operating procedure (SOP) is not the enemy of organization; it is the essence of organization.
>
> —*James Q. Wilson*

The previous four chapters presented a model of individual decision making with norms. While the exact character of this individual usually remained vague, frequently I implied that it was an individual person. With this chapter I begin my discussion of organizational decision making.

Since my basic concern lies with international politics and institutions I start from the basic premise that all key actors are organizational in character, be they IOs, NGOs, firms, or governments *all* main individuals in world politics are organizational in nature. Individual people are of course important but all of these persons are important because of the positions they occupy in various organizations. Central questions need to be addressed about people vis-à-vis their organizations, what I will call in the next chapter the individual–institution problematique (related to the principal–agent or agent–structure frameworks). However, in this chapter I treat the organization as a unitary actor. Organizations, like people, can be torn in different directions, have inconsistent or conflicting policies, interests, and values.

Throughout this volume I have quite consistently referred to "governments" rather than "states." This usage reflects the concern that we keep constantly in mind that the central actor in a theory of international institutions is government cum organization. In contrast, the use of the word "state" in the international relations literature often implies a conflation of the government with the country. In terms of international institutions, governments are but the most important of the many actors involved. Governments represent certain interests more forcefully than others; firms, NGOs, churches, all represent influential interests as well. Governments are without a doubt the most important players, but the government is *not* the country/nation.

I would like to thank Keith Krause and David Welsh for helpful comments on an earlier version of this chapter.

I argue in this chapter that the decision making with norms model in many ways fits much better at the organizational level than it does at the personal level. For example, I have spoken frequently of individuals choosing their norms; at the level of the person this is often not really a clear and explicit choice. In contrast, organizations have explicit procedures for adopting policies. All actors in the organization are supposed to carry out faithfully these policies, many of which long predate the arrival of the current leaders and bureaucrats of the organization. These policies have syllogistic expression and in governments are often formulated as law. Questions of precedent or when a particular policy applies fit naturally into the policy decision-making model. To the extent that policy is also law, the fit is extremely close. One need but examine any well-known book on legal thinking, the first topic is always syllogistic choice (e.g., Levi 1948; MacCormick 1978).

The second goal in this chapter is to introduce the punctuated equilibrium model of policy. This model proposes a very nonlinear life cycle for the typical norm, rule, or policy. There is the initial period of policy creation or adoption. These are big or small revolutions in the policy or norm structure as organizations adopt new areas of action, new basic principles, or new ways of dealing with old problems. This is followed by a period of consolidation, what I call policy fiddling. Like all inventions, new policies and new norms do not work well initially, due to unforeseen problems, such as lack of experience. Hence, naturally enough, bureaucrats and clients see problems to be fixed and ways to increase efficiency and effectiveness. This phase can be called incrementalist in that it is a period of relatively small changes. Often the policy life cycle ends with a bang as well. Revolutions, large and small, not only bring in the new but also sweep out the old.

I will argue that the punctuated equilibrium model of policy makes sense of what we know about the evolution of policy over time. For example, the concept of organizational inertia emphasizes the stability of most policies over most of their lifetimes. Yet, for example, students of American domestic policy have long known that major policy change occurs in fits and starts (e.g., Brady 1988). This too is exactly what the punctuated equilibrium model would lead us to expect.

In summary, this chapter applies the norms decision-making framework developed in part I to organizational decision making. It argues that the punctuated equilibrium model describes well the typical life cycle of policies or norms. Since international norms and institutions are after all just policies, once we have a policy model of governmental decision making we can then begin to consider how international policies get inserted into the policy structure of governments.

## Policy Decision Making as Organizational Decision Making

On a number of occasions I have described norms at the government level as policies. In American politics, and in principle, Congress establishes policy which the federal bureaucracy then administers. Bureaucratic decision making in this context means individuals applying mostly exogenously given rules, norms, and policies.

Nothing about political organizations makes them distinctive in this regard. Organizational theorists have frequently defined organizations as sets of policies, routines, and SOPs. Allison's classic article defined the organizational model in exactly these terms: "a government consists of *existing* organizations, each with a *fixed* set of standard operating procedures and programs" (1969, 698). By the time Allison published this article in 1969 organizational theories had already for a decade conceived of organizational decision making in this fashion. For example, March and Simon in their classic *Organization* define organizations in the same sense:

> Organizations are . . . assemblages of rules by which appropriate behavior is paired with recognized situations. (March and Simon 1993 [1958], 12)

James Wilson makes the same claim in the epigraph to this chapter, when he says SOPs are the essence of organization.

Organizational ecologists think about SOPs as the genes of organizations. Policies and rules describe the essence of an organization:

> We think that it is a reasonable first approximation to think of organizations as possessing relatively fixed repertoires of highly reproducible routines. (Hannan and Freeman 1984, 155)

The population of organizations, businesses, labor unions, and the like are analogous to various biological organisms struggling for survival and trying to reproduce themselves over time.

Given their conceptualization of an organization it is not surprising that March and Simon describe "organizational programs," i.e., policies, as follows:

> [L]et's call the first step the "program-evoking" step, and the second step the "program-execution" step. The bifurcation is characteristic of programs—a program includes a specification of the circumstances under which the program is to be evoked. (1993, 168)

The program[1] is the SOP or policy: it has the exact form of the syllogism I discussed at length in chapter 3. We have seen that these routines are the strategies that bureaucracies use to achieve their goals, strategies in the game theoretic sense.

Kier (1995) used the term "organizational culture" to express the importance of organizational norms on French military policy. Not surprisingly, I take the position on organizational culture that I proposed when linking norms and individual identity. If both culture and organizations are defined in basically the same terms, then organizational culture in many ways becomes redundant terminology. For example, Geertz describes culture in the same terms that we have seen are used to describe organizations:

---

[1] Recall that Simon is also a founding father of expert systems and artificial intelligence.

[C]ulture is best seen not as complexes of concrete behavior patterns—customs, usages, traditions, habit clusters—...but as a set of control mechanisms—plans, recipes, rules, instructions (what computer engineers call "programs")—for the governing of behavior. (Geertz 1964, 87)

Conceptualizations of organizational culture look much the same:

An organizational culture approach focuses on the way that the pattern of assumptions, ideas, and beliefs that prescribes how a group should adapt to its external environment and manage its internal affairs influences calculations and actions. In a sense, this approach focuses on "norms" that dominate specific organizations: culture is, in effect, a set of collectively held prescriptions about the right way to think and act. (Legro 1997, 35–36)

As Legro implies in his discussion, as well as in his case studies of militaries, many of these norms are instrumental ones about how best to fight wars and defend countries.

Clearly if organizations *are* rules and norms then decision making with norms is the obvious way to think about organizational action. All the machinery developed in part I can be directly applied to organizations. It is worth linking some of the characteristics of policy decision-making stressed in those chapters with facets of organizations that are emphasized in the literature specifically on organizations.

I have stressed that norms, policies, and rules are meant to be applied multiple times. This is the core distinction between a policy and a decision arrived at using a structure of norms. Organizations, like individuals, would be paralyzed by the costs and difficulty of doing cost–benefit analysis for each individual choice. They really have no option but to define rule-based strategies. A key characteristic of these strategies/rules is that they are intended to be applied frequently, often over various substantive domains and for extended periods of time.

Many people interpret a single government action in a policy sense: governments consider all their actions in terms of precedents. Even though it is the first time the problem arises, immediately questions arise about whether the government will act in the same way in future, similar circumstances. Governments avoid what might be a good choice in the current situation if they see that as a bad precedent. Halperin (1974) makes this point, not surprisingly, in the context of an organizational analysis of U.S. foreign policy (see also Anderson 1981). How many cases of humanitarian intervention occurred before lawyers, politicians, NGOs, and the UN were talking about a new norm? How many times has a foreign policy choice not been made because of fear of setting a precedent? These concerns make sense when one thinks of organizations and governments as consisting of routines, policies, and SOPs.

Another fundamental characteristic of organizations lies in the distinction between policy choice and the subsequent actions taken within that policy framework. One chooses a policy then applies that policy in many situations down the road. This process works in two important ways. One, well known, puts policy choice at the top of the hierarchy and actions within a policy framework at lower levels—implementation. This typifies the principal–agent approach. Another one, less well studied, affects the principals when they enter an organization. They too enter into an already existing policy structure and will be expected to carry out most of the already existing policy.

When a principal enters an organizational structure, she is not starting ex nihilo but working within an entity which existed before she arrived and one that will probably live on long after her departure. One might object that I am reifying an organization, but one talks about the law as having an existence independent of judges that apply it. The relation between individuals and institutions is the main topic of the next chapter, the key point here is that if we conceive of organizations as rules, norms, and policies then these exist as principals to all individuals in the organization. The action of leaders as well as outside actors then must be a part of a theory of policy change (or nonchange) within a given policy structure. But this is exactly what my individual model says: a person chooses new instrumental or moral norms but always keeping in mind the norm structure that these new norms must fit into.

In my discussion of instrumental and moral norms I emphasized that means and ends are blended together in a choice of policies. Implicit in any policy structure is a set of ends. Policies are the means, but one need not consider them as radically separate from ends. This contrasts with expected utility choice where the ends are exogenous and the object of the analysis is to derive the means. The refusal to radically divide the means from the ends characterizes much thought on organizational decision making. For example, Sikkink found in her analysis of U.S. human rights policy:

> While some policy makers advocated human rights policy solely from a principled stance, arguing that it was wrong or immoral to support repressive institutions, most mingled principled and causal reasoning in their justification of the human rights policy, arguing that it was both immoral and counterproductive for long-term U.S. interests to support institutions that violated human rights. (1993, 142)

When one looks at the content of various political ideologies it is hard to separate the means from the ends. Realists rejected human rights policies both in terms of their view of the content of national interests as well as the means of attaining those ends.

The extended example I gave in the previous chapter illustrates how the rules of war can be conceptualized as constraints on means (do not take certain actions), but how they can equivalently be taken as ends (the value of nonmilitary lives). The expected utility framework with its focus on means tends to use constraint talk, but formally maximization under constraints can be transformed into unconstrained maximization of a different preference function.

In summary, the rule-based decision-making model I have sketched out in preceding chapters has the characteristics that many theorists have ascribed to organizational choice. I discussed individual identities as a structure of norms, many have used that same ontology for organizations. I emphasized that a person's key norms are meant to be applied over long periods of time and that decisions get made using that rule structure. I have stressed that in policy decision making one does not radically separate the means and the ends, something many have found to be the case in organizational choice.

In many ways the decision making with norms model fits even better at the organizational level than at the individual one. Organizations make policy in a much more rationalized and explicit fashion than do individuals. Policy choice often rests formally distinct from policy implementation. Most governments separate legislatures from administrations: the separation between policy creation and policy implementation is fixed in organizational structures. Policies themselves are expressed in rule form because individuals, firms, and organizations need to know how the government will act in a variety of situations, hence the government has to announce its strategy and remain committed to it.

## The Biological Origins of the Punctuated Equilibrium Model

I have tended to assume in my discussion of norms and policies that they are intended to be used repeatedly for long periods of time. However, there is nothing inherent in the model that requires policies to be long-lived. In theory one could come up with a new policy structure for each decision faced. While impractical, we need to consider the modal life trajectory of a policy. I think there is a typical life course for a policy and this has major implications for a theory of organizational choice. The discussion above and in previous chapters really looked at how an individual decision gets made using norms, rules, and policies as the major input. I have not yet really dealt with the question of the evolution of norms, particularly in their organizational, policy forms.

I propose a punctuated equilibrium model of organizational choice, which argues for a nonlinear life cycle for the average policy. This model both in its decision making and biological existences stresses the nonincremental dynamics of policies as well as species. Traditional evolutionary theory, like traditional incremental organization theory, saw small, regular change as the dominant pattern. The punctuated equilibrium model suggests that the modal pattern varies between massive change and relative stasis. Since the model relies in its name and is very similar in substance to the biological, evolutionary model of punctuated equilibrium, it is worth introducing the organizational version by a discussion of its biological cousin.

For decades—since the 1940s—what Julian Huxley identified as the modern synthesis dominated the thinking of evolutionary biologists. Prior to this synthesis, a "bewildering array of evolutionary process theories existed, each touted by a different biological discipline seemingly bent upon establishing the primacy of its own phenomena and its own insights" (Eldredge 1985, 3). The modern synthesis involved combining Darwin's theory of natural selection with the discovery of how genes produce variation upon which natural selection can work. Perhaps most elegantly summarized by Gould (1983, 13), the synthesis emphasized "gradual, adaptive change produced by natural selection acting exclusively upon organisms [i.e., not species]." The standard theory thus saw evolution occurring everywhere, all the time, and in an incremental fashion.

It was from a group of paleontologists outside the core of evolutionary theory (often formal and mathematical) that arose the challenge to the gradualist vision of natural selection (see Eldredge 1995 for an account of the admission of paleontologists to the "high table" of evolutionary theory). The fossil record produces little evidence for the incrementalist position. That is, the literal geological record was more supportive of abrupt changes: most fossil species disappear looking much the same as when they appeared, while new species in any local area appear abruptly and fully formed. Traditionally—starting with Darwin—this was deemed the result of the rarity and poor quality of the fossil record.

In 1972 Eldredge and Gould proposed the punctuated equilibrium model, which instead of explaining away discrepancies between data and the standard theory devised a theory that matched more directly the fossil record (see Eldredge 1995 for a survey and overview). The punctuated equilibrium model portrays evolution as primarily the product of rapid speciation. The model suggests a process characterized by long periods of stasis punctuated by the sudden appearance of new, qualitatively different species. Unlike the standard model, the punctuated equilibrium model regards speciation and evolution as rare, occurring in specific and unusual circumstances.

As Gould recounts, scholars working in the modern synthesis only looked for gradualist evolution in choosing their cases for study. "Over and over again in my career I have bashed my head against this wall of nonreporting [of null results]. When Niles Eldredge and I proposed the theory of punctuated equilibrium in evolution, we did so to grant stasis in phylogenetic lineages the status of 'worth reporting'—for stasis had previously been ignored as nonevidence of nonevolution, though all paleontologists knew its high frequency" (1987, 37). With the punctuated equilibrium model in hand, biologists began to "see" long-term stasis in species as well as periods of rapid speciation.

The most novel of the rare speciation propositions was the suggestion that the birth and death of most species occur during periods of major environmental change and shock. The most famous of these is the claim that a large asteroid hit the earth about 60 million years ago causing the extinction of 65–70 percent of all existing species (Raup 1992). The evolutionary window-of-opportunity that this opened then resulted in the rise of thousands of new species.

Today, almost three decades after it was first introduced, the punctuated equilibrium model has been accepted by a majority of evolutionary biologists (Gould and Eldredge 1993).

For me the essential elements of the biological version of punctuated equilibrium are that species do not necessarily evolve in a linear and incremental fashion, but experience long periods of stability and experience change in a rapid and sometimes unpredictable fashion. Massive shocks are needed to upset that stability and provide windows-of-opportunity for new species to arise.

## The Punctuated Equilibrium Model of Organizational Policy

If we go back to the basic individual level decision making with norms model, particularly in the context of expert systems, a useful analogy emerges. In fuzzy logic expert systems one must first *create* some norms to solve the problem. But the initial set of rules is never optimal, one must then *fiddle* with them. Creation of a norm is a big policy change, fiddling with it is incrementalism. In fact Zadeh's basic idea when he invented fuzzy logic was to start with a model of a human expert. The systems expert formalizes the rules the human uses and then begins to fiddle with them to achieve as good or better performance on the part of a machine. This, after all, is the basis of chess-playing programs, which would be terrible without basic rules supplied by human chess experts.

I separate policy formation from policy implementation; the former concerns choosing norms while the latter involves decision making with norms. In individuals this separation is not so clear, one can make decisions that slowly evolve into routines, habits, and policies. But at the organizational level policy making is usually more conscious, systematic, and formalized than at the individual level. Since many if not most policies have instrumental and functional components we can use much of the cost–benefit machinery associated with expected utility models in making policy choices. Of course, this must be more like rule-of-thumb cost–benefit analysis than one-off decisions. One cannot propose policies/strategies that are sensitive to small changes in the structure of the game or situation. One must take into account that it often proves difficult to undo established policy. Once a policy is chosen the organization is committed, other actors cue off the policy, and the costs of breaking these commitments can be high.

Now, as one applies a new norm it becomes clear what the problems of the policy are, hence reason to fiddle. Sometimes because of dramatic failures, new ideas, new people, or whatever a large overhaul is undertaken. But a fundamental principle of organization decision making remains "if it ain't broke don't fix it." Herbert Simon elevated this to a major principle, if the policy works "satisfactorily" then do not change it. However, unlike the implications of the satisficing idea, I stress that in general fiddling goes on all the time. At any given time some policies and rules are seen as functioning fine, while others are being worked on.

Braybooke and Lindbolm emphasized that fiddling focuses on avoiding or eliminating evils: "The characteristics of the strategy ['incremental, exploratory, serial and marked by adjustment of ends to means'] support and encourage the analyst to identify situations or ills from which to move *away* rather than goals *toward* which to move.... Policy aims at suppressing vice even though virtue cannot be defined, let alone concretized as a goal" (1963, 102). One fixes only those policies and SOPs which do not work well. Kingdon (1984) and others have emphasized that policy making and agenda setting respond to perceived problems, something that must be fixed. In the theory of international institutions, various theorists have proposed that some sort of international shock is a prerequisite of institution creation (see chapter 9 for more on this). For example, the dramatic and highly publicized discovery of the hole in the ozone layer was crucial in the signing of the Montreal Treaty.

Much of the literature on organization behavior and policy making has emphasized the incremental character of bureaucratic choice. Braybrooke and Lindbolm (1963) and Wildavsky (1975), among others, have repeatedly contrasted organizational decision making with the postulates of expected utility choice arguing that the latter do not describe well what organizations do. The organizational ecologists (e.g., Hannan and Freeman 1989) take the same tack; organizations do not evolve; rather, they die as new organizations with different genetic makeups (i.e., SOPs) are created and succeed. Axelrod's work (1984) on the evolution of strategies fits in the ecological mold since the individual's strategy does not change over the simulation; what evolves is the relative size of each strategy subpopulation.

However, there is a fundamental problem with taking organization decision making as a purely incremental process. Since the 1980s Kingdon—and more recently Baumgartner and Jones (1993)—have questioned the strong incrementalist position; these scholars point out that sometimes policy shifts dramatically and rapidly.[2] A good theory of organization decision-making must be able to deal with both these empirical aspects of organizational policy. While incremental change remains probably the most frequent, large shifts do occur and because of their importance deserve careful attention.

It is possible, however, for policy to be created in an incremental fashion, what we can call "sliding into policy." I suspect that basic changes occur much more often in one fell swoop: the normal pattern is major rule change followed by incremental fiddling. There appears to be no specific research on this question in the policy literature (see Diehl and Goertz 2000 for a test in the context of enduring militarized rivalries), but my hypothesis concurs much better with the psychology of individuals and the dynamics of policies than large changes produced through incremental movement. If it happens, it happens big and fast. The collapse of communism in the USSR provides just the biggest and most recent example.

Figure 7.1 illustrates the difference between the incrementalist model of policy and the punctuated equilibrium one. The incremental model is one of small

---

[2]Braybrooke and Lindbolm (1963) recognize this in chapter 4 but then proceed to ignore it. Wildavsky (1975) discovered "shift points" but then proceeds to ignore them in terms of his theory; not only that, he explicitly excluded major organizational change and reorganization from his data.

FIGURE 7.1: Punctuated Equilibrium and Incremental Models

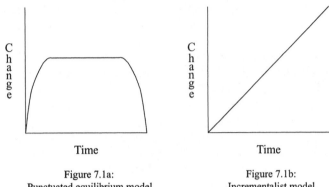

Figure 7.1a:
Punctuated equilibrium model

Figure 7.1b:
Incrementalist model

constant changes, indicated by the straight increasing line. One might object that such a line cannot continue forever, but if one examines Wildavsky's analysis there are no nonlinear (e.g., quadratic) terms that indicate a theoretical realization of that. In contrast, the punctuated equilibrium model exhibits radical growth at the beginning and rapid decline at the end, with relative stasis in between. The theories that generate these two lines have very different characteristics: the incremental model fits the linear model of regression analyses. The punctuated equilibrium model is a very nonlinear one with widely varying growth and decline rates.

Just as the gradualist model has dominated biological thinking on evolution so too has incrementalist thought held the center stage in research on U.S. domestic policy and budgeting. Wildavsky's (1975) work has perhaps been the most influential in establishing the incremental model. In his study of organizational behavior, he found that incrementalism described the behavior of bureaucracies well. Just as the punctuated equilibrium approach questioned traditional biological models so has the incremental model been challenged by those that note large shifts in the policy process. John Kingdon (1984) authored among the first and most influential of these studies. Kingdon's research suggested that the agenda-setting component is best conceptualized as independent streams of problems, policies, and politics awaiting periodic, albeit fleeting, opportunities for policy choice (largely based on the garbage can model of Cohen, March, and Olsen 1972). The likelihood of a particular condition becoming a public problem worthy of action, and for one policy solution to arise from amidst the primeval soup of possible policy alternatives to address it, only becomes significant if a coupling or linking of the problem, policy, and political streams occurs. When this confluence occurs, the item makes it onto the agenda of high leaders. For this to happen, policy windows occasioned by problem opportunities must open, viable solutions must be available and then be coupled to the problem by entrepreneurs operating within policy communities, and the political environment (e.g., the national mood or partisan predispositions in the U.S. Congress) must be amenable to policy change. In sum, Kingdon's overview of agenda setting portrays a decidedly nonincremental ebb and flow of items that appear and disappear with striking rapidity.

Kingdon's model of the policy-making process brought the idea of rapid change to the forefront, although he didn't use the punctuated equilibrium label and still regarded policy alternatives as arising incrementally. Other scholars were soon to challenge those ideas, and rely more heavily on the punctuated equilibrium analogy. Durant and Diehl (1989) explicitly adopted the moniker of punctuated equilibrium and argued that the elements of the foreign policy process can be characterized by rapid change and "pure mutation." Thus, some foreign policies, in their view, can be understood only by reference to a punctuated equilibrium process. Consistent with this is the idea that foreign policy attitudes of leaders and elites are relatively stable over time, and are disrupted only by dramatic shocks (Russett, 1990).

Starting from a punctuated equilibrium position, Jones, Baumgartner, and True describe the policy process as one that is characterized by rapid changes and long periods of stasis.

> Rather than making moderate adaptive adjustments to an ever-changing environment, political decision making is characterized sometimes by stasis, when existing decision designs are routinely employed, and sometimes by punctuations, when a slowly growing condition suddenly bursts onto agendas of a new set of policymakers or when existing decision makers shift attention to new attributes or dimensions of the existing situation. Complex interactive political systems do not react slowly and automatically to changing perceptions or conditions; rather, it takes increasing pressure and sometimes a crisis atmosphere to dislodge established ways of thinking about policies. The result is periods of stability interspersed with occasional, unpredictable, and dramatic change. (1997, 1)

Thus, they find that the incrementalist or gradualist story is not so much wrong as partially true. Incrementalism and stasis describe long periods of the policy process.

Jones, Baumgartner, and True (1997) empirically tested their punctuated equilibrium by analyzing U.S. budget allocations in the post–World War II era. They report dramatic changes at three points in the forty-eight-year period studied, with largely incremental change occurring otherwise. Importantly, the punctuated equilibrium model is compelling, even controlling for three rival explanations. Overall, they argue that stability interrupted by dramatic change is characteristic of processes throughout national government and not confined to a few programs or subsystems. They are not alone; others (Casstevens 1980; Mayhew 1991; Peters and Hogwood 1985) have found that short periods of intense policy activity leaves a substantial institutional legacy.

Military budgets provide one link between the domestic literature on policy and the concerns of international relations scholars. Here, as with other budgets, if one examines peacetime spending one tends to find incremental change. But a number of scholars (Russett 1970; Diehl and Goertz 1985) have noted a ratchet effect in military spending due to major wars: military spending increased dramatically during war, but rarely does spending return to the prewar levels in the aftermath of that war.

Stasis also characterizes much military policy decision making. For example, Rhodes (1994) in his analysis of U.S. naval weapons procurement (again looking at this over the period since World War I) finds that it can be best explained by the existence of a 15-capital ship rule, which itself dates from the Washington Naval Treaty of 1922. In spite of the many and well-known differences between the air, ship, and submarine divisions of the navy and the occurrence of World War II and the Cold War, all continue to agree on that basic rule. Much of the fighting goes on over what to do with excess money in times of affluence and what nonessentials to cut in times of shortage.

The punctuated equilibrium model of policy has dramatic implications for the research design and methodology of policy analysis. To evaluate the empirical validity of the punctuated equilibrium theory one must track policies over extended periods of time, ideally over their whole life cycle. At the very least one must cover the initial stages of a policy's life and track it for a significant period thereafter.

The punctuated equilibrium model hypothesizes that if you randomly study, say, ten years of a policy's life the chances are high that you will hit a period of stasis or incrementalism (one can see this in figure 7.1). One can contrast the punctuated equilibrium empirical analysis of Jones, Baumgartner, and True (1998) with Wildavsky's, both looking at U.S. federal budgets. Wildavsky chose about fifteen years from the 1940s until the early 1960s for no real strong theoretical reasons. Since Jones, Baumgartner, and True were *looking for* radical change periods they examined budgets over almost fifty years; Baumgartner and Jones (1993) looked at the rise and fall of issues over periods of up to 100 years.

It is well known that unless one has a theoretical reason to look for something one will often not find it. Even though people "know" about the fact, unless they fit into a theoretical framework they are often just ignored. Gould reports that a graduate student would never have been allowed to write a Ph.D. thesis on species that never evolved, since the traditional model took evolution to be gradual changes over time. Scholars of biological evolution traditionally did not look for stasis because their theories emphasized incremental change. A parallel has occurred in the policy literature. Wildavsky (1975) himself noted that occasionally large shifts occurred in budgeting forcing him to reestimate regression lines. Nevertheless, given his incrementalist framework he made little of this. Even though the punctuated equilibrium model stresses stasis as much as dramatic change Baumgartner and Jones (1993) emphasize radical change with the title "Agendas and *instability* in American politics" (emphasis is mine) because they are arguing in a context where incrementalist theories have dominated.

To keep a balanced perspective one must keep in mind that any model of punctuated equilibrium phenomenon must have two core characteristics. One, in the face of significant changes on key independent variables the dependent variable usually remains relatively unperturbed. This is the stability and stasis that policies exhibit over most of their lifetimes. Second, on rare occasions the model must produce dramatic and radical change.[3]

The model of institution creation I outline in chapter 9 and formalize in chapter 10 has exactly these two characteristics. To create a institution is to make a major policy shift. Institutions again are only policies, so in the terms of this chapter it is a model of major policy shifts. That model has very close links to this chapter since my theory of institution creation starts with Kingdon's agenda-setting model, which itself is closely linked to the work of Baumgartner and Jones. As I mentioned above, Kingdon's book was one of the first to emphasize the rapid rise of issues onto the agenda. What is less well known is that it also explains why most of the time there is little policy change. I will return to the punctuated equilibrium model again in chapter 9 to show why my model of institution creation has the two core characteristics that any punctuated equilibrium model must possess.

## A Punctuated Equilibrium Foreign Policy: Canadian Peacekeeping

Canada's foreign policy on peacekeeping and its history illustrate in one concrete case the punctuated equilibrium model of policy outlined above. Since most foreign policy analysis focuses on the United States it serves as a corrective to examine another industrialized country's foreign policy. American scholars often tend to assume, usually implicitly, that whatever is true about the United States is true about foreign policy in general. In contrast, I think that the United States is an outlier in general, though an important one to be sure.

Most foreign policy analysis directs attention toward actions rather than policy. Another tendency is for the analysis to center on just one event, often of topical interest. As an outsider one might imagine that given the prominence of peacekeeping in Canadian foreign policy that there would be a plethora of academic analyses of it. And in one sense there are, peacekeeping actions have generated a literature about them, very much linked to specific proposed, ongoing, or recent events. However, there are *no* analyses of the Canadian *policy* on peacekeeping. There are not even any comparative analyses of the many Canadian peacekeeping missions (beyond the off-the-cuff comparisons).

---

[3]Finnemore and Sikkink's (1998) discussion of international organizations has a strong punctuated equilibrium flavor to it.

All those who have adopted punctuated equilibrium-like frameworks (e.g., Kingdon, Baumgartner and Jones, Diehl and Goertz) have stressed the importance of thinking about policy over time. Canadian peacekeeping offers a classic example of a policy that has been applied literally dozens of times and has been around for over forty years.

As we have seen there are facts that all people "know" but which for a lack of an explanatory framework go unstudied. This was true of biological species that exhibited stasis, true of long-term international militarized rivalries, and policy shifts within an incremental paradigm. Canadian peacekeeping is but another example of this phenomenon. Students of Canadian foreign policy know the basic facts of the history, but since it does not fit into a standard worldview or methodology it is just basically ignored. A search of the principal Canadian international relations journal *International Journal* for the period 1956–1998 and the *Canadian Journal of Political Science* for all years until 1998 reveals only one article (Martin and Fortmann 1995) devoted to Canadian peacekeeping.

The first step in an analysis of Canadian peacekeeping involves asking about Canadian *policy* and its evolution over the decades. Here I take policy in the sense of a rule or SOP that is to be applied in multiple future occasions. In the case of Canadian peacekeeping there was no formal statement of policy, but that does not mean that there was no policy, but rather it was an implicit or tacit one.

One of the remarkable aspects of Canadian peacekeeping foreign policy is that the Canadian government has *never* refused a request to provide peacekeeping troops and has participated in virtually every UN peacekeeping operation over the decades since 1956. While Canada may never have had an official written-on-paper policy, obviously the UN and other actors saw that Canada did have a policy. The Krasner definition of a institution stated that it "guides expectations." Certainly most international actors had a common expectation about Canadian peacekeeping policy which guided their behavior; the Canadian government's response almost always conformed to those expectations.

A key point of this chapter identifies the ontology of a government with its policies, which exist independently of those currently in power. Canadian peacekeeping politics illustrates this nicely. Power has alternated between Tories and Liberals, and there have been a variety (nine) of prime ministers since 1956. I discuss the interaction between people and policies in the next chapter, but here I note that Canadian peacekeeping policy was in place when the vast majority of prime ministers took office. However they felt about that policy they were not all-powerful principals. Some prime ministers, such as Pierre Trudeau, had reservations about the policy, but did nothing to change it. Canadian leadership was not enthusiastic about participating in the UN forces in the Congo but felt that public opinion was strongly in favor. Certainly the path of least resistance was to continue with preexisting patterns.

The model of institution creation I present in chapter 9 takes as its starting point John Kingdon's (1984) influential agenda-setting framework. The key factors that explain institution creation—and by analogy policy formation—are: (1) problems, (2) solutions, (3) favorable context, and (4) power. One must have favorable values on *all simultaneously* for a major policy shift to occur. Hence policy creation is a highly contingent event.

The requirement of high values on all dimensions provides a theoretical structure that satisfies the criterion of any punctuated equilibrium model. Stability results from the fact that the absence of any one factor prevents change and maintains the status quo. Each factor is a necessary condition for policy creation. Change can occur abruptly when the four factors happen to coincide. For example, if three of the four factors are present then we can say that a window-of-opportunity is open. Supply the last factor and the structure changes dramatically. To illustrate this, if we consider that each factor has a 50 percent chance of being favorable and that each factor is independent of all the others, then we get policy change only 1 out of 16 times (the probability of getting four heads when tossing four coins).

The Suez Crisis and the Arab-Israeli war of 1956 set the stage for the birth of Canadian peacekeeping policy. Canada found itself with a severe problem in the form of a major disagreement between its two most important allies, the United States and the United Kingdom. The solution had been floating around for a while since Canada had participated in various UN operations in the late 1940s and early 1950s in the Middle East, India, and Vietnam. To use Kingdon's language, there was also a key policy entrepreneur at the right place and at the right time in the person of Lester Pearson, influential in Ottawa and at the UN. Oran Young (1991) has argued that leadership is necessary for rinstitution creation, and the Canadian case supports this in terms of state-level policies. The peacekeeping idea was certainly not going to come from the major or superpowers, and Canada was one of the few countries with any kind of experience with UN observation forces.

It was a solution that the United States and the USSR could support. Though there were numerous problems with implementation because of Israeli and Egyptian objections and obstacles, it was a balanced solution whereby neither side could be said to have a clear advantage.

This new policy was proposed and accepted, and it seemed to almost all to be a clear success. Peacekeeping troops separated the Israelis and Egyptians, and Pearson went on to win a Nobel Peace Prize.

That this first major application of what was to become Canadian policy was a success is important for the functionalist view of institutions. Success is a reason to continue along the same path. Success removes ammunition from critics. Again, if it is not broke, no reason to fix it.

Of course there are always opponents to any policy. As Baumgartner and Jones (1993) make very clear in their study of U.S. policy, critics need negative images and possible venues to pursue their actions. With Canadian peacekeeping, problems can arise through two generic channels, (1) the failure of UN missions that Canada is identified with, and (2) the pull and tug of domestic politics, particularly peacekeeping as an electoral issue. Once institutionalized there needs to be some major reason to change coming from one or both of these channels.

In the formative period of Canadian peacekeeping the international channel is blocked by the very favorable image of the role of Canada in the Suez Crisis. There are no international actors or blatant failures to encourage Canada to abandon its peacekeeping role.

The domestic channel is a less obvious one to look at (for traditional international relations scholars at least). Not surprisingly the Tories were not enthusiastic about peacekeeping (just like the Republicans in the United States who do not like such activities). Diefenbaker tried attacking peacekeeping in the 1957 elections, particularly in that it was not pro-British enough. Granatstein reports (1968) that it was soon clear that this was not a good election strategy. Even conservative, establishment newspapers such as Toronto's *Globe & Mail* (roughly the equivalent in Canada of the *New York Times*) supported peacekeeping activities. It appears that the Tories learned after this to avoid peacekeeping as an election issue, at least it does not appear in standard accounts of Canadian elections (e.g., Clarke et al. 1996).

As a rule foreign policy is never an issue in federal elections. As Major General Lewis MacKenzie, a prominent Canadian general and peacekeeper, asked rhetorically during a controversial time for Canadian peacekeeping: "Do you know of one other country that goes through leadership races and election campaigns time and again and never mentions defence policy?" (cited in Martin and Fortmann 1995, 378). In short, peacekeeping as an election issue did not occur.

Another potential counterargument is that the Canadian armed forces supported peacekeeping activities. However, this was clearly not the case. Peacekeeping was always a secondary and minor activity, NATO was the main preoccupation. The military consistently resisted special training for peacekeeping troops, and peacekeeping was certainly no way to make a career in the military.[4]

Initially then peacekeeping was a success and certainly was popular with the Canadian public. Later actions indicated the limits of this strategy; it was quite successful in maintaining truces but did little more to contribute to conflict resolution. But over the decades there was no real reason, domestic or international, to change policy. Even less so as time went by and Canada became quite identified with this policy.

The punctuated equilibrium model of policy stresses its stability, its ability to withstand shocks. The end of the Cold War provided one protracted shock to Canadian peacekeeping policy. Not only that, it was a period of fiscal constraint and Canadian troops were involved in a major scandal over murder and torture in Somalia. With the 1993 elections peacekeeping for the first time since Diefenbaker became an issue. Kim Campbell made criticism of peacekeeping part of her

---

[4]This changed slowly after the Cold War when the military began to see the popularity of peacekeeping as a means of maintaining budgets, but it continued to be true well into the 1990s.

election campaign. While it was probably not the major cause of her defeat—the worst in Tory history, leaving the party with only two seats in Parliament—her criticisms of peacekeeping went down with her ship to defeat. Martin and Fortmann report at the worst of the crises in 1991–94 over Canadian troops' behavior in Somalia and the general problems of peacekeeping in Bosnia the overwhelming majority, over 80 percent, of people polled were in favor of maintaining or increasing Canadian commitments to peacekeeping missions.

Martin and Fortmann (1995) discuss public opinion polls about Canadian defense policy in general and peacekeeping in particular. They report that at the founding of the UN 78 percent of Canadians were willing to send troops to maintain the peace. Polls conducted in 1986–89 about the priorities of Canadian armed forces consistently put peacekeeping at the top with about 25–30 percent; in contrast options like "prevent Soviet aggression" got around 15 percent.

Internationally, the post–Cold War has been a boom period for UN peacekeeping. Within a few years there have been more peacekeeping missions than during the whole Cold War period. So there is no reason in terms of the international situation for Canada to abandon its traditional role, which has now taken on much greater significance. Peacekeeping is now in.

The history of Canadian peacekeeping policy illustrates the punctuated equilibrium pattern. It was a special combination of conditions that led to its founding in 1956 and rapid institutionalization thereafter. For the following decades, through the Cold War and its demise, peacekeeping has remained a core part of Canadian foreign policy. It continues today to live a very healthy existence.

# Conclusion

> Looking backward today [1951] on these endless disputes between our government and the belligerents over neutral rights, it seems hard to understand how we could have attached so much importance to them.
>
> —*George Kennan*

For a historian of U.S. foreign policy Kennan makes an embarrassing admission. One important job skill of a historian lies in the ability to understand different cultures or times. Of course, Kennan belonged to the Cold War realist gang that was trying to overturn America's foreign policy heritage. Many of this gang, such as Morgenthau, Kissinger, and Hoffman, came from German—not American—traditions, and they found American foreign policy customs quite strange.

However, much of the core of pre–World War II U.S. foreign policy was founded in the direct aftermath of the American and French revolutions. Policies such as alliance-avoidance and the rights of neutrals were forged in the fire of revolution. These policies lived long and healthy lives before being destroyed by World War II. This is exactly the punctuated equilibrium model of policy, a long life that begins with major political events and ends likewise.

The Cold War realists stressed balance of power, flexibility, and alliance formation. American foreign policy for 150 years showed exactly the opposite traits. Instead of rejecting these facts about the history of American foreign policy as somehow aberrant and "against nature," the punctuated equilibrium model tries to make sense of them. It suggests that foreign policy is not the nimble dancing proposed by the classical realists, but rather a lumbering, straightforward moving military march. World War II did not so much derail American foreign policy as to put it on a new straight path of forty years of constancy in the form of the Cold War.[5]

Of course the classic realists focused on individual leaders rather than governments or foreign *policy*. The punctuated equilibrium model argues that, except in times of major policy formation, policies ontologically and historically precede leaders. The question then arises about individual choice in an already existing, institutionalized, foreign policy framework. This is the topic of the next chapter.

---

[5]The same issue arises for students of international war and conflict. Most wars and militarized disputes occur in the context of long-term rivalries. See Diehl and Goertz (2000) for an analysis and test of the punctuated equilibrium model for enduring rivalries.

# Chapter 8

# Individuals and Organizations

Les États sont gouvernés par cinq choses différentes : par la religion, par les maximes générales du gouvernement, par les lois particulières, par les mœurs et par les manières. Ces choses ont toutes un rapport mutuel les unes avec les autres. Si vous en changez une, les autres ne suivent que lentement ; ce qui met partout une espèce de dissonance.

—*Montesquieu*[1]

Government behavior can therefore be understood ... as *outputs* of large organizations functioning according to standard patterns of behavior ... government behavior relevant to any important problem reflects the individual output of several organizations, partially coordinated by government leaders.

—*Graham Allison*

The previous chapter argued that all key actors in the politics of international institutions are organizations, usually large ones, the key one being of course national governments. I treated the organization as a unitary actor, one defined by its policies, norms, and SOPs (like Montesquieu's states). That organization as a unitary actor resembled in many ways the individual decision maker I sketched out in part I. Notoriously, organizations are not unitary actors but involve the coordinated actions of many people. Hence, any theory of organizational actors must include a model of how individuals who have to apply rules interact with each other as well as with organizational norms.

In a dystopia the norms of the individual would match perfectly the norms and rules of the organization itself. The reality is that the match between system norms (institution, international institution, or organization) and individual policies varies widely. This poses problems—but also has advantages—for organizations. It is conventional to express this in terms of conflict between levels.

---

[1] States are governed by five different things: religion, general heuristics of government, specific laws, morality, and custom. These things all have a relationship with each other. If you change one, the others follow but slowly, which creates conflict everywhere.

The first conflict is between the organization and the leadership of the organization. Except for some rare, but important, cases leaders enter organizations that have established rules, norms, and culture. There may thus be conflict between organizational policy and the policy that leadership would like to establish. A second conflict can occur between leadership and those at lower levels in the hierarchy, what is often known as the principal–agent problem. To these two conflicts we can add a third, between agents and organizational rules and roles.

Since the key issue for me is the relation between the different norm structures of actors and organizations/institutions I shall refer to this general problem as the individual–institution problematique. By choosing this label I emphasize the link between individuals and their social, political, and cultural environments. The choice of the neutral term "individual" reflects my desire to address the fact that the individual varies depending on the focus of analysis. Since I consider leadership as a potential "agent" I prefer the terminology of individual in labeling the problematique. I choose the term institution because of my main focus on the relationship between governments and international institutions.

This problematique has received different names, usually corresponding to different theoretical perspectives, such as principal–agent, agent–structure, two-level games, and so forth. The individual–institution label fits better I think than the common alternatives which bring with them theoretical baggage and connotations that mislead. For example, some approaches imply—normatively or empirically—a particularly strong influence of the institution on the individual, this is the case of the principal–agent or agent–structure[2] perspectives. We need to leave open the extent of the influence of the institution on the individual.

Often the individual–institution relationship takes on very conflictual colors. Most extreme is the principal–agent framework which allows for little coincidence of interest between superior and inferior. We have seen the other extreme where coordination equilibria are completely in the self-interests of all players. Keeping with the fuzzy philosophy of this book, I propose that the conflict, both within individuals and between individuals and institutions, can run from extreme to none. At the individual level in this chapter we shall see that a person's professional identity and values can fit very well with her organizational role. At the same time it is possible for the principal to act against organizational norms and existing policy. Instead of starting with an a priori position we need models and minds open to a variety of possible configurations.

This chapter deals with the individual–institution problematique in its organizational manifestation. Unlike the principal–agent or agent–structure approaches which see two levels I shall analyze three levels, organizations, leadership, and bureaucrats and the relations between them. Figure 8.1 illustrates the basic framework where organizational existence is a given. Into this preestablished set of policies enter leadership and bureaucrats. There can be conflict or coincidence

---

[2] In theory agents also create structures, but as the Katzenstein (1996) volume exemplifies most scholars focus on structures influencing agents.

FIGURE 8.1: Individual–Institution Problematique: Organizational Version

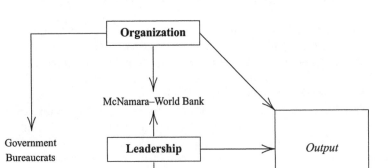

of policy norms between these various levels. I have intentionally chosen to illustrate the relations between different levels with examples that cut across the typical assumptions of the principal–agent or agent–structure frameworks. For example, when Robert McNamara enters the World Bank there is a conflict between his policies and the well-established norms of the bank; in my discussion of bureaucrats and governments I use the work of Brehm and Gates (among others) to illustrate that individuals often have personal value systems that correspond quite well to their organizational roles.

My perspective on these parallel sets of problems is to consider them all as *conflicts between norms*. Chapter 6 presented a choice procedure for the situation where norms provide conflicting advice. That discussion assumed that the conflicting norms belonged to a single actor, but I will argue in this chapter we can use the same conceptual framework for understanding choice when the origin of norms lies at different levels.

My approach was first to analyze conflicts between norms and then to consider how different norms might be weighted in the decision process. Chapter 6 did not make much of the weighting process, but that becomes key when one applies the basic framework to the individual–institution problematique. Weighting then becomes the relative power of the individual or institution norm in the final outcome. Sometimes the individual is more powerful than the institution, such as the U.S. government in many international institution contexts, or some agents in organizations like teachers in schools. This means that the final outcome depends relatively more on the individual norm than on the institutional one. Sometimes the institution is stronger and the output reflects more the content of that policy than the individual's.

Nevertheless the standard case will be one of some disagreement on policy. However, instead of seeing this as something distinctive of organizations, I have already made that assumption in terms of individual people. I assumed already in chapter 6 that a person would have conflicting values, rules, and norms. The whole purpose of that chapter was to understand decision making with norms when that arises. In fact I argued there that such conflicts were often positive in the sense that different rules represent different aspects of the choice that should be taken into account. I will propose that the same can be the case in organizational choice in this chapter using the relatively well-defined problem of armies and war.

Since I do not assume a priori conflicting norms one must empirically analyze the extent of conflict and the theoretical model must permit a range of conflicting values. Both the principal–agent and the agent–structure frameworks have assumed conflict, but this is really an empirical question. In the context of international institutions there are certainly governments who are quite willing to carry out directives of international treaties that they have signed. There may be agents in organizations that want to do their jobs well and in accordance with organizational policy.

The analysis of the extent of conflict is key both in international and organizational contexts. If all countries of the world were capitalist democracies then that would eliminate many potential conflicts between international norms, say on human rights, and national ones. The same is true for organizations, the goal of all leadership is to hire those whose individual values already match job requirements.

To use a different theoretical language, the functional view of organizations and individuals within them is a theory of identity politics. In this context it means the incorporation of role norms into one's personality. For example, U.S. trade organizations—international and domestic—clearly show the impact of role identities. Both in the case of the Federal Trade Commission (FTC) and the U.S. Trade Representative (USTR) important differences in policy arise depending on whether those in charge are economists or lawyers. One organizational revolution occurred in the FTC when under James Miller and Caspar Weinberger economists replaced lawyers as the dominant actors (Katzmann 1980; Clarkson and Muris 1981). Lawyers asked about violations of law and were instrumentally rational in terms of probability of success in court. Economists viewed mergers not in terms of law violation but in terms of whether the merger would increase or decrease competition. I discuss the USTR case below (233 ff.), but one cannot understand U.S. international trade actions without understanding that lawyers have dominated this particular bureaucracy.

Most of the time a new policy must be inserted into the structure of existing policy. This existing structure imposes not only constraints but also obligations and permissions. I think that much policy fiddling revolves around the integration of new policy into old structure. This can have a major impact on the success or failure of the policy itself. This is the point that Montesquieu was making in the epigraph to this chapter.

In short, this chapter deals with organizational decision making described in terms of conflicts between different structures of norms. The theoretical trick is to think of organizations, leadership, and bureaucrats as all being systems of norms, rules, and policies, which may conflict or coincide. Fuzzy logic decision making provides a way to combine norms into a final choice weighting the norm input of each according to its importance and influence.

## Conflicting Policies and Organizational Choice

All decision is a matter of compromise.

—*Herbert Simon*

The principal–agent approach to the individual–institution problem starts by framing the question in terms of a conflict of interest between principal and agent. While I discuss the extent of this putative conflict in the next section, the key issue here is that principal and agent are assumed to have opposing preferences. While the organization is reified in terms of the principal (something I obviously do not do) the expected utility approach makes the same basic assumption about the rationality of the two actors.

My approach transforms conflicting preferences into conflicting policy structures. However, in addition my framework also includes divergences on means as well as ends. In expected utility work this generally does not enter into the picture; in bargaining models differences on means never enter in. But in real organizations conflicts arise even though leadership and bureaucrats may have common goals; they can still differ on the best method for attaining them. Take Allison's classic discussion of the Cuban Missile Crisis (1971), Kennedy and his advisors might have had a common set of goals, but the views of McNamara, Ball, the army, navy, and air force did not at all agree on the best means. One can easily find expected utility work on aggregation of preferences but virtually nothing on aggregation of means.

In short, while the principal–agent framework assumes conflicting preferences I will speak of conflicting norms and policies. These conflicting norms include differences on means as well as ends. Hence the first step in my "solution" of the individual–institution problematique lies in the reformulation of the problem in terms of conflicting policy structures: the norms of the organization, leadership, and bureaucrats may not coincide.

The second step is *not* to assume that these are important conflicts. Going back to the Cuban Missile Crisis, McNamara and the navy may have had differences about the blockade, but they were legitimate differences about the best way to conduct the operation. This step has a corollary: the different policy systems can provide valuable input in the final decision. The navy obviously knows things about running a blockade that McNamara does not. McNamara has a grasp of diplomacy that the navy ignores. Here we pick up the potentially positive aspect of conflicting norms that the fuzzy logic decision-making methodology emphasizes. In terms of the final output one might want to take into consideration that organizations, leadership, and bureaucrats all have something of value to contribute. One then might want to arrive at a final choice that balances these various competing considerations.

Depending on the good or service produced one might want to *design* an organization in which the bureaucrats have a great deal of say in the final choice. After all, this was a major claim of the U.S. progressive movement in the late nineteenth and early twentieth centuries. It felt that government bureaucracies would better produce goods and service if the influence of politicians was reduced and that of professionals in the bureaucracy increased. The argument was that professionals were more devoted to the functional goals of the bureaucracy than were politicians who wanted to use bureaucracies for other ends.

Herbert Simon describes exactly this in his classic discussion of the principles of adminstration. He lists six commonly proposed principles and quite commonsensically shows that if you push them too far these principles begin to conflict. What happens in practice is that people try to find a balance between them. This all makes sense when expressed in a simple practical example:

> Closet space is certainly an important item in the design of a successful house; yet, a house designed entirely with a view to securing a maximum of closet space—all other considerations being forgotten—would be considered, to say the least, as somewhat unbalanced. (Simon 1997, 42)

The final big step consists of thinking of conflicting policy systems in organizations in terms of the methodology for dealing with conflicting norms in individuals outlined in chapter 6. In that context I assumed that the conflicting norms belonged to a single individual, but nothing prevents me from allowing these norms to arrive from different places, organization, leadership, and bureaucracy. In fact, we can go back to the extended discussion of the norms of just war theory (114 ff.). In the discussion of the Brunk et al. study I stressed that individuals have conflicts regarding the values represented by national security and the moral rules of war, and that most individuals tried to weigh these various concerns in their final decision. Here we can think of this in terms, say, of the rules of war that the U.S. Army has as official policy which may conflict with the policies of generals and frontline soldiers. The end result will reflect the impact of formal organizational policy as well as the norm systems of commanding officers and troops. As the epigraph to this section says: all decisions involve compromise. That is exactly what the fuzzy logic model of organizational choice produces.

However, once we move to the organizational context, we must make one major modification to the methodology presented in chapter 6. There the weight of each norm in the final choice was the value attached to that policy by the individual (not to be confused with how applicable a given norm is). For organizations we replace this by the relative power and influence that the organization's, leadership's, or bureaucrats' policy has in the final output.

In summary one can apply the same ideas expressed in figure 6.2 to the individual–institution problematique in its organizational version. One can replace "rule 1" and "rule 2" by organizational policy and leadership policy, and one can add bureaucrat policy to the figure since there is no limit to the number of applicable norms. The final decision is a function of how applicable its policy is and the power of the holders of the various relevant policies. The fundamental trick is to think of the individual–institution problematique in terms of conflicting norm systems.

In many ways the policy decision-making model that I first presented as a model of individual choice works better in the organizational context. This is because organizational policies and role norms are much more structured and explicit than those of the average individual. When a decision occasion arises almost all leaders and bureaucrats start by looking for relevant organizational policy and role norms, it is only after this that individual norms come into play. Justification of action relies almost exclusively in arguing for compliance with organizationally or professionally recognized norms.

## Conflicts between Individual and Organizations

As I have mentioned, the organization or government presents in microcosm the characteristics of the individual–institution problem. Within expected utility approaches this problematique has one expression in the principal–agent metaphor. Be it the administration as agent of the Congress, the navy as an agent of Kennedy we have a view of hierarchical relationships with chiefs and Indians. As we all know the Indians do not always obey the chiefs. As with all theoretical perspectives the principal–agent approach highlights some aspects of the individual–institution problem and hides others. Viewed through the lenses of my three-level framework it becomes unclear who the principal really is: should it be the organization or the leadership? The key issue for me is the fit between norms at different levels, in particular in this section, the correspondence between bureaucrats' norms and the organization's. This is most commonly expressed in terms of the match between role norms and individual's norms. For ease of exposition I will assume that role norms in the organization match those widely prevalent in society.

Brehm and Gates (1997) address the principal–agent framework in the context of American governmental organizations such as police departments and federal government agencies. The principal–agent literature provides their main theoretical interlocutor, however they treat the core concern in this section, the match between bureaucrats' personal policy systems and those of the organization and role within which they operate. Though they talk the expected utility language their critique of the principal–agent literature matches very well the argument I make here. Their core claim is that the principal–agent literature has radically misrepresented the nature of the agent. Agents not only have pecuniary and leisure preferences but they also have "functional" preferences: they *want* to do their job well. Brehm and Gates argue that both monetary and functional preferences matter; this fits well with the arguments of chapters 4 and 5 which suggested that people and polities had both instrumental and ethical norms. These functional preferences correspond in fact to role and professional norms, which are social institutions. So while they use the language of preferences I will talk about individuals' identities containing social role norms.

As Brehm and Gates remark, most of the principal–agent literature has a mean-spirited view of bureaucrats and agents. This literature focuses on a situation where superiors give orders that inferiors do not want to follow: it assumes a large conflict of interest. In this simple world, agents carry out and implement the principal's decision. In addition, there seems to be a normative assumption that agents *should* follow orders. I suggest that with a different type of decision-making model in mind and with a different type of organization as the archetypal model we can make much more sense of organizational policy making and implementation, and begin to see how to deal with other individual–institution problems.

Given its basic origins in economics, the principal–agent optic sees relationships in organizations via the archetypal category of the business firm with its relatively strict hierarchical relationships where bosses give orders to subordinates. Even more in its concern for "shirking" and "preferences for leisure" it seems to deal with factory-type relations. Basically chiefs give orders and Indians follow them because they want to get paid. The Indians do not really care about their jobs beyond what they get in wages. Given the *political* issues that interest me shirking is not a useful category. Many bureaucrats put in long hours, and work hard at their jobs. Feldman (1989) notes that many put in overtime writing reports that they know no one is likely to read. But as Brehm and Gates put it, agents may have policy disagreements with their chiefs. They may work hard but against the policy of the chief or on other policies that they prefer. According to the principal–agent conceptualization chiefs have different preferences from Indians, the principal must *make* the agent do what he does not want to do. But it is one thing to shirk and another to have a policy difference. Given the weak evidence for shirking as a problem at the level of important bureaucratic actors, we can ignore the preferences for leisure as a difference between the principal and agent.[3]

---

[3] In other contexts of course shirking does matter. I strongly recommend Peter Sellers's Ealing Studios comedy *I'm all right Jack* for an amusing treatment of the incompetence of capital and the shirking of labor.

Brehm and Gates have correctly emphasized that "sabotage" really means policy differences. Within an organization with existing SOPs and policy it may just as well be the principal who is sabotaging as the agent. The whole progressive movement in the United States began with a view that sabotage frequently came from above. Political concerns were prevailing over functional ones. Preferences of elected officials were running against the functional purposes of the bureaucracy. Instead of building roads one paid off political debts. The reform movement stressed that the actions of bureaucracies should be determined by the functions of the organization. Here we have a case where the bureaucrats' norms match better with the organization's than does the policy system of leadership.

The principal–agent framework identifies and merges the principal with the organization. To be a consistent methodological individualist requires that one question the identity of interests between the principal and organization. Principals are individuals just like agents. Be they elected officials or bureaucrats they enter a preexisting government with often well-established policies. If the principal wants to change all that she must fight the organization to change its rules. Just as agents have policy disagreements with principals so can principals fight with organizations.

When a principal gives an order the agent considers that within the organizational context and culture (see Smith 1994 for a wonderful analysis of this in the French army in the trenches of World War I). Not all commands are created equal. Those that the agent feels fit organizational policy, rules, and objectives may well be treated differently from those than run head-wise into organizational values. At the normative level, is it wrong for an agent in the civil rights department to resist an order of a Reagan appointee? Reagan himself felt the same about congressional orders regarding the contras in El Salvador.

Organizational functions and norms usually exist well before the principal or agent arrives on the scene. Within this context it makes a dramatic difference how the order of the principal fits with this preexisting rule structure. We can layer the organization–principal problematique on top of the principal–agent one. Conflicts and alliances can arise between and among all three levels.

Brehm and Gates find that typical views about the nature of the agent do not apply. This means that the *individual* level assumptions of the principal–agent model are flawed. It is worth citing in extenso the summary of their findings regarding federal bureaucrats, police officers, and social workers:

> Across all the variation in measures of performance, levels of government, and types of bureaucrats, we find striking convergence of our results. Subordinate performance depends first on functional preferences, second solidary preferences, and lastly on the efforts of the supervisor. . . . We also showed that functional preferences tended to affect both working and shirking, while not having a corresponding effect on encouraging work. . . . The strongest effects across the models for [police] officers in 1967 and 1977 were functional preferences and the officer's degree of professionalism . . . we found evidence of the role of solidary attachments and connections among fellows,

consistent with ideas of "corporate culture" as well as "police culture." A
higher degree of contact among officers yielded conformity in the patterns of
working and shirking. (1997, 195)

Brehm and Gates do not really develop this idea of functional preferences.
What does it mean to say one "likes the job" or that "one's preferences correspond to functional, job requirements"? In their discussion of police officers they
mention professionalization as a component of a good—productive—bureaucrat.
In terms of rules what they describe is in fact professional and role norms. To be
a professional means to act according to a set of rules and norms established for
that particular role. Hence one way to examine conflicts between individuals and
institutions is through examining differences between individual and role norms.
In normal times to follow role norms means to follow norms of the organization.
Hence we can reformulate the individual–institution conflict in the organizational
context in terms of divergences between individual and role norms.

Role requirements and professional norms usually have a functional character, society's view of how best to achieve certain goals. Role norms for teachers,
doctors, economists, and so forth relate to beliefs about how best to educate, heal,
produce efficiently, and so on. As we have repeatedly seen, goals lie inherent
in rule structures. Organizational role fits with organizational culture, it include
views about how best to achieve institutional goals (instrumental norms) and com-
prises what organizational ends should be. I mentioned Kier's use of the organizational culture concept in her study of the French military; culture there meant
commonly held instrumental beliefs about how best to protect France. Rhodes's
(1994) study of the U.S. Navy came to the same conclusion.

If organizations are routines, policies, and SOPs then the individual in an organization becomes a set of role and professional norms. I quoted March and
Simon in the previous chapter but left out part of the quote (the points of suspen-
sion), here is the whole thing:

> Organizations are *collections of roles and identities*, assemblages of rules by
> which appropriate behavior is paired with recognized situations. (March and
> Simon 1993 [1958], 12, emphasis is mine)

Any individual who takes a position in an organization enters into a structure of usually well-established norms for the organization as a whole as well as
specific role norms for her job. These role norms inform the individual what she
should, should not, and may do. For example, Hollis describes role decision making in just the terms which I have used to analyze decision making with norms,
what he calls a "normative explanation" and which involves:

> (1) the agent occupied a position with a role $R$ requiring action $A$, (2) the
> agent knew that $R$ required $A$, (3) the agent did $A$ because of (1) and (2). . . .
> We can read it as asserting that (1) and (2) caused him to $A$ in that he was
> so well socialized that he always acted on a normative syllogism with true
> premises. (1977, 74, 77)

To stress the importance of role is to endorse the aphorism: where you stand depends on where you sit. If role requirements determine behavior then we should see the same kind of consistency in behavior we find with norm-based decision making. Because role definitions change slowly, consistency in behavior *across* office-holders provides evidence for the importance of role definition. As Hollis and Smith (1986) emphasize, the kind of advice given the president in the Iranian hostage crisis was largely consistent with organizational role.

Role definitions are in part formally described (e.g., by law) but informal expectations in part dictate them. In chapter 4 I stressed that definitions of norms arising in the literature on convention and coordination games often see norms as expectation-controlling devices (it is also part of the Krasner definition of an institution). Role expectations do more than allow coordination, they also coerce. The violation of role norms often provokes sanctions, from other agents just as much or more than from a hierarchical superior, as Brehm and Gates found.

The principal–agent literature assumes that private preferences conflict with role duties. It is clear that individuals who play important roles have private agendas that influence their behavior, but what also happens is that the selection process tends to weed out the most blatant cases of conflict. A general principle is that a person with a sympathy for the military should be selected as secretary of defense: "only hawks can assemble the pieces of an office that needs a hawk with any consistency" (Hollis and Smith 1986, 283).

At the same time people do not tend to desire offices that conflict with personal values. The selection process works from both sides, people whose values do not fit well with the role set do not select those jobs. Recall that most professions require years of training; this process weeds out those whose interests and values match poorly.

Hence there is often little difference between role and individual norms. That was Hollis and Smith's point about hawks, the best choice for a bureaucratic position is someone who already fits the role/job requirements: in my terms people whose personal norms match the organization's. At the same time people will look for jobs whose identity matches theirs. This is exactly what Brehm and Gates found, the hardest and best workers were those who had strong functional (read role) preferences. That they also found that functional preferences were quite widespread means that organizations succeed in selecting people whose personal values fit with role requirements.

A great irony of the principal–agent literature is that its proponents are often the best example against the theory itself. As professors in universities they are bureaucrats, but very nonshirking, hard-working, and concerned about research and teaching; certainly preferences for leisure do not dominate the values of the majority. They would probably resist principals who tried to make them go against professional norms. Their effort seems only weakly related to their salary increases. In fact, many would give up salary to achieve APSR publications. Hence the expected utility scholar herself seems to fit quite well with the findings of Brehm and Gates about other kinds of bureaucrats.

But as Hollis and Smith argue, roles usually underdetermine choice. Normally there is a range of behavior that is consistent with role norms. Within this range one can expect personality effects to be seen. They also suggest that there may be conflicts in role norms; this too can make space for individual differences to surface. There may be scant resemblance between Orson Welles's King Lear and the local amateur's, despite the fact that they both speak the same words.

The central point here is that individuals often define themselves and their identities in terms of role and professional norms. Unlike the principal–agent literature I do not assume a priori that there is a conflict between the normative structures at the individual and role level. As Brehm and Gates found, it may be that the principal/role and agent have the same preferences. In my terminology the individual norms match well those required by the role.

Role norms—like all norms—represent a complex set of beliefs about how the world works and goals to be accomplished. As Hollis and Smith, and Brehm and Gates emphasize, bureaucrats often hold these same beliefs and values. The effective bureaucracies of the world—for example, Switzerland where I write this chapter—work not because they have solved the principal–agent problem with methods of supervision and sanction, but because it is easy to find people in Switzerland who have the appropriate personal norm structure.

Bureaucrats are obviously concerned about their salary and leisure time, but that is not the whole story. Most also believe that they should receive monetary rewards for doing their job well. But this does not mean that they do their job just for the money. Expected utility theorists claim that the shopkeeper is meritorious because it pays to be so. Bureaucrats believe the converse: if one is meritorious then one should be rewarded.

## Leadership and Bureaucrats: Organizational Output

> There are at least four rather distinct levels at which the analysis of the administrative situation may be carried out. At the highest level is the measurement of results, of the accomplishment of agency objectives. Contributing to these results are the elements of administrative performance. Subordinate to these, in turn, is input measured in terms of effort. Effort, finally, may be analyzed in terms of money cost. The mathematically minded will see in this structure a set of equations strictly identical with the economist's "production functions."
>
> —Herbert Simon

One can frame the individual–institution problematique in various ways. I have discussed it so far in terms of decision making using conflicting norm structures. But there is another approach to this issue, one that thinks in terms of institutional output or the production of goods and services. Decisions clearly are linked to output but there are nevertheless important differences. For example, an emphasis on output means one needs to be concerned about the nature of the goods and services provided, the technology of production.

Chapter 10 develops a production model of international institutions by focusing on the various functions that an international institution must perform well to produce its desired service, be it free trade, clean environment, human rights, or whatever. It also provides a formal model of this production metaphor in the context of international institutions. To ask about production is to pose questions about the performance of an international institution, and the same issue arises in the analysis of organizational output.

We can take two kinds of output as important, policy creation and implementation; the first is the modification of policies and norms while the second is how individuals in the organization use policies to produce goods and services. Not surprisingly, this distinction arises from the punctuated equilibrium model of policy developed in the previous chapter, which distinguished the policy creation phase from the long incrementalist one of policy application and fiddling. With an emphasis on output–policy or implementation–organization, leadership, and bureaucrats thus appear like capital and labor in an economic production function. Instead of trying to devise contracts so that the agent does what the principal wants, we want to design organizations and policies that produce the optimal output with inputs from leadership and bureaucrats.

How does the principal–agent perspective fit with a conceptualization of an organization as a system production? First, it becomes problematic who the principal, or agent, is. At virtually any given point in time *all* individuals in the organization are implementing *already* existing policies. To put it bluntly and baldly, everyone is an agent of production.

At the same time everyone is a principal. Policy is elaborated, interpreted, and specified at many different levels of an organization. Higher levels often set "guidelines" and general rules, agents translate them into specific policies, and then implement that.

Henceforth I will refer to policy implementation in terms of "agentness," and policy creation in terms of "principalness." This does not make everyone equal in policy creation or implementation but it does refuse the dichotomous, unbridgeable, and core distinction between principals and agents. It also makes sense of the fact that almost everyone is a principal of some and the agent of others.

Since everyone is an agent policy output results from the input of all concerned. We can take the team as the metaphor, the captain may be in charge, may decide the plays but she is also very involved in carrying out the plan of action. The principal–agent model assumes that the only input of the principal is supervision, monitoring, and sanctioning. One contribution to production may be supervision of others but there is no reason to limit principal input to these activities. They can also include, leading, training, do-it-yourself, shirking, etc. The psychological dynamics change completely if we think of the principal as leader of a production team rather than watch dog.

Of course one must permit differences between different bureaucratic actors in an organization. In particular one should include some measure of place in hierarchy, which corresponds roughly to the amount of power the principal has. But instead of erecting a dichotomy, I consider this a continuous function from minimal influence to complete control.

The same applies to policy making. Hierarchy is one essence of organization, another is specialization (Weber 1968 classically made these points). Instead of chiefs making policy we need a theoretical framework where all individuals provide input to policy making. We have no reason to assume that these individuals all have the same importance in the final policy product as delivered to the client, hierarchy is there to remind us otherwise. It may be more efficient to transfer some inputs from the principal to the agent, or vice versa, in order to achieve maximum output.

To jump ahead, this all makes even more sense in the realm of international institutions. Many actors create international institutions. Hierarchy in this context means differences in power, which of course is what it also means within organizations. Governments also implement international institution policies. Governments are simultaneously principals and agents within the context of international institutions.

With fuzzy logic philosophy in mind it does not seem odd to say that a certain actor is a .75 principal, while another is .50. In fact, this makes much more sense of the hierarchical character of organization. We can generally assume that the level of principalness decreases as we descend the organization ladder. Immediately we see that the typical principal–agent situation involves bureaucrats *both* with low levels of principalness. Take the examples of Brehm and Gates, the supervisors of social workers and beat police officers remain pretty low in the organizational hierarchy. If we take the common example of congressional oversight of regulatory commissions, we discover that in fact both have high levels of principalness.

I have suggested that degree of principalness decreases roughly with hierarchical level. However, it does not necessarily seem to be the case that the analogous principle applies to agents: degree of agentness does not necessarily increase as one descends the organizational ladder. The particular functional characteristics of the bureaucracy may give higher weights to supervisors and lower weights to agents, or vice versa. For example, the former can be the case when it is easy to monitor and sanction the actions of agents, for example, amount of sales, widgets produced, etc. But in the case of social workers output may depend more on the worker than the supervisor.

One might suppose that if an actor is .75 principal then it must be by consequence .25 agent, reproducing the dichotomous world of the principal–agent literature. Fortunately nothing in fuzzy logic requires this. Take the president of the United States and Congress, we might give both a high principalness score, say, .80 but in terms of agency we might give the Congress a low score, say, .10, while keeping the president very high at .85.

In summary, I propose that we treat all actors as to various degrees principals and agents. In terms of policy or organizational output—agentness and principalness—it proves more useful to think economically in terms of production functions. These typically consist of labor and capital, which we can replace by organization, leadership, and bureaucrats. The functional theory of institutions in chapter 10 takes just this sort of approach. There I consider different inputs horizontally across international institutions, but the same ideas apply here where inputs are conceived of vertically in organizations. In the present context organizations, leadership and bureaucrats contribute to output, but the relative importance of the two can very depending on the character of the actors and the service provided. For example, leadership can contribute as usual monitoring, sanctioning, and supervision, marginal rates of substitutability determine how much effect this has on total output.

By reformulating the principal–agent problematique into one concerning output and not compliance we have moved into the area of organizational design. Taking up the production function metaphor, we need to allocate activities between leadership and bureaucrats so as to maximize output. Like with capital and labor we need to find the optimal mix of organization, leadership, and agent policy. Things are complicated by the fact that organizational output is often conceptually and practically hard to evaluate. However, there is one interesting case—particularly for students of international relations—where there exists a long-standing debate over the relative weight of principal and agent in determining the quality of output: armies in war provide a good example of the issues involved.

One of the eternal discussions in the literature on strategy, armies, and war revolves around how much latitude should be given to lower-level commanders in the conduct of warfare. The question is how much should the leadership determine the actions of those in the front lines doing the actual fighting. Often there is policy conflict between those who look at the big picture and those who see a smaller picture. This policy difference gets expressed sometimes as the difference between tactics—lower level SOPs—and grand strategy. For example, Wilson claims that in the final analysis tactics are more important than strategy, basically because they lie at the end of the action chain:

> [I]n war, good tactics can often save a flawed strategy, whereas bad tactics can rarely make even an excellent strategy succeed. The French prepared, tactically as well as strategically, to refight World War I. . . . Had they adopted different tactics embedded in a more flexible organization, their strategic errors might not have counted so heavily against them. (1989, 18)

War fighting also proves illustrative since we can compare armies that use different relative mixes of agent and principal input. For example, in World War II the Germans left a great deal of initiative to lower-level commanders while the French insisted on much tighter control by the upper echelons (in contrast to the usual stereotypes of each culture). Creveld found that the German system was much more effective (since the Germans defeated quite easily the French), which he elevated into a general principle:

> [T]hose armies have been most successful which did not turn their troops into automatons, did not attempt to control everything from the top, and allowed subordinate commanders considerable latitude. (1982, 270)

This difference is not limited to World War II; these cultural differences can be seen already in the nineteenth century in Hutchinson's (1996) account of the development of the Red Cross. The Germans and Japanese trusted civilian groups to be efficient and capable of delivering healthcare services in time of war. In fact the Germans were quite successful in integrating (coopting) the Red Cross into the war effort. In contrast, the French military, which was quite elitist, fought the Red Cross idea because the military hierarchy did not believe that French civilians could do the job.[4]

In Vietnam one can contrast the U.S. Army which was much more hierarchical and top-driven with the U.S. Marines which permitted more lower-level initiative. Here too analysists have found that the marines were more successful in key aspects of the war, such as village protection and control.

Not surprisingly, differences in organizational design and culture can have dramatic effects on output. The army example illustrates that one needs to be concerned about shirking—dissertion—but just as much about agent input into the final decision. To formulate the principal–agent problematique in these terms means that you take seriously Brehm and Gates's functional preferences of agents. It only makes sense to allocate latitude to commanders if you think that they actually want to achieve organizational goals. The Germans quite clearly saw that one needed rewards for commanders who performed well, things like medals and promotions. But they also understood that other aspects were just as important. Creveld argues that the German soldier "fought for the reasons men have always fought: because he felt himself a member of a well-integrated, well-led team whose structure and administration, and functioning were perceived to be ... equitable and just" (1982, 163–64). It is not just the quantity of the rewards but also their quality that matters. Trust and esteem are just as important a payoff as an increase in salary. Brehm and Gates found that the consideration of peers was one of the three big factors explaining performance. Many have explained the differences in productivity between Japanese and American factories based on the better integration of workers into decision making in Japan than in the United States.

---

[4]One irony is that the French argument eventually won out since medical care during war was eventually taken over by the military everywhere.

The use of the concept of organizational output occurs a common part of organizational models, for example, Allison says in an epigraph to this chapter that "Government behavior can therefore be understood ... as *outputs* of large organizations." I shall return again in chapter 10 to the issues of output in the context of international institutions where I argue that international institutions are like governments and other organizations that produce goods and services. International institutions, like most government bureaucracies, are created to solve problems, hence one can ask of them how well they work and what determines the level of institutional output.

## Conflicts between Organization and Leadership at the World Bank

The previous chapter argued for an ontology of organization as a structure of norms, rules, and policies. Organizations, like law, exist in an important sense independent of the individuals that enter, act, and then exit. But of course organizations act through people, hence one must examine the fit between organizational norms and individual ones.

Not only do organizations act through individuals but individuals create and change organizations. The clash between organizations and individuals appears most clearly when new leadership enters with an agenda for change. The arrival of Robert McNamara at the head of the World Bank provides an example of the conflict between new leadership and a well-established and stable organization (and bureaucracy). In addition, this example illustrates the existence of multiple organizational levels. We have several actors in leadership roles in the form of the member states, the Executive Board, and the president. As the bureaucracy the bank has a large program and project staff, responsible for the choice and evaluation of proposals. Since its founding the bank as an organization has maintained over long periods—hence over changes in staff and president—consistent policies, yet important changes have occurred. Hence we can see the interactions between organization, leadership, and bureaucrats.

In the beginning the World Bank saw its role as capital lending to Third World countries. Its instrumental beliefs about promoting economic growth reflected the success of the Marshall Plan in helping European reconstruction. This led to a view that if capital shortages in the Third World were alleviated economic growth would ensue. Until the late 1960s bank lending consisted of loans for large capital projects like dams and power stations.

When McNamara entered the institution as president in 1968 he faced an organization and bureaucrats with well-established policies and roles. His new agenda included a transformation of the bank into a development institution, with a focus on basic human needs and poverty. It meant a radical redefinition of the role of economists and bankers in the bank as well as a basic reworking of fundamental organizational SOPs and routines. Hence, we have a perfect example of the leadership–organization conflict.

McNamara was the first World Bank president who himself did not come from a background in banking. His expertise was not even economics but systems management (instrumental rationality!). He applied this in the service of a number of different organizational goals, profit as CEO of Ford Motor Co., winning a war in Vietnam, and finally reducing poverty as head of the World Bank. He came to the bank with a clear agenda, one which mixed instrumental and moral values. He saw it as the moral duty of rich countries to aid poor ones, but also thought that poverty made communism more attractive.

McNamara's efforts to centralize and concentrate power in his hands indicates the high level of resistance he met on the part of bank economists and bureaucrats. Part of his effort involved selecting *new* personnel whose functional preferences matched the new policies of the organization. He brought in a large number of new staff with different backgrounds, with interests more in development and less in banking. All major attempts to change organizations and governments have used this tool of personnel replacement: it was the case for major political revolutions such as the French, Russian, and Chinese, as well as the minor revolutions of Roosevelt and Reagan.

Because the office of president already had a great deal of power in the bank hierarchy, and because he succeeded in concentrating more power in his hands, McNamara managed to transform some of the World Bank's basic policies. But a key factor was that there already existed pools of highly trained professionals that McNamara could tap to fill his bureaucracy. In this sense his values had to coincide with widely held values outside the organization.

The response of the bureaucrats gives an interesting test of the principal–agent model since they come from the same world—economics—as the proponents of principal–agent models. First of all, almost none responded to new and unpleasant job demands by shirking. But they did resent strongly what they considered as unprofessional demands instituted by McNamara. For example, traditionally the bank lent for capital projects where standard techniques of costs and revenue produced could be applied. All of a sudden they were to evaluate projects based on much fuzzier and harder to quantify criteria, some of which were noneconomic in nature such as environmental effects. McNamara asked them to violate their accustomed standards of professional rigor as well as traditional standards of evaluation.

Ascher (1983) describes the resistance of Bank staff to the introduction of these new policies. They influenced—sabotaged—policy in various ways. They introduced technical arguments against the new policies. They refused to gather the data to implement them. They generated a flurry of memos against the basic principles of the new line:

TABLE 8.1: Policy Change: World Bank Lending for Poverty

| 1968–70 | 1971–73 | 1976–78 | 1979–81 | 1982–84 | 1985–87 |
| --- | --- | --- | --- | --- | --- |
| Bank/IDA lending to poverty-oriented sectors (percentage of total) | | | | | |
| 5.0 | 15.3 | 27.4 | 29.5 | – | – |
| Bank/IDA lending to poor countries (percentage of total) | | | | | |
| – | – | 25.3 | 26.7 | 34.0 | 38.0 |

*Note*: data are three-year averages.
*Source*: Finnemore 1996.

Many professionals in the World Bank have been reluctant to incorporate new considerations in formulating development strategies if they require modes of analysis less rigorous than the traditional economic framework. The economist called upon to make decisions on the rate of return of a project will often balk at including factors for which only shaking data exist, such as the environmental cost, the indirect effects on the creation of employment . . . A more general lesson is that any new approach can be construed as a threat to the professional integrity of a perfectionist staff. (Ascher 1983, 428, 429)

The literature on the World Bank shows that the power struggle between leadership and bureaucrats revolved around policy. Asher claims that he found "ample cases" where policy resistance endangered the careers of bureaucrats. Also, the resistance depended very much on the professional beliefs and values of the bureaucrat. Staff with a "Chicago School" set of norms resisted more than staff with a "Sussex School" set.

In the process those bureaucrats most attached to old standards were probably the first to leave in search of jobs with a better fit with their professional norms. Transitional periods give good tests of role impact. Most of the time, as Brehm and Gates found, the fit between individual and role is pretty good.

Table 8.1 shows the change of policy in terms of the World Bank's distribution of funds to poverty sectors and the poorest countries. In 1965 these countries and sectors received little, less than 5 percent, by 1972 this had increased under McNamara's impetus to 15 percent, reaching almost 30 percent in the late 1970s. From the mid-1970s till 1990 we see incremental change in these global figures: the change from 5 percent to 25 percent is dramatic while an increase from 25 percent to 40 percent is incremental.

In terms of organizational output of services the World Bank fits well my framework of joint input of leadership and bureaucrats. The Executive Board (representatives of member countries) almost never vetoes a project and about as rarely initiates one. Of course, staff hesitate putting forward a project that they think the board would veto. But by the same token all projects that *do* get approval must be supported by bank professionals. This means that a project must satisfy *both* staff and board. This is exactly the formal model of institutional output described in chapter 10. Instead of the principal ordering the agent a more accurate model considers output in terms of the joint input of key organizational actors. In this regard the World Bank does not differ from the army example discussed above.

Studies of the bank confirm this fundamental aspect of organizational output:

> Because the staff has worked with a project all through the originating and consensus-forming phases, its share in influencing the approval decision is greater than that of any single Executive Director who does not hold his seat for a very long time and is, therefore, less familiar with the project than the operational staff. (Hürni 1980, 83)

> In practice, the Executive Directors veto a project only under extraordinary circumstances and have virtually no opportunity to initiate the consideration of specific projects. (Ascher 1983, 421)

In summary one must include agent inputs in any model of organizational choice at the World Bank.

But Hürni and Ascher underestimate the impact of leadership in their fine-grained look at agents. As the data in table 8.1 indicate, the bank massively shifted its lending to poor countries and poverty sectors. Without a doubt McNamara and his appointees succeeded in institutionalizing new, major, and long-term policies into the bank.

The punctuated equilibrium model emphasizes that policies do not change unless there is a problem. By the 1960s the large capital approach to development had attracted criticism; what had worked for Europe did not seem successful in the Third World. At the same time there had arisen institutes and approaches focusing specifically on Third World development with new ideas and which attacked the large capital projects typical of the World Bank. These new approaches focused on the basic needs of individuals such as health, education, and basic agriculture. A favorable political context for the World Bank consisted in the direction of U.S. domestic policy, in particular Johnson's War on Poverty and Great Society programs. That McNamara should wage an international war on poverty makes perfect sense in 1968, just as a Third World version of the Marshall Plan did in the 1950s. The World Bank case also shows the punctuated equilibrium pattern of abrupt policy change followed by incrementalism. Within a few years the character of the bank changed dramatically, but the World Bank of 1990 is clearly recognizable as only incrementally different from the 1970s one. The difference between the 1965 and 1975 bank is much greater than between the 1975 and 1990 one. The World Bank thus provides an example of how the punctuated equilibrium model works in an international organizational context.

# Conclusion

A key question in the institution literature is the effectiveness of international institutions. To use a preferred metaphor of this chapter the question becomes one of the output of the international institution. We can reformulate figure 8.1 as figure 8.2 to think about the individual–institution problematique in the international context. To do this we can map international institution ⇒ organization, leadership ⇒ governments, and bureaucrats ⇒ domestic actors. The functioning of the institution depends on the inputs from these three levels just like organizational output does.

I have examined briefly the various components of the organizational version of the individual–institution problematique in this chapter, but it is easy to find examples for the analogous international version. For example, it is clear that hegemons can exercise leadership and have an important influence on the content and performance of international institutions. At the same time the compliance of a *country*, say, in environmental institutions, depends a great deal on the interaction between the national government and domestic actors. Finally, the policy fit between some domestic groups and international institutions can be quite good, for example, domestic civil rights groups in authoritarian states.

As with organizations and individuals the key is to think in terms of interacting norm systems and the resulting policy choice. Be it individuals, organizations,

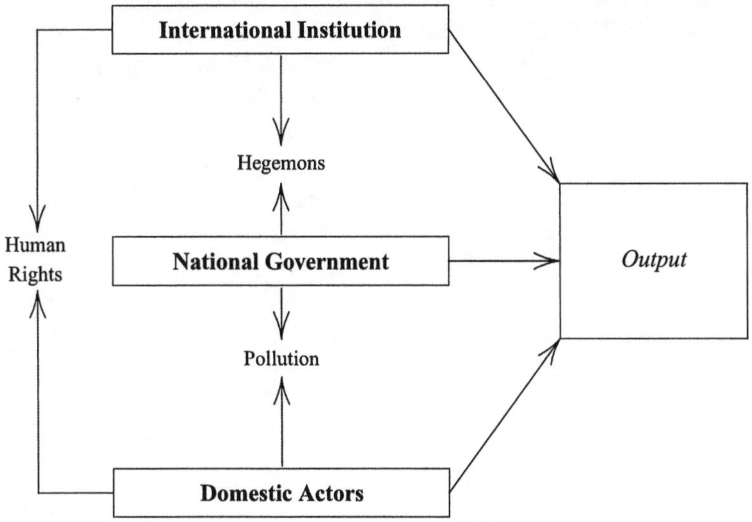

FIGURE 8.2: Individual–Institution Problematique: International Version

or international institutions we have the problem of conflicting norms. In the individual context I posed this roughly as instrumental versus ethical norms. In the organizational context it becomes conflicts among organizations, leaders, and bureaucrats. For international institutions it is conflicts among domestic actors, national governments, and international institutions. The relative importance and value of each norm determines its impact within an individual. However, once we move to organizations and international institutions the relative power associated with each norm determines its impact on the final choice.

Various metaphors such as principal–agent, agent–structure, and two-level games have informed thinking about the interaction of different levels. I find metaphorical and formal inspiration from the idea of production (economic production functions) and output. At the core of my functionalist approach lies the proposition that institutions exist because they provide services and goods, be they security, human rights, cleaner environments, free trade, etc. This is implicit when scholars view these issues through the lenses of collective *good* theory (see 10 ff. for more on that). In part III of this essay we shall see that the production function metaphor is more than that. Widely known scholars of institutions such as Elinor Ostrom have proposed theories that possess the formal structure of economic production functions (e.g., Cobb-Douglas). Not only that, we shall see that the mathematics of these models uses exactly the same fuzzy logic concepts that informed my analysis of conflicting norms in chapter 6.

Of course, I do not assume that organizations or international institutions actually achieve their goals or choose optimal methods. However, I think that one cannot forget that international institutions just like organizations have goals they want to achieve and that proponents work very hard to attain those goals in the best possible manner. But like the social constructivists argue, what those goals are and the "best" means of getting there depend on the cultural values and beliefs about the world of those who create and maintain those institutions.

# Part III

# International Institutions

# Chapter 9

# Creating International Institutions

How else would you do it?
*—(see page 192)*

Institution creation is policy formation at the international level. Governments occasionally decide to make joint policy decisions to regulate some aspect of their relations. These policies, rules, and norms that they decide upon have received the name "institution" in the world politics literature. Long ago in chapter 2 I defined institutions as a structure of rules and norms. This chapter focuses on the agreement on, hence the creation of a structure of policies. I say "agreement" advisably because as always the powerful tend to impose their views. In short, and statistical, terms the dependent variable is international institution creation.

I have divorced the ontology of institutions—rules and norms—from behavioral issues. Creating institution rules of course is an act, a behavior. What I continue to refuse to do is to assimilate that act to whether nations use institution norms in their decision making. When parliaments pass a law it is a law; the degree to which people follow it raises another set of questions, important ones to be sure. In practice these often go together, governments create institutions and then follow their norms, but to start from that point is bad theory and bad methodology (see chapter 2).

This dichotomy between creation and behavior mirrors a distinction I made in discussing organizations: policy creation often rests separate—often in organizational structure—from implementation. The punctuated equilibrium model of policy I proposed in chapter 7 for governments applies in the same sense to international institution policies. Institutional and social factors play a big role in policy and institution evolution. Hence we must not confound the creation phase with the fiddling and implementation phase of international institutions.

This chapter develops a theory of institution creation, which differs from a theory of institution evolution. This must be stressed because most approaches to institutions use the same basic theory for *both* institution creation and evolution. For example, Keohane's version of hegemonic stability theory uses the same power and interest factors to worry about "after hegemony" that he used to explain institution formation in the first place. Haas's analysis of the impact of epistemic communities in Mediterrean pollution institutions makes no distinction between effects at the beginning and during its evolution. I do not deny that power or lobbies matter in both institution creation and change, but they matter differently.

One needs to pose the question: what is the institution creation dependent variable? For the purposes of this chapter I take this to be the *explicit* agreement on a set of policies. This means a treaty signed by a significant proportion of the concerned states, and often the founding of an international organization to administer parts of the institution.

I do not assume of course that all relevant governments sign in order for an institution to come into existence. Part of the dynamics of the institution revolves exactly around why and when some governments finally sign on while others drop out. The United States has refused with some regularity to sign, at least initially, some institution-creating treaties, nevertheless these institutions were created. Also, quite often the United States joins the institution at a later date, as Nixon did, for example, when he signed chemical and biological weapons treaties (McElroy 1992).

The negotiations that lead up to these institution creation treaties can be quite lengthy. A good theory of institution creation can explain why some treaties are quickly negotiated and signed while others drag on for decades. These extended periods of negotiation prove key for *testing* theories of institution creation, since they permit us to examine the changes in causal variables over time.

To focus on explicit institution creation does not deny either the existence or the importance of tacit norms and rules. The focus of this chapter rests on the influential factors and the theory of institution creation. By limiting myself to explicit institution creation I avoid problematic cases of my dependent variable. I suspect that basically the same theory applies to tacit and informal institution creation. The rationale for limiting myself to formal institutions is pragmatic and not theoretical: first develop a theory for clear-cut cases before including ambiguous ones.

The existence of institution creation negotiations means that institution issues have made it onto government agendas. We can thus distinguish in a rough way between three stages:

(1) pre-negotiation activities by governments, epistemic communities, international organizations ⟹

(2) institution creation negotiations ⟹

(3) institution creation

Currently the institution literature focuses overwhelmingly on those institutions that make it all the way through this process (though see Underdal 1983; Young 1998). A real test of an institution creation theory requires data on the issues that drop out at the earlier stages.

This becomes even more important when we examine the structure of my theory. It makes very strong predictions about when institutions *fail* to form. A comprehensive test of ideas presented in this chapter thus requires studies on those prenatal institutions that were never born.

This chapter proposes a *theory* of institution formation. The interpretation of the word "theory" varies widely throughout the social sciences. In the context of this chapter I contrast a theory of institution creation with well-known *hypotheses*. To make this more concrete, we can take Young and Osherenko's study (1993) of the formation of polar environmental institutions. They examined and tested sets of hypotheses that arise from different approaches to regimes described as "power-based," "interest-based," and "knowledge-based" (see Hasenclever, Mayer, and Rittberger 1997 for a similar categorization). Thus they test a wide range of hypotheses, but in no sense do these hypotheses belong to one overarching theoretical structure. I propose to draw on ideas from these various categories and put them into a coherent and integrated framework: a theory of institution creation.

Some associate "theory" only with formal, mathematical, or deductive frameworks. The theory I put forth here can be formalized mathematically, something that I do in the next chapter. It turns out that the formal, functional theory of existing institutions I construct in the next chapter has the same mathematical structure as the theory of international institution creation presented here.

The theory I propose takes elements of functional as well as constructivist frameworks to create a hybrid approach. Institutions are policies which attempt to *solve problems*. I will talk constantly in terms of problems and their solutions; hence, one can describe my approach as a problem-solving view of institutions. By now this should not be surprising since in my discussion of individual and governmental norms and rules I have emphasized their instrumental aspects. As we saw in chapter 4, all norms have explicit or implicit goals that they serve. Here I use the language of "problems," but the idea is the same. Just as goals and interests vary so do problems.

To use a different language, problems are constructed. The constructivists are right, what counts as a problem or a solution depends on values, ideology, cultural traditions, and historical epoch. While some problems exist in an objective sense, e.g., lack of ozone in the atmosphere, these do not become "problems" in my model until some social group defines them as such and convinces others of that "fact."

By implication when something becomes a problem it means that actors think that government policies or institutions can provide solutions. Problems which are not "problems" can be called conditions. For governments, individuals, and organizations these conditions are constraints which people think cannot be changed. Bad eyesight is not a problem until someone invents eyeglasses.

A theoretical hybrid results from taking basically functionalist categories like "problem" and "solution" and interpreting them in a constructivist fashion. Also, there is no guarantee that the solution solves the problem, much less that it is the optimal solution. Following Kingdon, the way problems and solutions get "attached" to each other is very much a matter of social interaction, ideology, etc. For example, Kingdon stresses that sometimes solutions chase problems, as when advocates of market-based solutions look for government regulations to change. It may be that one group defines the problem while another generates the solution. For example, it may be environmental epistemic lobbies that create the problem of global warming while economists solve it with tradeable permits.

We all like to put ideas in boxes, as with this volume as a whole my ideas mix elements from different intellectual boxes. I tend to use a functionalist vocabulary, but my examples will all stress the constructivist content I give to this language.

## Determinants of Institution Formation

Given my emphasis on international institutions as policies it is not surprising that I begin with one of the most influential policy frameworks of the last decade. Kingdon's choice of problems, solutions and the importance of political context as components of his framework make it a natural candidate for building a model of international institution formation.

### Problem Creation

> To resolve a problem, the first thing you have to do is *make* it a problem.
>
> —*Panama President Torrijos to the U.S. ambassador about the Panama Canal*

Realists have always placed the pursuit of "national interest" at the core of their view of the international policy process, usually national interest of a particular sort, as we saw in chapter 4. To view international institutions as responses to problems shifts the perspective significantly. Since problems exist as a social phenomenon we start from a different level of analysis. Because problems come and go we have no eternal problems, only problems which international society sees as such at any given time in history. Institutions get created as responses to these problems, without a problem institution creation would be gratuitous, leaders have better ways to spend their time.

Problems make it onto the international agenda in different ways. So while the existence of a problem is necessary for institution creation there are different routes by which a problem arises for political action.

First of all, it is not necessarily the powerful—in the usual sense—that always define the problem or put it on the international agenda. In some cases leaders would even prefer that the problem never existed at all. Major events, crises, or shocks often occur outside the control of individual actors. These problems thrust themselves on governments demanding a policy response. The occurrence of World War II created a problem in terms of the construction of the postwar environment. The United States developed the atomic bomb as a weapon of war but as a side-effect the problem of the diffusion of nuclear weapons arose. So in many instances problems arise outside the control of any individual government, including hegemonic powers.

At the same time powerful governments can create problems. If the U.S. leadership decides that something is wrong then it becomes a problem for everyone else. If the U.S. government comes to the conclusion that government telecommunications monopolies are a hindrance to international trade then it gets on the agenda at WTO meetings. Hence the interests of the powerful can define what constitutes a problem for international action. This route we can call hegemonic problem creation.

Here we can see a contrast with standard hegemonic stability theory, which sees problems as essentially given and focuses only on the hegemonic actions to resolve problems. My approach does not take for granted that there is a "demand" for international institutions or that there are transaction costs that need to be reduced. The concept of "hegemonic problem creation" has the double advantage of implying that hegemons not only solve problems but also create them, and stresses the fact that what the hegemon sees as a problem may not be a problem from other points of view.

But hegemons are not the only group that create problems. Within the literature on environment institutions one finds a constant thread that claims that environmental institutions only come into being when the scientific community has reached a relative consensus that environmental pollution or degradation exists according to the norms of scientific research. Such consensus then creates a problem for policymakers. This appears with regularity in discussions of environmental institutions: "The identification of an ecological problem presupposes such [scientific] consensual knowledge ... shared knowledge is a necessary condition of institution formation" (List and Rittberger 1992, 803).

The key point is *not* whether there is an objective pollution problem but rather that politically influential scientists and relevant international organizations such as the UNEP (UN Environmental Program) agree that such a problem exists according to their definition of good science. One can contrast my position with Sprinz and Vaahtoranta (1994) who define national interest directly in terms of environmental degradation. I do not deny the reality of environmental damage, I only claim that for a theory of institution creation what matters is when this degradation gets defined as a policy problem for governments.

One cannot make sense of environmental policy by relying on objective measures of pollution. In 1965 environmental action was the concern of noninfluential scientists and fringe action groups. By 1975 governments all over the world were concerned with environmental policy. Nothing in the objective facts of pollution justify such a radical shift in affairs. Even more, the countries which had the worst pollution problems, e.g., Eastern Europe, were the least affected.

Many problems exist in an objective sense for decades or centuries before they become targets of policy action. If we are to believe the realists, war is the state of nature, hence wounded soldiers have been a problem for millenia. Tolstoy described with much detail in *War and Peace* the ordeals of badly wounded soldiers. But it was Henri Dunant who succeed in making these wounded a problem in the sense of putting it on the agenda of political elites across Europe, along with his proposed Red Cross solution. Dunant and other Genevois made this an international problem in the 1860s, eventually resulting in the Geneva Convention.

In summary, institution creation becomes possible when governments *see* a problem that demands attention. How that problem appears in their field of vision can vary. I have proposed three principal avenues by which problems get created:

1. exogenous shocks and crises such as world wars.

2. activities of powerful states, hegemonic problem creation.

3. international organizations, epistemic communities, influential individuals, and other powerful lobbies.

These routes to problem creation often direct attention toward real problems of international society. Again, I need to stress that many problems arise because of changing technology, changing domestic policy, changing economics, and changing values. These are real problems. But my model stresses that other just-as-real problems never receive attention. For example, Young (1998) mentions that important (objectively) problems like arctic haze have never become a prominent issue nor have the important issue of oil spills made it onto the agenda. Also, what one government considers a problem may not seem an issue for other actors. Problem definition is a social construction, at the same time it is an exercise of power.

## Solution Finding

My theory of institution creation places this event in a problem-solving framework. Institutions are thus policy solutions to problems that have made it onto the international agenda. Sometimes the chronological order is reversed. Kingdon emphasized that problems and solutions form separate "streams." Organizational decision making does not fit the classical "problem then solution" model. Often the solution has been around long before the problem arises or is recognized. Often problems float around without any solution being attempted—perhaps because all proposed solutions seem impractical. While many have noticed the novelty of the solution-then-problem aspect of Kingdon's model, for us the key thing is that it can happen in both chronological orders.

Important to the problem-solving approach is that we have a strong interaction, and often conflict, between the interests of actors and what counts as an appropriate solution to the problem itself. However, I leave this aspect to the next subsection on power. What is important here is that various groups propose different policies in response to the substance of a given problem. These policy responses often have a predictable form because of ideological and cultural values of the country or group involved. In this regard international institutions do not differ from domestic politics where we assume certain kinds of policy solutions from different political parties. In international, as in domestic politics, there are multiple ways to skin a cat.

Hence part of the debate is political, but another really revolves around the degree to which various proposals solve the problem and at what cost. Policy professionals play an important role in this process. Adler's (1992) discussion of the creation of the arms control solution to U.S.–Soviet security issues illustrates this quite nicely. These ideas arose in policy and intellectual groups only indirectly tied to politicians and official policymakers. Proponents made arguments that were instrumental and efficiency ones: they thought that the best way to manage the Cold War was through arms control agreements. Other policy groups felt that this was not a practical strategy and that straightforward arms acquisition and deterrence would better provide for U.S. security.

Finnemore's analysis (1996) of the Geneva Conventions and the Red Cross illustrates these points well. Almost all governments accepted this new problem, that of the war wounded, but there was much debate about the Red Cross solution. Most of the objections were practical, functional, ones. The French did not believe that civilians could do the job (Kier 1995 finds similar attitudes still present in the interwar period); the Dutch thought care for the wounded was the responsibility of the state; the British already had established medical units within the military; the Austrians already had a society devoted to these ends. In contrast a number of states, for example, German ones, found the Red Cross solution an attractive idea. The Geneva committee undertook massive lobbying efforts in their successful campaign to have their solution adopted by international treaty.

These examples illustrate both constructivist and functionalist points. These groups really try to solve problems, but the solutions cannot evade cultural and ideological beliefs about the world. Even in technical areas there is almost never a best solution, several competing ones vie for supremacy, each with its own advantages and disadvantages.

Hence it is important to emphasize that multiple policy solutions are frequently floating around for any given problem. The key point is that for institution creation to occur key actors need to see at least one feasible answer. Where this appears most clearly is in cases that might be described by Keohane as "harmonious," where all governments come to negotiations wanting to do something. Young and Osherenko's (1993) analyses of polar environmental institutions provide some good examples of this. One chapter discusses the formation of the institution to deal with the Svalbard Archipelago. All parties agreed that something needed to be done to regulate claims on these islands which lie in international waters. Original proposals were very long and complicated, and negotiations dragged on for years. It was then proposed to give sovereignty to Norway under a set of restrictions about taxation, nondiscrimination, etc. With this new, simple, and workable proposal on the table negotiations came quickly to a successful conclusion.

Genschel analyzes the difficulty the ITU [International Telecommunications Union] acting in the face of the demonopolization of the telecommunications industry in similar terms:

> Since 1970s the CCITT [telephone section of ITU] was under constant pressure to reform its basic structure . . . names of structures were changed . . . some new structures were added . . . but basically the CCITT's set-up remained unchanged. While this caution was due in part to the reservations of some developing countries, the more important factor behind it was that even the proponents of reform had no design for radical measures." (1997, 51)

Young and Osherenko's analyses illustrate well how small "details" can really block or delay institution creation. For example, Canada opposed part of the proposed polar bear institution because of the implications for sovereignty claims in other arenas. I have stressed that norms cut across issue areas—a major critique of the Krasner-definition of regimes. Here we see that in a very concrete way.

Young and Osherenko found that political leadership played a crucial role in environmental institution creation (the emphasis on the importance of leadership of various types has been a constant theme in Young's work, e.g., 1991; 1998). Some individual or group needed to be interested enough in the problem and the possible solutions to expend significant resources on organization and promotion. This may seem obvious but problems of collective action can be severe. Here the key point is that the institution must be quite important to *some* actors who have the interest and means to develop solutions. Leadership in this sense may in fact rarely come from the hegemon.

Nevertheless problems and solutions tend to go together. Sometimes the solution determines the perception of the existence of the problem. Things that cannot be changed—facts of life—often just do not register cognitively as problems. Long nights in Scandinavia are not a problem until escape becomes possible. Kingdon reports that topics in health care such as long-term care, mental health, and life style problems were not tackled because there existed no budgetarily or socially plausible solution.

I have proposed that institutions are solutions to problems. However, it is perhaps often the case that one solution is "no institution." I think this is particularly a propos in the case of hegemonic powers. There is a certain irony in this proposal given the prominence of hegemonic institution theory, but there are clear power-based reasons for this. Powerful states may prefer to go it alone since they have the power to do so and this gives them more control. Smith's discussion (1987) of the nuclear nonproliferation treaty illustrates this point exactly. When the United States was really hegemonic in terms of nuclear weapons it tried unilateral policies (the McMahon Act) to prevent other countries from acquiring such weapons. Once that failed it turned to the NPT. Young (1989) states that a number of U.S. analysts believe that "no institution"—i.e., open access—on deep-sea mining would be the best thing for American interests (see also Bräuninger and König 2000).

One can contrast the United States with Canada in this regard. Canada as a matter of course deals with international problems through international organizations and institutions. Canadian scholars (e.g., Keating 1993; McLin 1967) have argued that this is a natural move for "middle powers." Canada has acted as a political entrepreneur on numerous occasions as a way for it to resolve foreign policy problems. Once again I think the archetypal examples chosen by (American) scholars have taken the exceptional cases for core examples. I think it makes much more sense to assume that the more powerful the country the less likely it is to have recourse to an international institution as its foreign policy.

Nothing in this framework maintains that a given solution actually *solves the problem*. There are various reasons for this, most of them quite mundane in character. One whole set has to do with the implementation of policy which takes us outside this chapter into the domain of the next two chapters on the functioning of international institutions and the whole issue of sanctions. In terms of institution creation, I need but remark that like all human inventions there is no guarantee that they will work. In social as well as technical engineering it is only by seeing something work in practice that one knows whether or not it is achieving the designer's goals. As opponents of social engineering like to point out (see Hirschman 1991 for a nice discussion of this point) most designs have unanticipated consequences. But of course this is true of all proposed responses or nonresponses to problems.

In summary, policy alternatives can arise through the activities of various actors. Kingdon uses the term "policy entrepreneur" which I think fits quite well. These entrepreneurs can be individuals with influential organizational roles like the director of UNEP, or policy organizations like Rand and Harvard University in the development of arms control ideas, or NGOs in human rights and relief aid. Once again, hegemonic powers can be the source of solutions as GATT and Bretton Woods attest. Finally, small and middle-range powers have been quite active in promoting and finding institution solutions.

## Power Aggregation

Any theory of international relations that ignores power has serious flaws. The converse also holds: any approach that focuses overwhelmingly on power misses key elements. Power in a larger sense has not been absent from my discussion, powerful groups—I include epistemic communities as a powerful lobby—create problems. Powerful actors have access to resources to put forward possible solutions. Here I focus on power in the traditional sense as the ability to influence the policy option that is finally chosen.

Part of what counts as a feasible solution for a policy entrepreneur is a policy that will not provoke strong opposition from powerful actors. This of course may run in exactly the opposite direction from the solution to the problem in its own right. Dealing with pollution may be costly in both an economic and political sense. Hence feasibility in the sense of solving the problem may run up against feasibility in the power sense. Nothing really surprising about this, it occurs in domestic politics all the time.

The point here is that sufficiently powerful groups must come together behind one solution for an institution to be created.

I differ from most power theorists in permitting a wide range of power configurations to fill this role. I list the three typical ones in order of decreasing number of pages devoted to them in the literature:

1. hegemonic

2. oligarchical

3. mass-based

In rare instances a hegemon has the power and finds the institution solution attractive, so clearly this is one route to the power requirement. Examples such as GATT and Bretton Woods illustrate this and are well known to all.

Snidal (1985) has argued that small groups—usually of powerful actors—can combine to form institutions. I suspect that this is a much more common means of fulfilling the power requirement than the hegemonic route. For example, Japan and Europe supported the formation of a global climate change institution against the opposition of the United States (Paterson 1996). U. S. opposition had significant effects but the agreements were still signed. The same is true for the Law of Sea which came into existence after the United States pulled out under Reagan. More recently the Land Mine Treaty was signed over U.S. protests.

The mass-based route does not exist as an independent stream of thought so it deserves more commentary. By "mass-based" I really mean two different subroutes. The first is the impact of popular politics and public opinion within dominant countries that push leaders into institution policies. The second is the mass action by small and less powerful states that coalesces to get an international norm adopted.

In the first category we can include some hegemonic institutions such as the British imposition of antislave trade rules. This new norm certainly did not come at the instigation of British ruling elites, rather it arose from British civil society, in particular through the actions of nonconformist religious groups. Environmental institutions frequently have this character; in the early 1990s George Bush was briefly an environmental president for domestic political reasons.

This category clearly has hybrid characteristics but it is worth putting it outside the hegemonic institution category since these theorists resolutely take the government as the state as representing the country as a unitary actor with traditional realist interests. Hegemonic regime theorists rarely examine slavery, apartheid, decolonization, and other institutions that typically arise from important value changes within the populations of powerful states. The second subroute consists of coalitions of many relatively weak countries which, as a group, push new norms through. Often bigger countries sign on in the end but they are not really the creators and often do so quite grudgingly. This subroute overlaps with groups that have more impact in defining problems and solutions. The major impetus comes from smaller countries with larger ones coming in once they see that it cannot be prevented.

The period of decolonization provides some examples of this route. International norms about decolonization, national ownership of mineral resources, and the extension of territorial waters all came into being through coalitions of Third World governments. For example, this played a key role in Panama's regaining of the Panama Canal (McElroy 1992). One need only pose the counterfactual question about any major power giving up such territory in the nineteenth century to recognize the power of mass-based norms in the postcolonial period.

In short, institution creation requires the support of a powerful coalition of actors. How this coalition gets formed varies from case to case. I have distinguished between three archetypal paths in which the amount of power may remain roughly constant but the number of actors in the alliance increases. Keohane, Gilpin, and other hegemonic stability scholars have proposed hegemonic power as a necessary condition for institution formation. They are half right and half wrong: a large amount of power is necessary but it can be aggregated through various coalitions ranging in size from one to many.

**Context**

The three factors I have considered so far focus quite directly on the international institution itself; institution policies address certain problems and they need enough support to achieve treaty status. The fourth determinant—context—brings in the wider environment into the picture. Kingdon called this factor the "political stream" and for him it was the larger political context within which specific policy issues in health and transportation evolved. Young and Osherenko (1993) included this set of factors as well in their analysis of polar regime formation. For example, World War I had an impact on the creation of the Svalbard regime since it happened to have been included in peace negotiations. Having myself written a book (1994) on the ways and means international contexts influence government behavior I am particularly attached to this determinant.

One type of contextual affect that appears frequently in the institution literature is the idea that political shocks and crises open a window of opportunity for the creation of international institutions. Clearly the creation of the Concert of Europe, the League of Nations, and the United Nations responded to the system-wide wars that preceded them. Beyond major systematic crises this idea has been proposed for a variety of international institutions:

For climate change it turns out that the 1980s was the hottest decade on record with six of the hottest years ever. This obviously made people more receptive the problem of global warming. (Paterson 1996, 33)

The occurrence of a shock or crisis that is exogenous to the process of institution formation (though not necessarily to the issue area) increases the probability of success in efforts to reach closure on the terms of an international institution. (Young and Osherenko 1993, 9)

Crises or widely publicized shocks are probably necessary precipitants of environmental institution creation, but crises along cannot explain how or which collective responses to a perceived joint problem are likely to develop. (Haas 1993, 187)

Clearly many of these shocks overlap significantly with problem definition. Systemwide wars led many to feel that international business-as-usual had massively failed and that new policies were needed:

[W]hile violence on a grand and in some respects unprecedented scale— twenty-eight years of almost unbroken large-scale war and upheaval—proved to be one necessary condition of the transition from eighteenth- to nineteenth-century international politics, it was not really its main cause. . . . The transformation occurred first and above all in the field of ideas, collective mentalities, and outlooks. . . . What happened, in the last analysis, was a general recognition by the states of Europe that they could not pursue the old politics any longer and had to try something new and different. (Schroeder 1994, viii)

One sees this pattern often in institution creation: some dramatic event makes a problem very visible, particularly when the media get involved, and they force it onto the agenda. However, policy brokers need also to think that an international institution can solve the problem. Wars occurred in Europe for centuries before the League of Nations was created. World War II acted as a major impetus to the formation of many European institutions. European wars are not new, but in the 1940s and 1950s functionalists like Mitrany, Schumann, and Monnet had a new solution to the problem, the Common Market.

U.S. relations with the USSR during the Cold War were a vital context in the success of some environmental treaties. For example, Zimmerman et al. (1999) argue that the CITES and London Dumping Convention treaties were directly connected with detente in the 1970s. Later, the collapse of the USSR provides an analogous contextual factor. With the Cold War no longer a reason to support dictatorships and to block UN action, we have seen a dramatic rise in UN activity involving human rights, democracy, and the possible creation of norms like humanitarian intervention. This second spurt of activity follows the one made possible by World War II, which was followed by the formation of many institutions.

Perhaps the other major sense of "favorable context" comes from a number of governments taking similar policy actions. If such is the case, then change is in the air, decision makers are conscious of it, as are pressure groups. Debates and decisions in other countries make the media, cross-national contacts between similar interest groups get established. This all creates a climate favorable to institution formation.

Here we are clearly talking about the diffusion of ideas, policies, and values across the international system. Problems and solutions get identified within a specific worldview. As these sometimes spread across large parts of the system the stage is set for specific policy and norm creation. Decolonization was accompanied with anti-imperial values that argued for changes in international property norms. Environmental values diffused rapidly throughout industrialized countries in the 1970s. The 1980s and 1990s have seen the spread of liberal and market-based ideologies which promote old solutions and see new problems, notably in the realm of government regulation.

Policy diffusion is one means by which governments acquire new norms, while at the same time this creates a favorable context for international institution formation. The creation of one successful, say environmental, institution often will lead to the creation of others. For example, the success of the Med Plan for the Mediterranean led the United Nations Environmental Program to initiate nine other regional environmental institutions. We can see the same imitation effect from the success of European integration, which has spurred the creation of other regional free trade institutions. One cannot understand why NAFTA was formed without including the background of the spurt in European integration in the 1980s.

This contextual factor illustrates the incompleteness of hegemonic regime theory with its myopic emphasis on U.S.–created institutions such as GATT and Bretton Woods. My model makes the counterfactual proposition that without World War II such institutions would not have been created. As Russett (1985) shows, the United States was hegemonic in terms of material power already by 1910. The United States was hegemonic in Latin America without it moving to create institutions there. GATT and Bretton Woods were a response to problems in Europe brought on by World War II.

In summary, favorable international contexts are usually crucial for institution formation. In particular I have distinguished two common types of favorable contexts. The first, well known in the institution literature, consists of major shocks which open a window of opportunity for institution creation. The second, not well known in the institution literature, focuses on the diffusion of policies, values, and ideologies across many countries in the system. This too sets the stage for institution creation since many begin to see the same problems, have similar ideas about solutions, and hence can influence numerous governments.

# Necessity of Each Determinant

My theory of institution creation consists of four factors or determinants. As it stands this does not differ from a list of hypotheses about what influences institution formation. As of yet the theory has no *structure*. The purpose of this section and the next is to give these elements a theoretical structure.

The first step in giving theoretical coherence to these four factors is to propose that each is *necessary* for institution creation. This key theoretical claim has two forms which link individual determinants to institution creation as a whole:

1. if an institution is created then we find that determinant present.

2. if any determinant is absent no institution will form.

These two versions go in opposite directions, one starts from cases of institution creation and moves backward to see if a determinant was present, the other goes forward saying that if a determinant does not exist then institution creation does not occur. These correspond to the two forms a necessary condition proposition can take: (1) $Z$ is necessary for $Y$ and (2) not-$Z$ is sufficient for not-$Y$. These two propositions have the same truth values and are equivalent in classic Aristotelian logic (see Most and Starr 1989 for a discussion of this logic in the context of international relations).

Kingdon does not express himself in very formal terms but he quite clearly uses this necessary condition structure in his model as well:

> If one of the three elements [determinants] is missing—if a solution is not available, a problem cannot be found or is not sufficiently compelling, or support is not forthcoming from the policy stream [context]—then the subject's place on the decision agenda is fleeting. (187)

He uses the softer language of "the subject's place is fleeting" but the effect is the same (see the next chapter for a detailed discussion of this point).

One might consider claims of necessity as quite strong, and in a sense they are. However, the institution literature contains many examples of necessary condition hypotheses about institutions:

> For the United States to become a member of the ICO [International Coffee Organization], the executive branch's support for an international coffee agreement was a necessary, but not a sufficient, condition. (Bates 1996, 206)

> Low levels of concern, poor contractual environments and weak capacity are each sufficient to cause failures in collective management of environmental tasks. (Levy et al. 1995, 304)

> Our examination of leadership . . . suggests to us that leadership exercised by individuals is a necessary condition for institution formation . . . we continue to think that some factors are so central to the process of institution formation that they can serve as a basis for propositions stated in the form of necessary conditions. (Young and Osherenko 1993, 235, 247)

Why were the weapons [nuclear] not used? We have argued that the development of prohibitionary norms was a necessary condition for the limited use of
nuclear and chemical weapons. . . . *Norms structure realms of possibilities;
they do not determine outcomes.* . . . The bottom line is that these taboos
[nuclear and chemical] were a necessary condition. (Price and Tannenwald
1996, 145, 148)

The expectations created by the arms control epistemic community were thus
a necessary condition, though certainly not the only condition, for the forg-
ing of the ABM institution, and they preceded rather than followed the units
of effective modification—namely, the creation of normative behavioral patterns and the formal creation of the institution. (Adler 1992, 145)

This is not all: if you examine some of the quotes I used in discussing the four
determinants many of them use the necessary condition concept. Also, the next
chapter will demonstrate that discussions of collectives goods and institutions use
this concept as well.

The examples above also illustrate that the necessary condition idea cuts
across theoretical boundaries. Prominent individuals in the constructivist and epistemic community literatures use this idea. Not only that, hegemonic regime theory
is most often interpreted in necessary condition terms:

As applied to the last century and a half, this theory—which will be referred
to as the "hegemonic stability" theory—does well at identifying the apparently necessary conditions for strong international economic institutions, but
poorly at establishing sufficient conditions. (Keohane 1980, 137)

[C]ollective action is still possible but *only* when the United States takes the
lead—when, in short, it still chooses to as leader. (Strange 1987, 574)

[T]hree prerequisites—hegemony, liberal ideology [in the hegemon], and
common interests—must exist for the emergence and expansion of the liberal market system. (Gilpin 1987, 73)

The strongest and most widely discussed hypothesis of the power theorists
states that the presence of a hegemon is a necessary condition for the emergence of institutional arrangements at the international level. (Young and
Osherenko 1993, 9)

Hegemonic stability theorists suggest that cooperation is only likely to exist
and persist while there is a hegemon to support it. (Haas 1990, 165)

Keohane gives some credit to the theory of hegemonic stability without, however, accepting its "crude" version which argues that a unipolar distribution
of power is both *necessary* and *sufficient* for a institution to merge and persist
in any given issue area. Neither of these claims, according to Keohane (1984,
chapter 3), is ultimately tenable. (Hasenclever, Mayer, and Rittberger 1997,
38)

While scholars frequently use this necessary condition structure, its theoretical and methodological implications do not seem to have attracted much attention.

As the Hasenclever, Mayer, and Rittberger quote illustrates, some people have denied that a given factor is really necessary, but this is about as far as things ever go. By the time we have finished this and the next chapter we shall see that a complex theoretical structure underlies this common idea.

The necessary condition formulation for my four determinants has a number of methodological implications. There exist two means of testing a necessary condition hypothesis corresponding to the two ways in which the hypothesis can be formulated (see Braumoeller and Goertz 2000 for an extensive discussion of testing necessary condition hypotheses). The first selects cases of institution creation and determines if the determinant was present. Given that the institution literature tends to select on the dependent variable of institution success this tends to be the way necessary condition hypotheses get generated (see Dion 1998 for necessary conditions and selecting on the dependent variable).

But in fact the second version of the necessary condition presents in many ways a stronger test. The absence of any one of the determinants implies institution creation failure. This is a stronger claim than what one gets for the presence of a necessary condition, which predicts neither success nor failure. Hence a stronger test of my theory of institution creation relies on gathering data on institution formation failures, something which we have little in the way of case studies of.

In summary, I propose that each determinant must be present for institution creation. This structure has important implications for theory and research. In the next chapter I shall go into much more theoretical detail including a formalization of these ideas. This discussion also has implications beyond just my theory of institution creation since the necessary condition concept is widely used in the institution literature. My analysis in this and the next chapter not only make clear my theory but indirectly make explicit implications of many other hypotheses about institutions.

### Two-Level Theory

The previous subsection emphasized that each of the four determinants must be present for institution creation. This is only half the story since my model is really a two-level structure. If the basic level is constructed in necessary condition terms, in contrast the next level is not constructed at all in those terms.

In my discussion of each determinant I stressed the *different* ways or paths through which that slot could be filled. For example, a hegemon can provide the power requirement, but oligarchical or mass-based means work as well. This is true for all four determinants. The slot must be filled, but there are multiple means by which that can occur. Let me briefly review the discussion of the determinants with this in mind.

I.      Problem.

      A.  international organizations, epistemic communities, and other nongovernmental actors.

    B.  crises and shocks.

    C.  hegemon.

II.   Solution.

    A.  policy entrepreneurs.

    B.  middle powers.

    C.  hegemon.

III.  Power.

    A.  hegemon.

    B.  oligarchal.

    C.  mass-based.

IV.  Context.

    A.  crisis, shock.

    B.  policy diffusion.

Kingdon emphasized that these determinants—what he called "streams"—evolve independently. He was saying in part that each slot can be filled by different actors or events: one group might define the problem while another might provide the solution.

Hegemonic institution theory thus becomes one possible configuration whereby the problem, solution, and power slots are filled by the same actor. Unlike some critics of hegemonic regime theory, I do not need to argue that it is wrong, rather it becomes one particular institution creation configuration (which of course still needs to have a contextual factor to be completed).

This two-level theoretical structure has elements of rigidity and flexibility. Requiring that each determinant be present provides a rigid foundation; but allowing multiple means of filling each structural prerequisite permits a wide range of institution creation possibilities. One can fault many prominent approaches to institutions because they were constructed with one or two archetypal examples, be they empirical such as the WTO or the Med Plan or be they theoretical such as prisoners' dilemma or coordination games. It is a simple job to criticize these approaches since one can easily find examples where the archetypes do not work.

In contrast, I start from the position that a good theory of institution creation must start by recognizing the variety of international norms and institutions that one sees in practice. My model permits different actors and events to play different roles and multiple roles at one time in the process of institution creation. For example, Paterson (1996) found that epistemic community lobbies were crucial in the problem-definition stage but had little impact on the final solution. Within my model this is not surprising but rather to be expected.

## Joint Sufficiency of All Determinants

The two-level necessary condition approach provides one cement linking the four determinants in a coherent theoretical structure. This section completes the construction of this theoretical edifice by proposing that the four factors in addition to being individually necessary are *jointly sufficient* for institution creation. In other words, if we find that these four factors happen to occur at the same time an international institution will be formed.

The presence of necessary conditions of course does not imply sufficiency, this must be added as a separate hypothesis. In this I also follow the Kingdon model:

> the rise of an item [on the agenda] is due to the joint effect of several factors coming together at a given point in time, not to the effect of one or another of them singly . . . It was their *joint* effects that were so powerful. (188)

He expresses clearly the idea that several factors must come together *at the same time*—i.e., joint effects—for an item to make it onto the agenda. Since he is explaining the success of an agenda item he is talking about sufficiency effects.

Beyond sufficiency in general there are two aspects of my model that merit some discussion: (1) it is not sufficiency in general but a specific model that has multiple necessary conditions which are jointly sufficient, (2) the emphasis on the conjunction of factors as key in the sufficiency explanation.

### Multiple Necessary and Jointly Sufficient Conditions Models

I illustrated above that necessary condition hypotheses arise with considerable frequency in the institution literature. In contrast, it is almost impossible to find sufficient condition ones. Now, of course one can transform a necessary condition hypothesis about institution creation into a sufficient one about institution formation failure (see above page 182) but since almost no one studies institution creation failure this remains an unexplored option.[1]

Beyond sufficient hypotheses in general I am concerned with one kind in particular, where multiple necessary conditions are jointly sufficient. Table 9.1 illustrates this with a two necessary condition model. Sufficiency occurs when both variables are present, necessity means that if either is absent then institution creation does not occur (see Ragin (1987) for a good exposition of the logic and implications of this for social theory).

This is all a matter of elementary logic and not controversial as such. One question is whether we can find examples of this theoretical structure in the institution or related literatures. I will argue in the next chapter that this is in fact a common approach to institutions and collective goods, for example, collective security.

---

[1] The democratic peace gets frequently expressed in the two forms: (1) nondemocracy is necessary for war and (2) joint democracy is sufficient for peace.

TABLE 9.1: Multiple Necessary and Jointly Sufficient Conditions for Institution Creation

| $Z_1$ | $Z_2$ | Institution |
|---|---|---|
| 1 | 1 | 1 |
| 1 | 0 | 0 |
| 0 | 1 | 0 |
| 0 | 0 | 0 |

In the context of this chapter I can note two examples of this structure. Ostrom's (1991) prominent work on common pool resource institutions proposes that there are eight necessary conditions for the proper functioning of such institutions. However, she says nothing about sufficiency; but if you put her data into a table such as table 9.1 you will discover that the sufficiency hypothesis fits perfectly.

Deterrence theory provides another example. While this may seem remote at first glance from institution theory, many institutions have as their major function the *prevention* of certain actions (Nadelmann 1990), hence they try to deter governments, firms, and other groups from doing certain things. According to Harvey, standard deterrence theory has four necessary conditions which are jointly sufficient: "(1) clearly define the behavior deemed to be unacceptable ... (2) communicate to challengers a commitment to punish violations ... (3) possess the means (capability) to defend the commitment by punishing adversaries who challenge it, ... (4) demonstrate their resolve to carry out the retaliatory actions if the challenger fails to comply" (1998, 676). He notes—along with others who look at necessary condition methodology such as Dion (1998) and Braumoeller and Goertz (2000)—that this version of deterrence theory has not been correctly tested.

But in general sufficiency claims are rare, more common is a relatively long list of necessary conditions from which one can then imply a jointly sufficient hypothesis. I shall give examples of this in the next chapter, but the Ostrom proposition shows why this makes intuitive sense. If in fact all eight necessary conditions were present we would expect that the likelihood that the common pool resource institution works is very high. The same intuition applies to the four necessary conditions for deterrence success, if all these were present one might suppose that deterrence would work.

## Conjunctural, Configurational, and Contingent Explanations

All this talk of necessary and sufficient conditions may seem like the positivism that social constructivists reject (it is, though see the social constructivists" hypotheses above, page 182). However, the theoretical concepts that the constructivists like to use such as conjunctural, contingent, and configuration also apply to my theory. Kingdon's model has been praised and criticized for this emphasis on path dependence and contingency. He says that only when the three streams *happen* to coincide does something make it onto the agenda. Hence it is the conjunction of factors which is sufficient, but this conjunction is a very contingent event.

Some, including Kingdon and the inventors of the garbage can model (Cohen et al. 1972) that Kingdon used as his starting point, stress how haphazard this process is. For many this means we can have no rigorous theory, not to mention the implication that the process is "irrational." I will formalize the core of this model in the next chapter, so obviously a rigorous theory does underlie much of the model (also Cohen et al. 1972 have conducted computer simulations which also implies a certain rigor). Within international relations, constructivist theories accent historical contingency, path dependence, and the like. All these adjectives describe my theory of institution formation. These scholars tend to think like many critics of Kingdon that this excludes rigorous and/or formal theorizing; this whole volume belies that opinion.

The emphasis on configurations of factors is often taken as typical of the comparative method. For example, Ragin describes the comparative method as such: "causation is understood conjuncturally. Outcomes are analyzed in terms of intersections of conditions, and it is usually assumed that any of several combinations of conditions might produce a certain outcome" (1987, x). We can contrast this with those that come at comparative politics from a statistical, regression framework such as King et al. (1994); here one finds no mention of conjunctions, configurations of variables, or contingent events. When I give my examples of necessary condition hypotheses or multiple necessary and jointly sufficient ones they come from qualitative and comparative scholars. My interpretation of Kingdon's model fits what many think of as typical of comparative thinking:

> A comparativist might argue that social class and party preference are strongly related to each other in a sample of British voters not *simply* because Great Britain is an industrial society but also because it has a long history of class mobilization and conflict which *coincided* [my emphasis] with the development of its current political system. In effect, this explanation cites three *convergent* [my emphasis] conditions: (1) a history of class struggle, (2) coinciding with polity maturation (3) in a country that has been industrialized for a long time. It is their *combined* [my emphasis] effect that explains the enduring individual-level relationship between social class and party preference. (Ragin 1987, 14)

> In statistical work it is a standard procedure to probe for interaction effects, and then to weigh the explanatory contribution of the interaction—itself turned into an explanatory variable—compared to the effects of other variables. . . . In *States and Revolutions* I proceed in an entirely analogous way . . . I show that arguments proposed by other theorists do not differentiate the social revolutions from the political and failed social revolutions.

Then I spell out and validate through the same comparisons my own argument based on combinations of causal conditions. (Skocpol 1986, 188–89)

Notice that in both these examples Ragin and Skocpol are using configuration and conjunctural explanations to answer *sufficiency* questions. They are looking for an explanation of why something occurred. Given the comparativist's interest in explaining specific events the question she poses is a sufficiency one. So when I require my four determinants to be jointly present I am answering the institution creation question in a comparativist fashion.

The contrast between Young and Osherenko (1993) with Stokke (2001; see also Stokke, O. et al. 2000) in this context is illuminating. Young and Osherenko was a significant advance in the institution literature because it was one of the first studies to test clearly multiple hypotheses drawn from differing theoretical perspectives. However, each hypothesis—leadership, interest, power, or contextual—is considered in isolation. There is no sense of a configural argument. Stokke in contrast includes a variety of factors and specifically looks for configurations—using Ragin's Boolean methods—that explain his dependent variable. My interpretation of Stokke's results is that in cases of high costs (what he call "inconvenience") there are different configurations than in cases where costs are low.

I think one can see clearly that my model has functional and constructivist characteristics. This has both a theoretical and methodological component. Functionalists tend to privilege formal theory along with statistical testing methodologies. Comparativists tend to stress contingency, conjunctions, and configurations of factors. My model has both these sets of characteristics.

## Two Warnings

To use the language of necessary and sufficient conditions often brings along with it an accompanying freight of ideas. These ideas often seem "obvious" but at the same time they do not result from considered reflection on the issues.

One methodological piece of freight is to assume the principle that one counterexample suffices to reject a necessary condition hypothesis. Given their distaste for quantitative methodologies Young and Osherenko find this an attractive characteristic of a necessary condition approach:

> There is an understandable tendency among students of institution formation to concentrate on formulating hypotheses that focus on bivariate relationships. . . . Especially when cast as necessary or sufficient conditions, these hypotheses are powerful. . . . They can be stated in a clear and precise manner. Equally important, they are comparatively easy to test. Every case should conform to the expectations raised by such hypotheses, which makes it possible to engage in testing without resorting to the deployment of statistical techniques. Because the numbers of truly comparable cases are always small in dealing with international phenomena such as institution formation, the appeal of hypotheses stating necessary or sufficient conditions

from the point of view of testing is not just understandable, it is almost ir-
restible. (Young and Osherenko 1993, 246)[2]

There are good reasons not to accept this position. One reason lies at the
theoretical level where key concepts are usually quite abstract, hence vague, and
open to a variety of interpretations on a more concrete level. For example, many
theories use the concept of democracy, when we get to an operational level this
concept can receive quite different content (contrast Jaggers and Gurr 1995 with
Przeworski and Limongi 1997).

Another reason to object to this position is that a number of cases fall into
the gray zone, the boundary between dichotomous categories. It is just not clear
how to categorize these cases. For example, is Great Britain a democracy in 1812
(an important case for the democratic peace) or South Africa in 1970? Related
to this is the tendency of make all variables dichotomous even if the underlying
indicator or concept is continuous. Again the literatures on the democratic peace
and the requisites of democracy illustrate the tendency to dichotomize even when
continuous data are available.

Data error provides a third reason to refuse the one counterexample and reject
principle. This should be kept separate from the gray cases which can really be
gray. Data error means the true value can move in and out of its correct category.
Even very modest amounts of error can produce counterexamples, a good test
should take this into account (see Braumoeller and Goertz 2000 for a measurement
error analysis of Bueno de Mesquita's *War Trap* necessary condition hypothesis).

In summary, theoretical controversy about concepts, gray zone cases, and
measurement error are three good reasons to disagree with Young and Osherenko.
There exists a rapidly growing literature on the specifics of testing necessary condition hypotheses (see the chapters in Goertz and Starr 2002) in addition to some
classics (Ragin 1987; Most and Starr 1989), yet this has yet to filter into comparative methods textbooks, e.g., King et al. (1994).

A second, and related, error lies in considering all variables in my model
as dichotomous ones. My model draws heavily on ways of thinking common in
comparative and qualitative methods. At the same time, given the fuzzy logic
philosophy that lies behind most of this volume, it should not come as a surprise
that I take as my starting point variables which are continuous on [0,1]. The
qualitative, comparative tendency is to dichotomize variables (e.g., Ragin 1987,
but see Ragin 2000). Even if the concept is continuous and continuous data are
available scholars still dichotomize, as the democratic peace and the requisites of

---

[2]Note that Young (1998) has explicitly given up on using necessary and sufficient condition hypotheses as a general way to frame his research agenda. However, he continues to make necessary
condition claims: "Emergence of a champion is a necessary condition for an issue to move to the top
of the agenda" (53). "Under the circumstances, it is probably accurate to say that there would have
been no AEPS [Arctic Environmental Protection Strategy] in the absence of the dedication and en-
trepreneurial skill exhibited by the key HODs [Head of Delegation] at a number of points during this
stage." (110) "it is also fair to say that the whole idea of pursuing multilateral cooperation in the Arctic
would have been a non-starter in the absence of the winding down of the Cold War" (188).

democracy literatures illustrate. In short, one should view my four determinants as ranging from "not present at all," i.e., zero, to "completely present," i.e., one. The model I develop in the next chapter takes *all* variables to be continuous on [0,1]. It implies that when a necessary condition is only weakly present, i.e., near zero, one expects to see a few counterexamples. One should view all necessary conditions in a continuous sense, it is rather the exceptional case where something is really dichotomous. While this may seem odd and very counter-intuitive I shall provide some examples that support an intuitive conceptualization of necessary conditions as continuous variables.

The two errors to avoid—one counterexample and reject, and dichotomous variables—are thus very closely related. Again these errors become clear once one combines a comparative, qualitative theory with formal and mathematical considerations.

## Conclusion

I have taken John Kingdon's model of agenda setting and modified it to form a theory of international institution creation. This theory makes clear propositions about when institutions form and when they fail to form, resulting from the various necessary and sufficient condition hypotheses contained in it. In the decentralized international system one needs a critical mass to attain institution creation. This occurs when a minimal number of individual governments come to believe a problem exists and that an international institution provides a solution. Because it is a decentralized system policy brokers must be present to bring problem, solution, and actors together. That is the model I have proposed. Institution creation occurs when a rare confluence of favorable values on all dimensions arises.

This theory uses elements of both functionalist and constructivist approaches. The problem-solving framework itself directs attention to the fact that leaders and actors look to institutions as solutions to what they perceive as problems. At the same time problems and solutions result from political action, lobbying, values, and the culture of the various participants. There are no objective problems or optimal solutions.

To develop this model I have eschewed the rational actor language of the functionalists as well as the sociological/philosophical language of the constructivists in favor of a language of problems, solutions, values, and ideologies. Sylvan and Majeski (1996) have characterized American foreign policy decision making as a "problem-solving culture"; I propose that this is the way to address international institutions, in terms of "problem-solving" and "culture." Of course this means that what counts as a problem or a solution depends heavily on cultural values, ideology, tradition, etc., Kingdon (1984, 140–41) expresses this very well:

The component of ideology, based on the participants' view of the proper size of government, has a cross-national aspect. . . . Programs that are commonplace in other countries, such as nationalized railroads, national health insurance, and public ownership and operation of sizable portions of the housing stock, are not even considered live options in the United States. . . . One of my transportation respondents illustrated graphically the different mind set:

> I was just talking to somebody from Sweden. In Sweden, they designed their system so that they would have various modes of passenger transportation all coming into the same terminal, and various modes of freight transportation all coming into the same terminal. They coordinate these things very nicely. When I asked this man how they do that he replied, "How else would you do it?"[3]

---

[3] See Kelman (1971) for more on U.S.-Swedish differences.

# Chapter 10

# A Functional Model of International Institutions

Anarchia is a perfectly circular island, and each citizen owns a wedge-shaped slice (not all equal) from the center to the sea. Like the Netherlands, Anarchia is protected from occasional storms that threaten to flood the land. But since Anarchia has no government, everyone makes his own decision as to how high a dike to build. While the height of each citizen's dike is perfectly visible to all, the customs of Anarchia forbid enforcement of any threat, inducement, or contract whereby some parties might influence the choices of others. In times of flood the sea will penetrate the sector belonging to whichever citizen has constructed the lowest dike, but the topography of Anarchia is such that no matter where the sea enters, damage will be suffered equally over the whole island. The economists of Anarchia have long realized that flood-protection for their island is a public good. Many centralized schemes for motivating individuals to build dikes of the socially optimal height have been discussed, but Anarchia's citizens find any such social planning intolerable. It so came about, however, that the United Nations generously paid for an analysis of the situation by the well-known international consulting firm of economists Arthur "Dam" Little & Co. to everyone's surprise, the conclusion was that Anarchia's citizens have voluntarily invested in dikes (and therefore have provided themselves with the public good of flood-protection) to almost exactly—98.17 percent, to be exact—the socially efficient amount.

*—Jack Hirschleifer*

In the previous chapter I used the language of problem-solving to discuss issues of institution creation. When an institution is formed usually this means the creation of international institutions and organizations. In this chapter I would like to examine the issues of the *functioning* of international institutions. Young gives as part of an "agenda of questions that require consideration in the analysis of any international institution . . . (3) *Conditions of operation.* What conditions are necessary for the institution to work at all? Under what conditions will the operation of the institution yield particularly desirable results? (4) *Consequences of operation.* What sorts of outcomes (either individual or collective) can the institution be expected to produce? What are the appropriate criteria for evaluating outcomes?" (1989, 206–8).

In order to examine these issues I make a semantic shift. Instead of speaking in terms of problems and solutions I use some separate but overlapping frameworks for analyzing the functioning of international institutions and institutions:

1. Functionalism in the biological and sociological sense.

2. Institutional economics.

3. Institutions as providers of collective goods.

4. Production of goods and services.

I combine these to talk about the production of (collective) goods. In many ways this should not be controversial, most scholars discuss institutions in terms of n-person prisoners' dilemma or collective goods. For example, Keohane (1984) uses transaction cost ideas, he talks of supply— production of collective goods—and uses much functional language. North (1990) sees the state performing many key services such as the enforcement of contracts, creating transportation infrastructures, and the like. Hence one way to think about how well an institution works is to examine how well or how efficiently it produces (collective) goods.

Much of the literature on prisoners' dilemma and the like focuses on what I call the "financing" of collective goods. Starting with the work of Olson (1971) and Schelling (1984) economists and game theorists have looked at the provision of collective goods in terms of the contributions of individuals to the production of these goods and the individual benefits derived from them. Here in contrast I focus on the *production* of (collective) goods. The analogy of a business firm illustrates this important distinction. One problem for an entrepreneur is obtaining financing, a second problem is creating a firm that actually makes a profit. The literature that follows Olson and Schelling usually assumes the creation of a money-making collective good institution follows automatically if financing is available. I suggest that we need for international institutions both a theory of financing and a theory of the firm.

This emphasis on production joins two important streams of the institution literature: (1) concern with the effectiveness of an institution and (2) issues of institutional design. Going back to the business analogy, one wants an international institution that efficiently uses resources to maximize services and goods provided to the international community.

The stress on the production of (collective) goods also leads us into a different branch of the economic literature, the study of economic production functions (Chambers 1988). In its standard formulation production function analysis examines the optimal mix of labor and capital needed in order to produce a given good. This is a *design* decision: how is the firm going to best use its resources to produce a good?

Again I can contrast this with the literature on collective goods. How institutions actually produce a collective good is rarely present in these theories. Usually output is directly, additively, and linearly related to the number of contributors or contributions. One goes directly from individual contributions to output (see figure 10.2 below). Ironically, there is *no* institution present in the theory of collective goods. Ostrom's American Political Science Association (1998) presidential address has this tension, since she defines the "social dilemma" in terms of individuals, but at the same time she is vitally concerned with institutions. Hirschleifer's fable at the head of this chapter illustrates perfectly the economic approach where institutions do not appear in the production of collective goods.

In summary, this chapter presents a theory of institution effectiveness in terms of a theory of institutional production of goods and services. Obviously, it does not address all the factors that influence institution performance, for example "financing" and traditional collective action problems remain, but it does address aspects of international institutions that are crucial and relatively ignored by scholars.

## Institutional Economics and Functionalist Theories

This section focuses on the general overlap between institutional economics and functionalist thought. This goes against the general trend which stresses the differences, and usually the weakness of sociological functionalism. Many scholars such as Harsanyi (1969), Barry (1978), and Elster (1978) have contrasted functional (read sociological) theories with expected utility ones. But in spite of the many attacks on functionalism from expected utility thinkers, they can in fact coexist. For example, expected utility modelers in biology such as Maynard Smith (1982) would certainly describe their biological theories as functionalist. Functionalism need not be amorphous à la Talcott Parsons. The economic approach to institutions describes them in functionalist terms: what is the function of a stock market? Functional language appears naturally in discussions of biological organisms and machines, components of which serve clear instrumental roles in the functioning of the whole.

Institutional economists, sociological functionalists, and biological functionalists stress the benefits of a particular institution, norm, or biological part for society or the organism as a whole. Any specific analysis probes the role that the institution plays in the maintenance of the society or overall economic efficiency. For example, many examples can be found of international organizations that reduce transaction costs, for example, a stable monetary system with clear rules for currency exchange makes international trade easier, thus allowing more profitable international trade to be made (for an interesting historical analysis see Milgrom, Weingast, and North 1990). North says: "The major role of institutions in a society is to reduce uncertainty by establishing a stable (but not necessarily efficient) structure to human interactions" (1990, 6). I propose that one cannot escape functionalist language and categories when analyzing any given institution.

A major difference, however, lies in the relation of parts to wholes. The sociological version of functionalism looks at parts at the institutional level: the institution is analyzed into its component parts. In contrast economic institutionalism focuses on individual actors and their relation to the institution. This chapter focuses on the aspect of functionalism that examines the relationship between the parts of the institution, not between the institution and actors that support it. By doing so I look at different but related aspects of how well an institution functions. One can think of this in terms of "institutional engineering" just like functionalism in biology looks at biological engineering due to natural selection. In particular I examine components of an international institution that are core to its functioning.

A functionalism that sees societies and institutions having necessary core components forms at a basic, fundamental part of the sociological classics of functionalism. Going through these works one easily finds claims of this sort:

> The functional view of culture insists therefore upon the principle that in every type of civilization, every custom, material object, idea and belief fulfills some vital function, has some task to accomplish, represents an indispensable part within a working whole. (Malinowski 1936, 133)

> [A] social system must somehow provide for the minimum biological and psychological needs of a sufficient proportion of its component members. On a more strictly social level, there seem to be two primary fundamental foci of its functional prerequisites. One lies in the coordination of the activities of the various members. . . . The second focus is on adequacy of motivation. The system can only function if a sufficient proportion of its members perform the essential social roles with an adequate degree of effectiveness. (Parsons 1948, 159)

> Durkheim's definition is that the "function" of a social institution is the correspondence between it and the needs (*besoins* in French) of the social organism. . . . I would like to substitute for the term "needs" the term "necessary conditions of existence," or if the term "needs" is used, it is to be understood only in this sense. It may be here noted, as a point to be returned to, that any attempt to apply this concept of function in social sciences involves the assumption that there *are* necessary conditions of existence for human societies just as there are for animal organisms, and that they can be discovered by the proper kind of scientific enquiry. (Radcliffe-Brown 1952, 178)

For me the key theoretical aspect of this kind of functionalism lies in its claims that these factors are *necessary* for institutions to work properly. Malinowski calls them "indispensible parts," Parsons speaks of "essential social roles," and Radcliffe-Brown explicitly uses necessary condition language. These examples illustrate the language of necessary condition theory with its frequent references to "prerequisites," "needs," "requirements," and so forth. If something "must be present" for an institution to function then we have a necessary condition.

The necessary condition explanatory structure forms perhaps the core of functionalist theories. This comes out when one examines philosophers' attempts to synthesize the essence of functional explanations. For example, Hempel's influential description (1965, 361) of functionalism defines it as follows:

> $s$ functions adequately in a setting of kind $c$ only if condition $n$ is satisfied. (Major Premise)
>
> At time $t$ system $s$ functions adequately in a setting of kind $c$. (Minor Premise)
>
> *therefore*
>
> Some one of the items in class $I$ [whose members satisfy condition $n$] is present in $s$ at $t$. (Conclusion)

In additional to its syllogistic form (!), the major premise states that system $s$ functions well *only if* $n$ is satisfied. The expression "only if" signals in canonical form the presence of a necessary condition.

Nagel's well-known discussion of functionalism contains the same sort of description. Here is an example in the context of biological functionalism: "The function of chlorophyll in plants is to enable plants to perform photosynthesis ... Accordingly, the initial, unexpanded statement about chlorophyll appears to assert nothing that is not asserted alternatively by 'A necessary condition for the occurrence of photosynthesis in plants is the presence of chlorophyll'" (Nagel 1961, 403, 405).

This language and thought seems leagues away from the approach of those working in institutional economics. However, if one examines the literature, particularly actual case studies, necessary condition claims along functionalist lines arise quite frequently:

> Assurance games most clearly apply to disasters that can be prevented only with reciprocity practices. There will be no protection unless everyone contributes. Each has an effective veto over the provision of the good. Each perceives herself as making a difference, as being the "weak link" who can make or break the chain. (Levi 1988, 59)

> Legislative approval of the policy bargain is a necessary but not sufficient condition for contingent consent ... contingent consent has at least one further condition: the existence of institutional arrangements that enforce government's commitments. Without a policy bargain, the policy lacks legitimacy. Without appropriate institutional arrangements, the policy lacks credibility. (Levi 1997, 109)

> By "design principle" I mean an essential element or condition that helps to account for the success of these institutions in sustaining the common pool resources and gaining the compliance of generation after generation of appropriators to the rules in use. ... I am willing to speculate ... [that] it will be possible to identify a set of necessary design principles and that such a set will contain the core of what has been identified here. (Ostrom 1991, 90–91)

One cannot have the productivity of an industrial society with political anarchy. But while . . . a state is a necessary condition for realizing the gains
from trade, it is obviously not sufficient. (North 1984, 260)

Notice that Ostrom uses the language of institutional engineering in the context of
the functioning of common pool resource institutions. Levi is interested in how
well a given government can produce tax income. The "weak link" metaphor
that Levi uses provides another expression of the necessary condition idea: an
institution works *only if* all the links are strong. As we shall see below my formal
model captures the theoretical core of this common metaphor.

## Necessary Conditions for Collective Security

I have focused so far on the overlap between functionalism and institutional economics. The third framework for thinking about international institutions uses the
concept of collective goods and prisoners' dilemma to think about institutions. At
the same time it is useful to examine the intersection of the functionalist, economic
institutionalism, and collective good frameworks in one concrete case. Collective
security provides a good specific example since the literature on the topic is an
amalgam of these three frameworks and illustrates many of the points I have been
making (or will be making). Scholars have discussed collective security in necessary condition terms for over two decades. Finally, as its name indicates, many
think about collective security in terms of the theory of public goods.

I note that collective security has a clear function: its purpose is to solve
the security problem. We can evaluate this institution on how well it produces
security for its various members. The product of this institution in a positive sense
is security and in the negative sense it is the absence of war or major military
conflict. The problem-solving language I used in discussing institution creation
fits naturally with the functionalist language used here to analyze the output of
international institutions.

Some problems have consistently been treated in necessary condition terms,
often over decades. Such is the case for collective security. Of course not everyone
uses this conceptual tool, but it does reappear consistently, often without any real
consciousness of the implications of this decision on the part of the participants.

However simple the collective security approach may seem upon superficial
acquaintance, the truth is that it assumes the satisfaction of an extraordinarily
complex network of requirements. The first group of prerequisites includes
those of a *subjective* character, related to the general acceptability of the responsibilities of collective security; the second group may be characterized
as a category of *objective* requirements, related to the suitability of the global
situation to the operation of collective security. (Claude 1971, 250)

Three [pre-]conditions must be present if a collective security organization is
to take shape and function effectively. . . . The first condition is that no single

state can be so powerful that even the most robust opposing coalition would be unable to marshal preponderant force against it. . . . The second condition is that the major powers of the day must have fundamentally compatible views of what constitutes a stable and acceptable international order. . . . The third condition is that the major powers must "enjoy a minimum of political solidarity and moral community." . . . It is important to note that these four features encompass two of the three necessary conditions for collective security outlined [above]. (Kupchan and Kupchan 1991, 124, 144)

[six key issues for the discussion of collective security include:] (1) collective security requires a substantial diffusion of power . . . (4) collective security cannot survive in the absence of an outside threat, (5) collective security requires states to commit themselves to an inflexible course of action that is insensitive to context and self-interest (Downs and Iida 1994, 36)

Though I do not pretend to do an intellectual history, I think one can pinpoint the key work that established the necessary condition idea and set some of the terms of the theoretical debate for the following decades continuing into the present. Innis Claude's influential discussion in *Swords into Plowshares* established the tradition of necessary condition discourse on collective security. I think one could trace many traits of current discussions to his treatment of the problem.

Downs provides a particularly good example of how easy it is to adopt necessary condition traditions. In another context, deterrence, he objected to the use of necessary conditions: "The search for necessary conditions is problematic because the utility of a necessary condition is poorly understood. There are an infinite number of necessary conditions for any phenomenon. For example, it is true that all armies require water and gravity to operate, but the contribution of such universals is modest" (1989, 234). However he seems to have no objections to their employment in the collective security context. The above quote from him on collective security comes from his introduction to an influential book on the topic; there he frequently adopted necessary condition language, naturally enough because that is the way people have discussed the problem since Claude.

Claude's work on collective security is not the only one to use the necessary condition theoretical structure. Deutsch's influential study (Deutsch et al. 1957) on security communities uses the idea to structure its analysis. Throughout the whole volume Deutsch and his colleagues probe for necessary conditions for successful security communities: "Altogether we have found nine essential conditions for an amalgamated security-community: (1) mutual compatibility of main values; (2) a distinctive way of life; (3) expectations of stronger economic ties or gains; (4) a marked increase in political and administrative capabilities of at least some units" (58).

Collective security proves a useful example since for most people it was an international institution that failed. Other international institutions have had more success in dealing with security problems. Many think that the Concert of Europe was successful in reducing the frequency of war (the nineteenth century being a particularly peaceful one). This fits naturally with my emphasis on the distinction between institution creation and functioning.

In summary, I focus on a functional theory of international institutions and institutions which takes necessary conditions as its core structure. No doubt other institutional structures exist, the models I develop do not fit everything. However, they do address an important class of ideas that has been floating around the unconscious of institution scholars. I make them explicit and formalize them. Once it is clear how a necessary condition functional model of institutions works then it becomes easier to identify institutionals that do not belong to the necessary condition class of structures.

## Sufficiency and the Output of International Institutions

Necessary conditions for the proper functioning of institutions gives us perhaps the key elements of institution effectiveness but as of yet it provides no clear set of propositions about the production of collective goods such as security. Of course, as we saw in the previous chapter, we have a negative result since the absence of a necessary condition implies that the institution does not work at all. But we have no positive result in terms of the effectiveness of the institution when all conditions are present.

Mitchell (1994) conducted one of the best and most thorough studies of institution design and effectiveness. He stresses the interrelated character of the elements of a institution structure in terms of the working of the whole:

> [D]eterrence-based strategies often require the successful completion of a complex chain of actions to be effective. The initial discharge standards [oil pollution discharge standards for oil tankers] subinstitution faced problems at almost every step of the process: detecting violations, identifying violators, prosecuting violators, and imposing potent sanctions. . . . Successful deterrence strategies must ensure that the whole legal chain operates smoothly, since the breakdown of any link can significantly impair its effectiveness. (Mitchell 1994, 456)

Note that Levi (see above page 197) used the same link-in-a-chain metaphor. This chain metaphor proves quite apropos in the context of institutions whose main purpose is proscription or deterrence (Nadelmann 1990). Lebow expresses a standard theory of deterrence as a chain with four links: "The commitments in question appeared to meet the four necessary conditions of deterrence: they were clearly defined, repeatedly publicized, and defensible, and the defending states gave every indication of their resolve to use force in defense of them" (1989, 32).

But the weakest link idea focuses on the negative aspect of the absence or weakness of crucial elements. It does not help much to explain output when key factors are present. Here I think it is useful to speak of each link having a "sufficiency effect." Each link has a positive influence on the output or production of the (collective) good.

The concept of an sufficiency effect helps make sense of the idea that when all necessary conditions are present—particularly when there are a large number of them—they are likely to be jointly sufficient. If each necessary condition has a reasonably large sufficiency effect then when we "add up" all these effects we get a well-functioning institution.

Ostrom provides a good and typical example of how sufficiency hypotheses lie implicit in necessary condition ones. Nowhere does she make the move from her eight necessary conditions to joint sufficiency. However, if we examine her data we see that they fit perfectly the joint sufficiency claim. This makes intuitive sense, if all eight necessary factors are in fact present—each with its own sufficiency effect—we would expect that the probability that common pool resource institutions work well to be high.

Mitchell was probably not completely aware of how appropriate his language was. If necessary condition models do not exist in the consciousness of scholars as special theories, the sufficiency hypothesis lies buried even deeper. Nevertheless I think the examples of Mitchell, Ostrom, and collective security—not to mention Deutsch on security communities—show that the joint sufficiency hypothesis fits naturally as an interpretation of many institution theories.

I suspect that scholars like Ostrom have hesitated to make sufficiency claims because they see sufficiency to mean "guarantees 100 percent" that the institution exists or works; J. S. Mill certainly thought sufficiency meant this when he said that "the consequence invariably follows." In the next section I argue that one need not make this interpretation of sufficiency, and in fact it is better not too. Once we formalize these models a lot of these misconceptions disappear.

## Toward Formal Models: The Machine Metaphor

I have arrived in my model of institution functioning at the same theoretical structure I proposed for institution creation, multiple necessary conditions which are jointly sufficient. I have argued that these ideas lie half-exposed in the literature on regimes and institutions. It is time to refine this raw material. This section presents a different metaphor—the machine metaphor—which I think helps overcome some of the hurdles in thinking about necessary and sufficient conditions.

First and foremost is the dichotomous conceptualization of necessity and sufficiency: either $Z$ is necessary or not. For example, Ragin (1987) treats necessary and sufficient conditions in this fashion (see Ragin 2000 where he relaxes this assumption). In addition, the dichotomous conceptualization underlies most of the institution examples cited above. Many would object to saying something is 95 percent necessary. However, I defend exactly that position. Since fuzzy logic pervades this volume, not surprisingly it touches the concept of a necessary condition as well. Instead of saying that a necessary condition variable can only take 0 or 1 values I propose that it can take on *all* values in the [0,1] continuum.

The machine metaphor makes sense of crucial parts taking on values from zero to one. All machines have essential parts without which they do not function. These parts are necessary conditions in an engineering—and functionalist—theory of the machine. If they have value zero, i.e., do not work, then the machine functions at level zero. This is the dichotomous view of functionalism and necessary conditions. But it makes perfect sense at the same time to claim that an essential part works poorly, say at only 5 percent of normal. The result: the machine as a whole does not function well. A car with sporadically firing spark plugs still runs but not fast. Translating "works poorly" means that the essential part takes on a value between zero and one, in this case near zero. Obviously this is just what I proposed above, necessary conditions can take all values in the [0,1] continuum. Sufficiency is how well the car runs, clearly here too values in that continuum apply. The machine metaphor is a necessary and sufficient condition model with all variables taking on values between zero and one.

The machine metaphor illustrates the difference between most economic theories and functionalist ones. An engineer develops theories about how machines work, an economist thinks about costs. A principal difference between business and economics is that economists assume things that entrepreneurs must find ways to do: creating a business that makes money is a nontrivial matter. A entrepreneur must succeed on many fronts for her business to work and make a profit, these factors rarely interest economists.

The machine metaphor permits—by analogy—one to make sense of probabilistic necessary and sufficient condition claims. Kingdon in the exposition of his agenda-setting model never, and probably quite carefully, used necessary and sufficient language. Using probability language softened his claims, and he wanted to emphasize the unpredictability of the process. Nevertheless he invokes the machine metaphor when he says that the absence of a factor makes the probability of an item making the agenda is very low. When he says that the probability is high when all factors coincide then he makes the sufficiency hypothesis. Cioffi-Revilla (1998) develops models very similar to the ones presented here within a probabilistic framework. Dion (1998) also talks about probabilistic necessary conditions which have values less than 1.00.

Once we see necessity and sufficiency falling in the [0,1] range probability talk comes quite naturally. Something which is .95 sufficient easily translates into .95 probable. A value of .05 on a necessary condition variable means that agenda success is very improbable. The machine metaphor is still there, just expressed in probabilistic language.

Of course some factors are really dichotomous. Nothing I have proposed excludes this special case. But I want a general formal model, not one limited to a special case. The basic problem arises from the cognitive difficulty of nondichotomous necessary or sufficient conditions. The machine metaphor helps remove this cognitive block. I can now turn to developing formal, functional models of international institutions.

## Formal, Functional Models of Institutions

The first step in formalizing a functional model of institutions consists in defining necessary condition theories in general. The key characteristic of these explanations lies in the property that when a necessary condition is absent the effect does not occur. Formally,

$$\text{if} \quad Z_i = 0 \quad \text{then} \quad Y = f(\mathbf{Z}, \mathbf{X}) = 0 \tag{10.1}$$

where $\mathbf{Z}$ consists of a vector of necessary conditions and $\mathbf{X}$ is a vector of generic[1] independent variables. I propose that any potential necessary condition model must satisfy this condition. Equation (10.1) just requires that when a necessary condition $Z_i$ is absent, i.e., equal to zero, then the whole institution fails, i.e., equals zero.

$Y$ represents the "output" or effectiveness of the international institution. Obviously, effectiveness has multiple dimensions (e.g., Sand 1992; Young 2000; Helm and Sprinz 2000; Underdal 1992). Two main kinds of effectiveness dominate discussions. One focuses on the extent to which the institution actually addresses or solves the problem for which it was designed, for example, do environmental treaties actually result in reduced pollution. The second, and the one I emphasize, looks at the degree to which the relevant actors conform to the rules and norms of the institution. Given my emphasis on norms in this volume in general and on institutional engineering in this chapter, it is clear that compliance (another version of effectiveness) means following rules, but there is no guarantee that the rules are well designed to solve the problem in question.

Since I consider necessary conditions in the range $[0,1]$—and following the machine metaphor—one would also like $f(\mathbf{Z}, \mathbf{X})$ to be small if any $Z$ is close to zero, indicating that if an essential part works poorly so does the whole institution. We need not require this specifically since as long as we take continuous and well-behaved functions we shall get this property.

Equation (10.1) categorizes necessary condition models in general, but my functional model has *only* necessary conditions. Hence we must restrict ourselves to a subclass of necessary condition models which contain only necessary conditions:

$$\begin{aligned} Y &= f(Z_1, Z_2, \ldots) \quad Z \in [0,1], \quad \text{where} \\ Y &= 0 \quad \text{when any} \quad Z_i = 0, \quad \text{and where} \\ Y &= 1 \quad \text{when all} \quad Z_i = 1 \end{aligned} \tag{10.2}$$

The obvious example of such a model, but not the only choice, uses a multiplicative form. Such a model satisfies the fundamental requirement for a multivariate functional model, that the poorly or nonworking part makes the whole

---

[1] These "generic" variables can be thought of as factors that influence the performance of the institution without being crucial to its functioning.

function poorly (or not at all). Hence, a basic model is:

$$Y = Z_1 * Z_2 * Z_3 \qquad (10.3)$$

This emphasizes that multiplication often characterizes necessary condition models. If we take $Z_i$ as dichotomous variables we get table 10.1 (see below page 207).

Most people would probably feel that a claim that $Z_i$ is *more necessary* than $Z_j$ contradicts the meaning of "necessary." Equation (10.2) implicitly weights each variable equally, probably the usual understanding of "necessary." However, one can easily give differential weights to each necessary condition by adding parameters as exponents, giving us:

$$Y = \alpha * Z_1^{\beta_1} * Z_2^{\beta_2} * Z_3^{\beta_3} \qquad (10.4)$$

With equation (10.3), we assume that all factors equally affect the dependent variable. However, it seems reasonable in the case of institutions to assume that some factors will play a bigger role than others. Equation (10.4) expresses this through different values of $\beta_i$. Since all the $Z_i$ lie in the interval $[0,1]$ if $\beta_i > 1$ then this factor is more important, since it reduces the reliability of the whole more than components with $\beta$s less than one, for example, $.25 = (.5)^2 < (.5)^1$. If $Z_i$ is a less important factor, then its $\beta$ is less than one, for example, $.71 = (.5)^{.5} > (.5)^1$. In this case the importance of $Z_i$ is mitigated, even though $Z_i$ has low importance itself, its impact on the whole is not so severe. If all the $\beta_i = 1$ then we have equal weights for all parameters and equation (10.4) reduces to equation (10.3).

The limit case of $\beta_i = 0$ provides a test of nonnecessity since $\beta_i = 0$ implies that $Z_i^{\beta_i} = Z_i^0 = 1$, $Z_i \neq 0$. This means that $Z_i$ has no impact on the functioning of the institution, regardless of the actual value of $Z_i$ (except zero when it is undefined) its contribution to the functioning of the whole is always the maximum, one.

The necessary condition model presented in equation (10.4) *does not* decompose into simple bivariate necessary condition hypotheses. The only clear-cut bivariate hypotheses occur when $Z_i$ equals zero. Particularly when there are a sizable number of necessary conditions, the value of each part can be fairly high and the functioning of the whole fairly poor. In the case of an institution designed to take care of a collective action problem, if we assume eight necessary conditions functions à la Ostrom, each working at 50 percent, then the institution as a whole works poorly— $(.5)^8 = .004$— virtually not at all.

### Necessity and Sufficiency Effects

The variables in this class of models have two effects. In their role as necessary conditions they function to *limit* the output of the institution; in the limit—when they are zero—they force the institution to a grinding halt. At the same time their presence contributes positively to output; what I call a sufficiency effect.

I suggest that the necessity effect be defined in terms of the limiting or barrier-setting characteristic of the factor.[2] This emphasizes the characteristic of a necessary condition that its absence (or low value) reduces the production of the whole to zero (or very low levels), while the presence of a necessary condition only says that production may be greater than zero.

I propose that the necessity effect be defined as:

The Necessity Effect. The necessity effect of $Z_i$ is the maximum output attainable given that all the other variables are at their maximum (i.e., 1.00).

$$Z_i^{n.e} = \max f(\mathbf{Z}) \quad \text{where} \quad Z_{j \neq i} = 1 \qquad (10.5)$$

This defines the barrier beyond which one cannot increase output with increasing $Z_i$ itself, stressing the limiting role of the variable in the model.

Sufficiency effects deal with how much an increase in $Z_i$ results in an increase in output $Y$. Here instead of the limiting role of a necessary condition we see the positive contribution of $Z_i$ to the level of sufficiency. The sufficiency effect answers the question: how much more $Y$ do I get when I increase $Z_i$ by $\epsilon$? Hence we can define the sufficiency effect as follows:

The Sufficiency Effect. The sufficiency effect is the marginal increase in $Y$ due to the increase in $Z_i$.

$$Z_i^{s.e} = \partial f(\mathbf{Z}) / \partial Z_i \qquad (10.6)$$

The sufficiency effect is the marginal contribution of $Z_i$ to the output $f(\mathbf{Z})$ holding all other values of $Z$ constant. In mathematical terms this is the partial derivative of $Y$ with respect to $Z_i$.

These definitions capture the spirit—and the letter—of the necessity and sufficiency concepts. I will return to these effects when I discuss figure 10.1 where we can see these effects graphically illustrated.

## Institutions and Production Functions

I have spoken continually in this chapter about the output and production of (collective) goods. This may seem just another example of the imperialism of economic language in the institution literature (like the "supply" and "demand" for institutions). In contrast here we find a very close link at the mathematical level:

What I have defined as a functional model of institutions has the same form as the Cobb-Douglas production function in economics.

---

[2] See Goertz (1994) for a general discussion of the characteristics of barriers in international politics.

The Cobb-Douglas production function has a venerable history, going back to the 1920s (Cobb and Douglas 1928). As its name indicates it tries to model the *production* of (industrial) *goods* as a mixture of Kapital and Labor inputs:

$$Q = \alpha * K^{\beta} L^{1-\beta}, \quad \beta \geq 0 \quad \alpha > 0 \tag{10.7}$$

It is clear that this[3] is exactly the functional model I described above. However, one must be careful since not all production functions have the characteristic I have required for functional models.[4]

Since I came to economic production functions via necessary conditions and functionalist ideas it is interesting to examine the economic production function literature (e.g., Chambers 1988) for expressions of necessity. There the idea of necessity gets expressed through the term "essentiality": labor and capital are essential to production. If there is no capital there is no production; if there is no labor also no production (hence the power of strikes).

These functionalist/production models have two key characteristics. The first is that they are nonlinear. Both the multiplicative form and the parameters in the exponents make the model very nonlinear. Second, the model is very interactive in nature. A change in one variable (say to from near one to near zero) can have a dramatic impact on the whole. For example, if one variable goes to zero the whole institution collapses. The necessity and sufficiency effects can be large because of the tight and closely knit structure of the model.

In summary, both at semantic and mathematical levels there exists a close relationship between functional models of institutions expressed in terms of necessary conditions and classic production function models in economics. Both look *inside* the institution or firm to try to understand how goods and services actually get made. Both argue that there are key, essential, components to this production process. Thus in spite of many differences, at the core there are remarkable resemblances between economists' view of production and sociologists' view of institutions. Any concrete (economic) analysis of an institution makes reference to the functions it serves for individuals or society at large. I have but tried to formalize these common threads into a continuous cloth.

## Fuzzy, Formal, Functional Models

In my discussion of economic production functions I have taken the Cobb-Douglas as the archetypical model. However, not all production functions satisfy the criteria of my functionalist model expressed in equation (10.2). Also, other functions

---

[3] In the special case of $(\beta_1 + \beta_2 + \beta_3) = 1$ the function is said to be linearly homogeneous. This is actually the most common expression of the Cobb-Douglas production function. Used in such a form, Cobb-Douglas statistical models are tested with restricted least squares (Greene 1991, 211–16).

[4] For example, the constant elasticity of substitution model (Arrow et al. 1961)—known to noneconomists as the generalized mean—does not fulfill our necessary conditions criteria. The constant elasticity of substitution production function, $[\sum_{i=0}^{n} \beta_i (X_i)^{\rho}]^{1/\rho}$ does not equal zero when $X_i = 0$.

TABLE 10.1: Simple, Formal, Functional Model of Institutions

| $Z_1$ | $Z_2$ | $Y$ |
|---|---|---|
| 1 | 1 | 1 |
| 1 | 0 | 0 |
| 0 | 1 | 0 |
| 0 | 0 | 0 |

which do not appear in the economic production function literature fulfill the requirements of my functional model. It would be nice to characterize the class of institutional production models.

One way to get an intuitive start is to go back to table 9.1 discussed in the previous chapter, reproduced here as table 10.1, which deals with simple dichotomous variables. We can think of it in terms of logic and set theory. In particular we can think of it as a truth table. The logical function which corresponds to table 10.1 is the "and" logical operator or the intersection operator in set theory. In other words, $Z_1$ *and* $Z_2$ give the truth value $Y$.

We really want continuous instead of dichotomous variables so we can use the fuzzy logic of the "and" or intersection operator since it functions on variables continuous on [0,1]. Hence from an unexpected direction fuzzy logic enters again into my analysis. I can use fuzzy logic mathematics to characterize the class of functional institution models I have outline above, including production functions like Cobb-Douglas.

Figure 10.1 illustrates some common fuzzy intersections all of which satisfy the requirements of equation (10.2). Included of course is the basic multiplicative model of equation (10.3). Notice that all the surfaces have output $Y = 0$ at the two axes. This means that when either $Z_1$ or $Z_2$ equals zero then production is zero. Note as well that if one $Z_i$ is close to zero then so is $Y$. This fits the machine metaphor; the poor working of part $Z_i$ makes the whole machine $Y$ run badly. We can see the values in table 10.1 as representing the corners of the cubes in these figures.

An important theorem of fuzzy logic (Klir and Yuan 1995, 65, Theorem 3.10) gives the limits to how large and how small my institutional production functions can be. The smallest function is called the "drastic intersection": $i(Z_1, Z_2) = Z_1$ when $Z_2 = 1$, $Z_2$ when $Z_1 = 1$ and zero otherwise (figure 10.1a). The largest is the minimum of $Z_1$ and $Z_2$ (figure 10.1b). Hence the class of institution production models has clearly defined limits and contours.[5]

Above (page 205) I defined necessity and sufficiency effects. These can be visualized in figure 10.1. The sufficiency effect of $Z_1 = z$ is the slope of the surface along the $Z_1$ axis at value $z$; this is the marginal effect of an increase in

---

[5]The constant elasticity of substitution (generalized mean) produces values larger than this class but approaches it from above. When $\rho$ equals infinity the generalized mean is the minimum function.

FIGURE 10.1: Fuzzy Institutional Functions

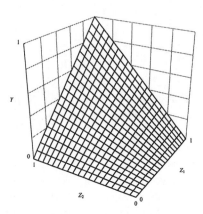

Figure 10.1a: Product

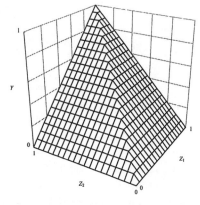

Figure 10.1b: Minimum

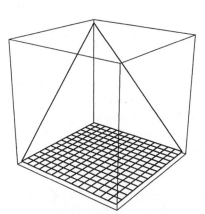

Figure 10.1c: Drastic Intersection

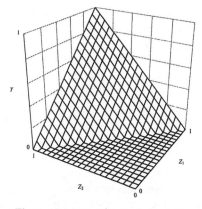

Figure 10.1d: Max$(0, Z_1 + Z_2 + 1)$

$Z_1$ on $Y$. The necessity effect is more subtle, it can be seen by looking at the *largest* value $Y$ can take on for a given value of $Z_1$: since all the surfaces are increasing this is the value of $Y$ when $Z_2 = 1$ which appears at the back wall of $Z_2$. This emphasizes the barrier-like quality of each necessary condition since no matter what value of $Z_2$ the output $Y$ cannot go higher than that back-wall value.

It may be surprising that fuzzy logic, which has played such a central role in the early chapters of this volume, should reappear again here, but the relationship is even more intimate than the mere use of fuzzy logic. If one goes back to my discussion of the structure of conflicting norms in chapter 6, I explored how one could use fuzzy decision making to model the common situation where two or more norms apply to a given situation. What the fuzzy logic decision-making procedure did (see figure 6.1) was to take the *intersection* of the two rules. The intersection is *exactly* what the institutional production model also uses!

So at a very basic level the same mathematical theory of institutional decision making applies to the actual functioning of the institution. This theoretical, structural, and philosophical unity provides one good reason to look at the production of (collective) goods in this functionalist fashion. I discuss below other production functions that are more common in the economic literature on collective goods, but I argue that these have little empirical foundation since they tend to ignore that institutions produce almost all collective goods. Fuzzy logic provides me with a philosophy, mathematics, and decision-making framework that undergirds this whole volume. The link between the individual and organizational decision-making models of early chapters uses many of the same basic ideas I put forth to understand the creation and functioning of international institutions.

## Collective Good Production Functions: A Review

With my institutional production function model in mind it is useful to examine briefly the literature on n-person prisoners' dilemma and collective goods that dominates most thinking about (international) institutions.

The typical economic model of a collective good starts with individuals as consumers purchasing two products, one a standard good, the other a collective good. Because of the peculiarities of collective goods, notably nonexcludability, a given individual gets to enjoy the collective good purchases of others. Within this setup then it is quite natural to consider the total amount of collective good provided as the *sum* of the purchases of all individuals.

Thus the standard—and overwhelmingly most common—move is to assume that the amount purchased is the amount produced. Hence the production function is a simple additive one. Figure 10.2 illustrates this where we see the direct input of four individuals being directly linked to level of production of the collective good. For example, in her American Political Science Association presidential address (1998) Ostrom defined "the social dilemma" as production of this particular

FIGURE 10.2: Additive, Direct Production of Collective Goods

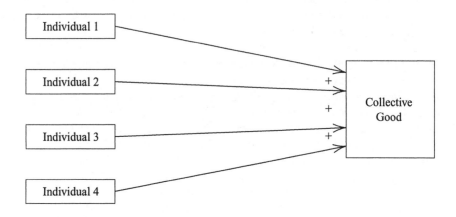

sort. This also underlies Schelling's (1984) well-known treatment of collective action problems. Finally, this is the dominant model in the formal modeling literature on collective goods (Cornes and Sandler 1996).

However, there does exist a small literature on alternative production models, one of which is of special interest to me. In the epigraph to this chapter I provided the fable Hirschleifer (1983) used to introduce what he called the weakest-link production function to the literature on collective goods (see also Cornes 1993; Cornes and Sandler 1996).[6] Obviously, I have already used this metaphor to describe the necessary condition class of production functions. There have been some applications of this model to international relations, notably by Conybeare (Conybeare et al. 1994), who examined which production function best fit the NATO alliance.

The story Hirschleifer used to motivate his proposal illustrates quite well a key point of this chapter. He told a story about N individuals whose fields were protected by a dyke and who were each responsible for maintaining the section of the dyke that bordered on their fields. Obviously the dyke is a collective good since others benefit from an individual's maintenance of her part of the dyke. The weakest-link model applies because if one section fails the whole dyke fails and everyone's field is flooded.

---

[6]The other important production function is known as the "best shot," which in fact can be related to a fuzzy logic model that uses the generalized union operator instead of the intersection one that gives the weak-link class. The maximum which is the operation used in best-shot models is just one of the class of fuzzy unions. One can generate a figure analogous to figure 10.1 for this class of production functions.

FIGURE 10.3: Institutional Production of Collective Goods

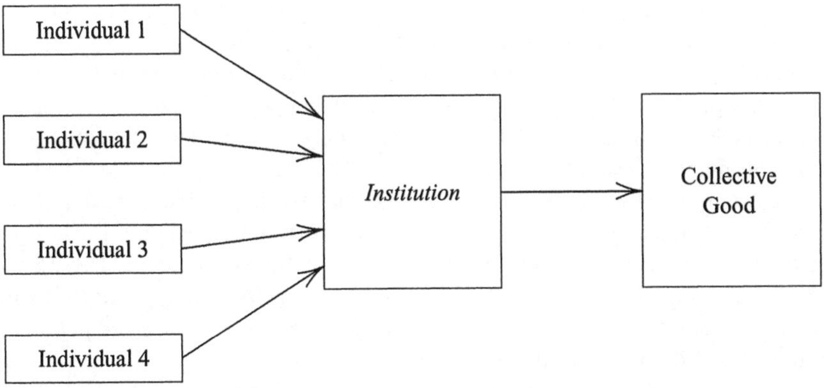

We can contrast this fable with what we know about common pool resource institutions, notably from Ostrom's work. In reality, such a dyke would be maintained by a social institution. Individuals might well be responsible for maintenance, but the whole production of maintenance would be determined by the rules of the institution. Individuals would contribute (or not) to the institution, but the institution would also monitor and sanction those same individuals. In short, most cases do not have the direct production function illustrated in figure 10.2 but rather the collective good is produced by an institution as illustrated in figure 10.3. The key fact is that an institution "intervenes" in the production process. One cannot assume a direct relationship between individual contributions and production à la figure 10.2. I referred earlier to the idea expressed in figure 10.2 as the finance model, it is like the assumption that if one invests money in a firm then one will automatically reap a profit, which ignores all that a firm needs to do to make profit a reality.

In the context of the economic literature on collective goods this chapter argues that the general class of weakest-link models should be the dominant production function while the additive one should be relegated to relatively rare special cases. The weakest-link literature uses only the minimum function, but we have just seen that there is a wide class of models that fit the metaphor. Most interesting in this context is the Cobb-Douglas production function which is rarely used as a weakest-link model (e.g., Arce M. 2000).

# Monitoring and Sanctioning as
# Institutional Functions

I have outlined the formal structure of my functionalist model of (international) institutions. For this mathematical structure to be useful we need to fill it with content, in other words we need to give political substance to its variables. Here economic production functions can serve as an analogy. Normally they contain two variables Labor and Kapital: what sorts of concepts do we put into an institutional production function?

Ostrom, Mitchell, Lebow, and Jacobson and Weiss provide a starting point. Each have argued for necessary functions for the effective operation of institutions. Table 10.2 summarizes their proposals. I continue to include Lebow and deterrence since many institutions have deterrence roles. Taking Mitchell's oil pollution institution, we can ask how deterred oil companies are from polluting: how much deterrence does the institution produce? [7]

Two functions I think stand out in these lists: monitoring and sanctioning. Whatever the output, the institution needs to monitor compliance with institution rules and norms, and needs to deal with violations. This parallels economic production functions with their use of labor and capital, which are necessary for all kinds of production and are not tied to the production of specific goods and services.

Ostrom picks out monitoring and sanctioning for particular attention: "Most robust and long-lasting common-pool institutions involve clear mechanisms for monitoring rule conformance and graduated sanctions for enforcing compliance" (1998, 8). Game theorists have picked up on the same themes: "Institutions may play an important role in overcoming the adverse effects of incomplete information. Role specialists may be created to whom authority is delegated to administer the rules of the game, to monitor the adherence of members to these rules, most important, to identify and publicize transgressions by errant members. . . . Thus institutions need not be granted any sanctioning power to facilitate stable cooperation. Rather they need only provide the information that is required for effective decentralized punishment by members" (Garrett and Weingast 1993, 179). If we look at the work of transaction cost economists, monitoring and sanctioning are always central to the role of economic institutions such as governments. The minimalist, night watchman state enforces contracts and sanctions the violations of property rules and criminal law.

One may object that international institutions have weak sanctioning capacities. If those institutions also have low output then there is no contradiction with my model. I refer the reader to the next chapter which delves into this issue in

---

[7]To these I can add the proposition of Levy et al. that "Low levels of concern, poor contractual environments and weak capacity are each sufficient to cause failures in collective management of environmental tasks" (1995, 304). Not all these factors lie within the institution, but the structure of the argument is exactly the necessary condition one I am developing in this chapter.

TABLE 10.2: Functions of Institutions

| Ostrom | Mitchell | Lebow | Jacobson/Weiss |
|---|---|---|---|
| Monitoring | Detecting violations | Clearly defined threats | Sunshine methods |
| Graduated sanctions | Identifying violators | Repeatedly publicized | Positive incentives |
| Clear boundaries | Prosecuting violators | Defensible | Coercive measures |
| Congruent rules | Potent sanctions | Resolve to use force | |
| Conflict resolution means | | | |
| Rights to organize | | | |
| Nested units | | | |
| Collective-choice arenas | | | |

detail. I note in contrast that Ostrom, Mitchell, Lebow, North, and Jacobson and Weiss all include sanctions as key. As with almost all issues, I think it is better to start with standard cases, if international institutions have specificities as social institutions then so be it. One should not populate the core concept family with nonstandard examples (a critique I made of the Krasner definition of regimes).

## Ways to Monitor or Sanction: Substitutability

The case studies of Ostrom, Mitchell, and Jacobson and Weiss illustrate that while monitoring and sanctioning are necessary for the proper functioning of institutions there exists a variety of ways to perform these functions and some of these may be better than others. Mitchell's analysis of oil pollution institutions (1994) demonstrates this very well. He describes two institutions for the prevention of marine tanker oil discharges, one which worked well and another which did not. The badly functioning institution was structured so as to make monitoring and sanctioning very difficult. The successful institution in contrast incorporated monitoring into standard inspection procedures and sanctions occurred at the level of the inability to get insurance if a ship did not pass inspection.

The possibility that there are multiple machines which do the same basic thing I call the "substitutability" of different techniques and rule structures. My institutional model has two levels (1) the necessary functions, e.g., monitoring and sanctioning and (2) the various, substitutable, means of performing these roles. There is wide substitutability *within* a given function such as monitoring, but little substitutability *between* different functions, e.g., between the monitoring and sanctioning that compose an institution. My functional models require an adequate value on all necessary variables. However, there exist a variety of means of achieving a high value on an essential dimension.

At the structural level my models allow limited substitutability between dimensions:

when $Z_i = 0$ no substitutability is possible

when $Z_i > 0$ limited substitutability is possible

For example, if $Z_i = .5$ and it declines to .4, increases in the other $Z_i$ values can compensate for this, at least partially. However, at zero no substitutability can occur, $Y$ will be zero no matter how much one increases the other $Z$ values.

The general class of functional models I discussed above permits a certain range of substitutability effects. However, *all* possess the property of no substitutability when $Z_i = 0$; this is the necessary condition property that lies at the core of functionalist models. The necessity effect determines the limits to the substitutability since it puts an upper limit on how much $Y$ is produced for a given value of $Z_i$. In general, most models also possess the property that substitutability is quite limited for values of $Z$ close to zero. This comes as a result of imposing the property of continuity on the general class of models I discuss.

The issue of substitutability appears in various guises in the international relations literature. Most and Starr (1989) express the same idea with their concept of foreign policy substitutability. The most sustained discussion occurs in the context of the substitutability of arms and alliances both of which are means to increase power (Morrow 1993; Diehl 1994; Sorokin 1994; see the special issue of the *Journal of Conflict Resolution* 44[1] 2000). Here too we see the two-level model: at a more general level lies the concept of (military) power, governments traditionally have two means to increase this, arms acquisition and alliance formation.

If multiplication forms perhaps the typical necessary condition structure then addition expresses very well the substitutability idea:

$$Z_i = \alpha_1 S_1 + \alpha 2 S_2 + \alpha_3 S_3 + \dots \qquad (10.8)$$

Any $S_j$ can compensate for the absence of any $S_i$.[8] Equation (10.8) formalizes the idea that one can use a variety of means to achieve an institutional function $Z_i$. Ostrom's work illustrates that, for example, monitoring of a common pool resource depends on the physical characteristics of the resource, what works for Spanish irrigation does not for Swiss pastures.

The two levels of my model have quite different formal structures. At one level it is necessary conditions formalized by mathematical operations like multiplication, intersection, and logical "and." At the second level lies substitutability, no necessity, and the use of mathematical operators like addition, union, and logical "or." Cioffi-Revilla and Starr (1995) analyze and develop formal models with exactly this structure.

---

[8]The range of the $S$s and the $\beta$ values can limit this compensation, but nothing in the general model puts bounds on it.

My two-level model is really no different from that implicit in economic production functions like Cobb-Douglas. One can have different forms of labor; for example, slave labor versus paid, as in the debate about the efficiency of slavery as an economic system. Likewise, sources of capital vary such as markets, autofinancing, and the state. The two levels of economic and institutional production function models are basically the same.

The key point here is that one must not confuse the different levels of the model. All institutions must monitor and sanction, but there are lots of ways to fulfill these functions. At the base level we have the *necessity* of each factor, at the next level one finds *substitutability* of means to achieve each particular subfunction of the institution.

## Putting It All Together

The time has come to put all the elements of my functional model of institutions together. I have frequently referred to Elinor Ostrom's work on common pool resource institutions, hence it seems appropriate to use her work as my example. As I noted in table 10.2 she proposed eight necessary conditions for the proper functioning of common pool resource institutions. She has specially emphasized the monitoring and sanctioning functions which I have also taken up.

Figure 10.4 illustrates the structure of my model using the contents of Ostrom's work. To indicate the interconnectedness of the monitoring and sanctioning elements the arrows from them link up before arriving at the institutional output. Also, I have indicated that interdependence by marking that relationship as multiplicative, i.e., "and."

In contrast, substitutability within the sanctioning and monitoring functions means that different common pool resource institutions have solved these problems in different ways. Ostrom in her case studies describes two common techniques used to fulfill these functions. For monitoring, one method uses the members of the institution itself as monitors. The second solution engages paid workers to perform this task. Obviously, a given institution could use some combination of these two. For sanctioning, two common solutions are (1) some official body is charged with examining claims and assessing fines or (2) having monitors levy fines. As with the production of industrial goods, much depends on the physical specifics of the resource to be managed.

Jacobson and Weiss implicitly have a two-level view as well. "Sunshine methods" are described as "monitoring, reporting, on-site inspections, access to information, and NGO participation." "Positive incentives" and "Coercive measures" are the two sides of the sanctioning coin. There are various ways to do each of these. Positive incentives include "special funds for financial or technical assistance, training programs, or access to technology." Coercive measures

FIGURE 10.4: A Functional Model of Institutions: Common Pool Resource Institutions

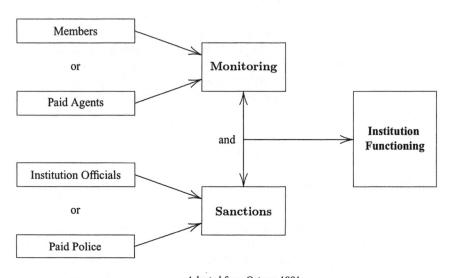

Adapted from Ostrom 1991

take the form of "penalties, sanctions, and withdrawal of membership privileges" (1999, 542).

The formal model I propose is not new with me. I argued in the previous chapter that it underlies Kingdon's agenda-setting ideas. In international relations Harvey Starr gets the same theoretical structure by taking opportunity and willingness as two necessary condition variables and adding foreign policy substitutability to this basic structure. Cioffi-Revilla and Starr (1995; see also Cioffi-Revilla 1998) have formalized this and they produce results very similar to those that I have sketched out here.[9] Cioffi-Revilla and Starr proposed this as a general

---

[9] Cioffi-Revilla and Starr state some axioms which clearly illustrate the similarity of their model to those discussed here:

AXIOM 1 (First-order Causality: Political Necessity). *A political behavior event* **B** *in* **U** *[universe] occurs when* **W** *[willingness] and* **O** *[opportunity] occur. Formally,* **B** *is defined by the causal equation:*

$$B = W \text{ AND } O$$

*where the Boolean AND connective stands for the formal logic conjunction (i.e.,* **W** AND **O** *are necessary conditions for* **B***).* (452)

framework for the understanding of foreign policy. I find it to be quite useful in the study of institutions and institutions.

In summary, I think my functional model of institutions captures the core of Ostrom's framework. I have formalized it and linked it to other functional ideas via the production metaphor. As Ostrom's, Mitchell's, and Jacobson and Weiss's work shows, institutions must perform certain functions to be effective. The literature on collective goods has not really internalized the empirical fact that most collective goods are produced by institutions. Again the difference between a business school and a department of economics illustrates this distinction. To become an entrepreneur requires skills not taught in most economics departments. Obviously, economists and game theorists have much to offer in analyzing when sanctioning will work or not. But one cannot just assume that once individuals agree to pay for an institution that it will automatically be able to deliver the goods.

**Back to Regime Creation**

It is quite obvious that the functional model of institutions I have developed in this chapter has exactly the same theoretical structure as my theory of institution creation. I have used a different language to discuss this structure, more appropriate to the institutional content of this chapter, particularly with its emphasis on production functions but the formal, mathematical theory remains exactly the same in both cases.

The two institutional functions of monitoring and sanctioning correspond to the four dimensions or determinants of institution creation (1) problems, (2) solutions, (3) power, and (4) context. I claimed that each must be present, each is necessary for institution creation. I make analogous necessary condition claims about monitoring and sanctioning for the successful working of international institutions.

This chapter speaks of substitutability in terms of how each core factor can be fulfilled, in the previous chapter I preferred the language of social constructionism. I never assume that design is optimal nor do I assume that institutions function at 100 percent, so I can fill boxes in both the institutional creation and functioning models in a social constructivist fashion.

---

This corresponds to what I have called the structural level of analysis. They go on to define what they call "second order causality":

AXIOM 2 (Second-order Causality: Political Redundancy or Substitutability). *Political willingness and opportunity occur in alternative ways (*canonical modes*). Formally,*

$$W = W_1 \text{ OR } W_2 \text{ OR } \ldots W_m$$
$$O = O_1 \text{ OR } O_2 \text{ OR } \ldots O_n$$

*where m and n are the number of alternative modes for* W *and* O, *respectively.* (454)

They then go on to develop the characteristics of probability models with this structure.

While my models of institution creation and functioning have identical structures the content of them is certainly not the same. In my discussion of individual and organizational decision making I proposed the punctuated equilibrium model of decision making. This model argued that one should make a clear distinction between the initial choice of a norm for use in decision making and the fiddling with the norm that takes place as the result of experience and changing conditions. The same distinction lies at the difference between my theories of institution creation and institution functioning/output. It is never clear when a institution is created whether or not it will work. Mitchell's work makes this point forcefully. If students of international institutions studied failure more often this would seem obvious.

In short, *structurally* and *mathematically* my theories of institution creation and functioning are identical, but in terms of their content they are quite different.

## Punctuated Equilibrium and International Institutions

The punctuated equilibrium model of organizational and individual choice made an important distinction between the initial choice of a rule and resulting fiddling in attempts to improve the rule. This chapter and the previous one apply the punctuated equilibrium idea to international institutions. The chapter on institution creation focused on explaining when institutions will be chosen for international society, which we know from chapter 2 are composed of norms and rules. This chapter was devoted to analyzing some of the key factors that determine how well the institution serves its goals, the implementation phase.

The functional components of the punctuated equilibrium model—along with common sense—imply the institutions that governments form to govern their affairs are not guaranteed to work. Just as on the state level, there is no assurance that new policies will address the problems they are intended to deal with. Creating international institutions is exactly analogous to the creation of policies by individuals and governments. They are designed to solve problems but only experience will tell how effective they are.

The punctuated equilibrium model then addresses how decisions are made with new policies. Similarly, this chapter has dealt with how effective international institutions are in practice. Just as individuals and governments want a coherent set of norms so do international institutions. In particular they want rules that produce effective sanctioning and monitoring of the basic norms of the institution.

The punctuated equilibrium model then works at the three levels (1) individual, (2) organizational, and (3) international basically in the same fashion. The core of the model is decision making with norms and rules. For much of part I I took policies and norms as exogenous, but clearly many states take their policies from the international institutions that they belong to. Those norms can be directly plugged into their organizational decision making since they have the same logical form at all levels. In addition to the core of norms, the punctuated equilibrium model separates policy adoption—at whatever level—from implementation. We expect the same pattern of rapid change and then stasis at all levels from individual to international.

# Chapter 11

# Sanctions and International Institutions

Covenants without the sword are but vain breath.

—*Hobbes*

The previous chapter argued that sanctioning norm violation was a key function of most institutions. Beyond that some—notably sociologists—incorporate sanctioning into the concept of a norm itself. Yet, a major difference between international and other societies lies in the lack of a centralized sanctioning body, both at the general level of the United Nations as well as in the issue-specific international organizations. There are of course exceptions such as the IMF and the WTO, but as a rule formal international organizations have relatively little in the way of direct sanctioning power.

It is clearly understood by most analysts of international institutions that local governments must implement international rules and norms. The same is true of sanctions. We need to examine the general role of norms in the sanctioning behavior of individuals, organizations, and governments. I will argue that norms do play a key role in their sanctioning decisions.

I suggest that it is interested parties that are likely to sanction. However, I will continue to understand "interests" in the broader sense I have developed in earlier chapters. A core proposition will be that when an actor's interests are harmed it makes a great deal of difference if this harm comes about through norm violation or through norm-following behavior. To attack someone's interest within the rules of the game provokes no sanction and gives no reason for international institutions to intervene. However, actions which cause the same level of objective harm but which violate norms provoke a stronger reaction on the part of the harmed party as well as providing the occasion for the intervention of international organizations and other actors. Hence norm violation matters in three ways: (1) the directly harmed party reacts more strongly and vigorously, (2) the international institution whose norm is violated can enter or be called into the affair, and (3) other states can be called upon by the individual or the institution to take action against the norm violator.

If realists are right and international norms do not matter then all that counts is the actual level of damage to government interests. If students of international norms are correct then the fact of norm violation changes the behavior of the harmed party and relevant third parties, both individuals and institutions. But before turning to an examination of these questions we need to examine some conceptual issues regarding norms and sanctions with particular reference to the international relations literature.

Durkheim makes a distinction crucial to the discussion of norms as equilibria or convention: "The violation of a rule generally brings unpleasant consequences to the agent. But we may distinguish two different types of consequences: (i) The first results mechanically from the act of violation. If I violate a rule of hygiene that orders me to stay away from infection, the result of this act will automatically be disease. The act, once it has been performed, sets in motion the consequences, and by analysis of the act we can know in advance what the result will be. (ii) When, however, I violate the rule that forbids me to kill, an analysis of my act will tell me nothing. I shall not find inherent in it the subsequent blame or punishment. There is complete heterogeneity between the act and its consequence. It is impossible to discover *analytically* in the act of murder the slightest notion of blame. The link between act and consequence is here a synthetic one" (1953, 42). Durkheim explicitly rejects self-sanctioning systems as eligible for the qualification as a social norm. His point (i) rejects cases where sanctions follow "mechanically" from the act of violation, but this is exactly what happens in game-theoretic models of norms as (coordination) equilibria.

We have seen that a prominent way norms have been investigated within game theory is through the concept of an equilibrium strategy. Repeated prisoners' dilemma has a number of equilibrium strategies, such as tit-for-tat, always defect, and others. From this point of view violations of the norm (i.e., equilibrium strategy) are *self-sanctioning*. That is what equilibrium means: no actor individually has an incentive to deviate from the norm, if she does her payoff goes down. The decrease in payoff is the de facto sanction for violating the norm. Here the sanctioning mechanism is built into the structure of the situation, there is no need for recourse to some special system of sanctions. In a similar fashion markets are automatic sanctioning mechanisms. Hirschman (1970) called this mechanism the exit option: if prices are too high then buyers exit and choose other producers; the loss of sales thus sanctions the overpriced producer. Sanctions are implicit in the system itself. But all this seems to ignore the situation of most interest: when actors have an incentive to violate a norm.

I see no reason to exclude coordination and convention norms from consideration just because norm violation automatically brings sanctions. But neither do I require all norms to be equilibria of some sort. The most interesting kinds of norms are those that some individuals have an incentive to violate. In this sense I believe Durkheim is correct that most common, and most theoretically important, cases are when sanctions do not occur automatically but must be the result of a decision which takes the norm violation as a major input.

More generally, how can sanctions fit within an expected utility framework? Probably the most common response is that they are incorporated into the payoffs. The likelihood of sanctions can determine in part the payoffs, or enter into a cost-benefit analysis. If sanctions are likely then the average payoff is lower and conversely if the risk of sanctions is low. Hence, one does not really need the concept of sanctions at all, since that factor is already counted in. Within expected utility theory one must justify a particular payoff matrix. Sanctions certainly influence preferences about outcomes, but once the game defined the sanctions disappear into the game structure. Coleman takes exactly this position: "In general, I will have little to say about compliance with norms, because, in this theory, compliance or noncompliance is merely the result of the application of the principle of maximizing utility under different constraints" (1990, 286).

However, a tension exists in game theoretic work between sanctions and equilibrium approaches. For example, Niou and Ordeshook provide a typical equilibrium framework:

> It follows that constitutions are best conceptualized as mechanisms that co-ordinate society to an equilibrium of rules. A constitution is stable and self-enforcing if it establishes a set of self-fulfilling expectations about due process, rights, and legitimate ways of making collective decisions. (1994, 222)

But then they move to a sanctioning perspective, and implicitly a nonequilibrium position:

> In focusing on a hegemon's coordinating functions, we see why that role need not evaporate in the event of the hegemon's decline. If the equilibrium achieved under the hegemon is sufficiently advantageous to all states, the ex-hegemon may continue to as the primary instrument of coordination long after it loses its near-predominant status or even after it loses its status as the leading power. What does disappear with the hegemon's decline, however, is its ability to punish individual states unilaterally and the expectation that it will do so. (224).

It is not clear how sanctioning and coordination roles work together in one model, since coordination usually means equilibrium *selection* which is self-enforcing while sanctions imply equilibrium *imposition* which appears in the payoffs and requires the continued presence of the hegemon. The same uneasy mix of equilibrium and sanction appears in Koremenos, Lipson, and Snidal's introduction to a special issue on international institutions:

> [I]nstitutional rules must be "incentive compatible" so that actors create, change, and adhere to institutions because doing so is in their

interests. Consider an institution that can be sustained only through sanctions and whose members must apply these sanctions themselves. This is an equilibrium institution only if the members who are supposed to apply sanctions actually have incentives to do so. Incentive compatibility does not mean that members always adhere to rules or that every state always benefits from the institutions to which it belongs. It does mean that over the long haul states gain by participating in specific institutions—or else they will abandon them. (2001a, 768)

Coleman provides another language which expresses the exogeneity of sanctions. Instead of being incorporated and then hidden in payoffs one talks about expected utility maximization "under constraints'. Constraint language appears frequently in the economic literature on institutions (see Koford and Miller 1991 where it furnishes the dominant metaphor). Again, hidden somewhere is the notion that if the constraint were to be violated sanctions arrive to reduce the payoff to the constrained maximum.[1] To cite Douglas North: "Institutions . . . are the humanly devised constraints that shape human interaction" (1990, 3). However, the constraint approach avoids a bunch of interesting questions: when, where, and why do people, institutions, or governments sanction? Since constraints are exogenous these questions never receive the attention they deserve.

One might want to assume initially that there will be those who are tempted to violate any norm. There are temptations to violate most laws (otherwise, so it goes, there would be no need for laws). Laws and sanctions reduce the temptation. Domestic society also informs us that laws still work even though they are violated on occasion. International norms may be distinguished from domestic ones, not because there are no sanctions, but because the sanctioning mechanisms are different. If sanctioning is by definition key to the concept of a norm and if sanctions do not exist in international affairs then we should perhaps start calling international norms something else.

δε

Another paradox regarding sanctions in the institution literature lies in the borrowing of the transaction costs approach from institutional economics. North regularly includes sanctioning as part of transaction costs:

> The costliness of information is the key to the costs of transacting, which consist of the costs of measuring the valuable attributes of what is being exchanged and the costs of protecting rights and policing and enforcing agreements. (1990, 27)

> It is . . . measurement plus the costliness of enforcement that together determine the costs of transacting. . . . It is because we do not know the attributes

---

[1] As I discussed in chapter 5, within linear programming constraints can always be transformed in to optimization goals, in expected utility terms, constraints can always be incorporated into the payoffs.

of a good or service or all the characteristics of the performance of agents and because we have to devote costly resources to try to measure and monitor them that enforcement issues arise ... Enforcement poses no problem when it is in the interests of the other party to live up to agreements. But without institutional constraints, self-interested behavior will foreclose complex exchange, because of the uncertainty that the other party will find it in his or her interest to live up to the agreement. (1990, 32–33)

Hence when Keohane borrows the transaction cost concept he quietly ignores this particular—but important—cost.

What is less problematic for North, but more so for Keohane, is that institutions and organizations actually do provide enforcement and thus contribute to reducing transaction costs. North basically lumps sanctions and information under the rubric "transaction costs," implicitly assuming that these are no major differences between the two which would require a radically different theory of sanctions as transaction costs as opposed to information as transaction costs. The case of international relations suggests that, at least in one situation, institutions reducing one kind of transaction cost are much easier to create.

ᵗᵃ

This discussion of sanctioning in conceptions of norms in expected utility modeling and institutional economics forefronts a number of essential points. One is that, as in jurisprudence and sociology, sanctions again form part of a common conception of norms and rules. Two, institutions provide enforcement of the rules. Three, only rarely do sanctions enter explicitly into expected utility models; norms are equilibria and payoffs are assumed to include sanctions.

For theoretical and empirical reasons a discussion of international norms must take seriously the issue of sanctions and enforcement. We cannot assume well functioning institutions that reliably enforce norms. Hence we must hunt, theoretically and empirically, for actors—not just governments—that sanction international norm violation. We cannot take sanctions as exogenous either as constraints or hidden in payoffs. We need to ask why actors sanction when it inevitably means paying costs.

## A Methodological Interlude

The act of sanctioning a rule violation falls in the middle of a temporal sequence of events. A skeletal view must include: (1) norm violation, (2) knowledge of the violation, and then (3) sanctions. One must know a crime has been committed and the identity of the thief before she can be put in jail. I chose "monitoring" and "sanctioning" as the two components of my functional theory of institutions in part because monitoring is necessary for sanctioning. The bureaucratic organization of these two components often separates them, monitoring—police—is separate from the sanctioning—the judiciary.

In my methodological remarks on the ontology of institutions I stressed the need for data on compliance and noncompliance with institution rules. This kind of data form the basis for the analysis of sanctioning. Unfortunately these kind of data usually do not exist—though in a few cases, notably environmental institutions, some efforts have been made (Sprinz 1996; Weiss and Jacobson 1999).

The key methodological point remains that sanctions occur midway through a series of events. To jump to the middle without a consideration of compliance and monitoring definitely produces a biased view. With these caveats in mind we can consider the issues surrounding, and some of the data on, economic sanctions.

Sanctions fall in the third slot of the temporal sequence outlined above, hence the universe of cases for testing uses all situations where the first two parts of the sequence have occurred. The population of interest thus consists of all norm violations. One would then compare this instances which resulted in (economic) sanctions in contrast with those which did not. The emphasis on norms defines the population of cases: all norm violations.

Most work on economic sanctions focuses on their effectiveness, in statistical terms they lie on the independent variable side of the equation. This itself implies a contrast either with no-sanction cases or even better with the efficiency of other foreign policy tools. If the sanction variable is dichotomous then examining *only* cases of sanctioning will never produce any useful results (since the sanction variable is identical with the intercept parameter). A continuous sanction variable will generally, however, provide valid results and one can extrapolate to the no-sanction case.

Morgan and Schwebach (1995) provide a rare example of a study that includes no-sanction cases. They focused on economic sanctions in the universe militarized disputes, hence they can examine crises and disputes that do not involve economic sanctions. They find that when one does so economic sanctions do not seem to have much effect. They examined as well only sanction cases where sanctions did seem to matter, in the sense that as the costs to the target increased so did impact. If nothing else, their study illustrates the importance of selection effects. However, given that they look at *militarized* disputes, all their cases by definition involve the use of military sanctions (this is the criterion by which their data are gathered). Hence, it becomes hard to disentangle effects. The most one can say is that economic sanctions do not add much when military means are being employed.

In contrast, I look at sanctions in the context of norm violation, in statistical terms again, as dependent variables. The literature on sanctions provides some hints about the questions that interest me but these cannot be but more than suggestive. We have significant information about economic sanctions but for a valid study we would need no-sanction cases, otherwise we cannot make useful comparisons (selecting on the dependent variable problem).

# Why Sanction?

The norm approach to sanctions thus differs dramatically from the literature on instrumental economic sanctions. In the economic literature sanctions are the independent variable, in the norm approach they become the dependent one. Instead of asking how effective sanctions are, one poses the question about why sanctions are imposed.

I have already remarked upon the curious absence of the analysis of sanctions or enforcement in the institution literature. In some ways where sanctions arise frequently is somewhat peculiar as well. In the foreign policy literature sanctions in the generic sense rarely come up. As we shall see below hegemonic institution theory and the concept of reciprocity implicitly involve sanctions, for example, "defection" in the tit-for-tat strategy can be seen as a sanction, but the sanctioning terminology is rarely used. Similarly in the security literature, one reads about threats but rarely of sanctions per se. The only sustained analysis in the world politics literature has been in the study of economic sanctions. Nevertheless, to qualify sanctions as "economic" suggests other kinds of sanctions—military, above all—but again there appears to be little work on military sanctions as distinct from compellence and deterrence.

The literature on economic sanctions is considerable, including major studies by Hufbauer, Schott, and Elliot (1990), Martin (1992), and Drezner (2000). Can this literature inform an analysis of sanctions in relation to international norms?

The Hufbauer et al. and Martin studies treat different but complementary aspects of economic sanctions. Hufbauer et al. focus on the conditions which determine when economic sanctions are effective. That is, *given* that there are sanctions, what is the success rate? what influences the success rate? Martin concentrates on *producing* sanctions, particularly sanctions conceived of as a public good of some sort, which often requires various states to coordinate efforts in order for them to be effective, e.g., trade sanctions. Martin's work thus follows directly in the wake of Keohane (not surprisingly since she was his student) posing the question of the provision of public goods and the possibility of international cooperation. Both Martin and Hufbauer et al. think about economic sanctions in instrumental terms.

The "why" question has two interpretations. The first refers to the act which provoked the sanction, for example, a norm violation. The second contrasts the economic sanction tool with other possible responses in terms of their efficiency in achieving exogenous goals.[2]

As Martin makes clear in the first paragraph of her preface, she links in no way sanctions to issues of international norms:

> This project developed from discussions about two theoretical and substantive puzzles in international politics: the conditions for international cooperation and the uses of issue linkage. An interest in these two subjects made a

---

[2] Again case selection rears its head, since to evaluate the efficacity of economic sanctions one needs to compare them with other foreign policy tools.

study of international cooperation on economic sanctions an obvious choice. Economic sanctions are a common example of issue linkage in international politics, as states attempt to use economic levers to achieve political gains. (xi)

Clearly economic sanctions are not linked to norm violations, they are tied to other political issues. Linkage is possible because sanctions are a tool used to gain other (political) ends. Martin suggests that her study should be of interest "to academics and others attempting to understand and utilize this foreign policy tool" (xi). Economic sanctions as a unified object of study comes from the commonality of the means and not the ends.

However norm violation lies half-hidden as a theme throughout her study. In fact, she starts out—the first page of her book—with it:

> When Saddam Hussein's Iraq army invaded Kuwait on 2 August 1990, nearly every state in the United Nations was outraged. Beyond posing a severe economic challenge by consolidating control over vast oil reserves, Iraq's action violated one of the entrenched norms of the international community—a norm against forcible acquisition of disputed territory. (3)

If the index is any indication, the theme of norm violation remains undeveloped since neither "norm," "principle," nor "international law," merit mention, while "international institutions" gets passing notice in the introduction. On the other hand, international institutions occupy a significant place since she is concerned with the role of hegemons and institutions in coercive cooperation.

Martin does find that institutions play an important role in facilitating cooperation on sanctions. As we have seen North (1990) emphasized sanctions as part of the transaction costs that institutions can reduce, but Martin does not adopt this framework for her analysis of institutions (Douglas North does not appear in the bibliography nor "transaction costs" in the index). One can ask the "why" question of institutions: why should an institution become involved in economic sanctions?

One plausible response is that someone has violated a norm that forms part of the international institution. Recall that I have defined institutions as "structures of norms." Hiding in the background of an institutional analysis of sanctions is the violation of the norms that fall within the rule domain of the institution. One needs to pose not only the question "why institutions?" but also the question of "which institution?" For example, in the case of U.S. human rights policies in the late 1970s Martin emphasizes that it was institutional norms and policies that were used as reasons for *not* involving the IMF and other international financial institutions in sanctioning human rights violations. Human rights are no norms of the IMF.

As Martin stresses, an important aspect of the sanctioning problem at the international level is convincing other states to apply sanctions. Often for sanctions to be effective they must be applied by many actors simultaneously. More generally this sanctioning can be thought of as a second-order game. For example,

Axelrod's definition of a norm (see above page 33) invokes sanctions. In his simulation of the evolution of norms the costs of sanctioning outweigh the benefits individually (there are no centralized sanctions in his model). Hence, as with most public goods, sanctions are under-provided because individuals have no incentive to do so.[3] At this point Axelrod introduces a "metanorm": sanction those who do not sanction. With this metanorm in place sanctioning works. But the risk of infinite regress appears: is it in one's self-interest to apply the sanction in the metanorm? Or is it the same problem displaced one level? The point, however, is important, the failure to sanction itself may be subject to sanctions. The hegemon has enough power to sanction at both levels: the original violation and no-sanctioning behavior. Here too is where institutions come into play since they provide forums where pressure can be applied on no-sanctioners (in addition to their sanction coordinating function).

A complete view of the problem means moving beyond a focus just on sanctions to the original situation that provoked the application of sanctions. Coleman (1990) in his extended discussion of sanctions sets this up as two linked games. The first game is the basic situation where, in my terms, one can follow the norm or violate it. If one of the n-players violates the norm then the other n–1 other players face what might be called the collective security problem. They now are playing the sanctioning game; depending on the payoffs and the actions of the n–1 players sufficient sanctions may or may not be provided (Axelrod's procedure is basically the same).

The economic sanctions literature only examines this latter game, the implicit assumption is that the first game resulted in an action to be sanctioned. Though sanctions rarely appear explicitly in the game theoretic literature, examples like Coleman and Axelrod suggest the two-part game formulation is the appropriate one for thinking about sanctions in the expected utility framework.

🙚

The question "why sanction" appears to admit only one response in the literature on economic sanctions, an instrumental one. However, such is not the case if one examines the justification for sanctions in domestic society. Here the terminology shifts and one speaks more frequently of punishment (Hart 1968; Ten 1987). There are two answers to the "why" question discussed by virtually all those who have studied the problem. One is what I call the deterrence rationale, which sees punishment as a way of affecting the future behavior of the offender and other potential offenders by making it clear that the payoffs of law violation are clearly negative, replicating the logic of international deterrence. If punishment serves not to deter potential offenders then it is useless—or worse, since precious resources are wasted in a futile procedure. The rationale for punishment clearly calls upon a

---

[3]Here again we see the additive, noninstitutional provision of collective goods critisized in the previous chapter.

TABLE 11.1: Sanctioning Rationales

| | | Target | |
|---|---|---|---|
| | | Offender | Others |
| Motive | Instrumental | Offender deterrence | General deterrence |
| | Morality/Culture | Retribution | Vindication of social norm |

*Adapted from*: Miller and Vidmar 1981, 148

cost-benefit framework for justification. As Dr. Brodsky, the conditioner of Alex in *A Clockwork Orange*, says, "We are not concerned with motive, with higher ethics. We are concerned only with cutting down crime" (Burgess 1972, 126).

The second approach can be called the retributive; it is the law of *lex talionis*, the Old Testament eye-for-an-eye. Here it is a question of justice and morality. From this perspective the offender *deserves* to be punished regardless of whether such punishment will reform her or deter others. It is not a utilitarian calculation in the usual sense but rather a choice based on a moral norm. Retribution may also serve other "functions" but that is not why it occurs. Unlike the forward-looking character of deterrence, retribution looks backward. The former projects future effects of a punishment decision, while the latter conditions the choice on past behavior.

Western, and probably all, systems of punishment combine the two. For example, there is the principle of proportionality between crime and punishment, this is a moral principle which overrides deterrence calculations: the punishment cannot be much more severe than the crime even though that might have positive deterrent effects. Western societies find it repulsive that the hand of a thief is cut off. At the same time, in European history capital punishments and floggings were public and the rationale was quite explicitly a deterrence one.

The controversy over capital punishment in the United States revolves around these issues. Numerous social scientific studies have been conducted to ascertain the deterrent effect of capital punishment (see Baldus 1980 for a survey of social science evidence in law). But lack of evidence for a deterrent effect never suffices for its elimination, there must be a moral convergence around its banishment before it can succeed. An examination of Supreme Court opinions reveals a complex mix of moral and utilitarian arguments. Justices in favor of capital punishment will claim it has deterrent effect in the face of virtually no (social scientific) evidence for their position. Those opposed to it would probably be so even in the face of evidence that it did have a strong deterrent effect.

We are back to the relations between instruments and goals, which has repeatedly arisen in the course of this essay. Most recently it was in the context of organizational decision making where it appears hard to distinguish between the policy goal and the means used to get there. All norms—like all strategies—imply goals, Western law is a complex blend of inputs from both concerns. This is why fuzzy decision-making logic remains central to my enterprise; it provides a formal and plausible way to combine different norms, and hence different values into one choice.

Nossal (1989) explores sanctions as punishment in the international context. He notes as well that punishment does not fit the standard instrumental framework that undergirds most of the sanctions literature. Not surprisingly, for him sanctions involve "wrongdoing." In his concept of sanctions, punishment and wrongdoing form the core: "I argue that two distinguishing characteristics [of economic sanctions] can be identified: first, international sanctions are imposed for acts of wrongdoing; and second, they are punitive in intent" (305). Nossal is not alone in thinking about sanctions in terms of norm violation; Doxey uses the same language: "It is still possible—and desirable—to preserve our understanding of sanctions as penalties linked to real or alleged misconduct" (1987, 4).

This means that norm violation is key to understanding when sanctions are applied. Thus we might expect to see cooperation on international sanctions correlated with the degree of international consensus about the norm which is violated. A related hypothesis would be that purely instrumental applications of economic sanctions receive much less cooperation. So one would expect less cooperation on sanctions over Soviet gas pipelines than South African apartheid.

Hence we can see the instrumental–wrongdoing/morality dimension which appears in domestic politics also applies to thinking about international affairs. One cannot help but think that Israeli reprisals against Arab states contain a good dose of punishment as their motivation. After major international wars punishment of the losers always is a popular option. For example, when at the Congress of Vienna some diplomats argued that France should be punished Castlereagh said that the allies should seek "security, not revenge" (cited in Webster 1919).

If one examines the cases of economic sanctions in world politics it is clear that many times they have been used when moral norms have been violated, such as in South Africa, Rhodesia, and human rights. Hufbauer et al. and Martin lump all these together because the reason for applying economic sanctions is completely exogenous to their studies. Table 11.1 suggests that deterrence may not be the only reason for sanctions nor the only criteria for evaluating them. In the "morality/culture" row one finds that sanctions also support, vindicate, and maintain the social norm.

Of course, one can argue that punishment sanctions serve the instrumental goal of maintaining and supporting a certain normative order; an order which gives other benefits. Nossal says something like this: "what prompts a state to invoke 'sanctions'—not merely the instruments of economic coercion—is the perception that the target state has violated norms of moral behavior valued by the sender and thus deserves not only concrete penalties but also a public proclamation of the

TABLE 11.2: Realism and Norm Sanctions: Actions Which Harm National Interests

Response

|                  |              | Sanction | No Sanction |
|------------------|--------------|----------|-------------|
| Action           | Violation    | 20%      | 80%         |
|                  | No Violation | 5%       | 95%         |

target's impiety" (Nossal 1989, 306). But here I think one must return to internal explanations that I have explored in the context of morality and organizations. It is within the values and goals of the individual that lie the explanation of much sanctioning. The constitutive norms of organizations and individuals drive them to act consistently in many domains (external constraints of course always enter into decision making). Not surprising those that support capital punishment domestically support punitive measures abroad. Those that are racists domestically oppose sanctions against South Africa and vice versa for civil rights activists (Hill 1993; Murray 1997).

This book systematically argues that in many respects international politics does not differ from domestic. The economic sanctions literature shows that this assumption has gone unquestioned. What is a vigorous debate in the domestic literature on sanctions finds absolutely no parallel in the international relations literature, it does not even exist negatively: everyone assumes that moral values play a role in cases like South Africa, but the discussion still revolves around efficiency (with some exceptions like Klotz 1995).

ᨃ

The classic—and jejune—distinction between realism and idealism rested on the conflict between international norms and national interest. We have seen that usually those who create international norms choose ones which correspond to their interests. Hence any simple-minded contrast between international norms and national interests is bound to fail in many circumstances, since following the norm does promote government interests. But this has important implications in terms of case selection, largely because of the focus on norm violation.

Adopting for the moment the realpolitik interests versus norms distinction, one must consider the crucial "no barking dog" case. Realists advise leaders to ignore norms whenever doing so serves national interests. However, if the focus is on actions which harm a government's interests, then we need to examine the whole gamut of such actions. In particular, actions by other states which conform to international norms, but which harm national interests. According to the pure realists one would expect sanctions in these cases as well; since norms do not matter, one sanctions *all* actions according to their impact on national interests, regardless of their relation to international norms. If we take as our universe of cases all actions which have negative effects we can consider two cases, those which conform to international norms and those which do not, as illustrated in table 11.2 with some hypothetical data.

Notice that norm violation rarely gets sanctioned, but harmful actions which conform to international norms are even less likely to be sanctioned. All the cases of norm-conforming but harmful acts are the nonbarking dogs. If calculation is based purely on the impact of the action on national interests we should not see any difference between the two rows. If the hypothetical data were real, one would conclude that norms were part of the cause of sanctions, even though sanctioning of norm violation is rare. As always selection effects can dramatically change the interpretation of data.

The case of Iraq and the United States illustrates this point. Realists use it to point out the irrelevancy of international norms; Iraq invades Iran and the United States supports it, while the invasion of Kuwait brought United States reprisals down upon it. If we examine it from Hufbauer and Martin's view, the invasion of Iran does not fall into the universe of cases while Kuwait does. For me both clearly constitute norm violations. Since Hufbauer and Martin focus on means we can ask why U.S. support of the Iraqi invasion of Iran was secret and provoked a mini-scandal, while the United States went to the UN and coordinated sanctions with other states in the Kuwait case. It seems clear that the United States could not openly support a flagrant violation of international norms in the Iran invasion, and could not expect support from other Western countries. In contrast, the norm violation gave good reasons to many countries to support U.S. and UN efforts against Iraq in support of Kuwait. The difference in tactics seems nontrivial and clearly related to international norms.

The same has been found by those who study territory, international norms about colonies, and military conflict. Huth (1996) found that not only was there no correlation between power and territorial dispute initiation, but that often weaker powers initiated disputes. This is clearly related to the norm of decolonization which made legitimate such claims, reduced negative reactions against even military action (e.g., India in Goa), and increased the power of the weaker state (e.g., Panama vs. United States): "Challengers who have disputed colonial territory have rarely encountered active opposition from the international community" (Huth 1996, 99). Goertz and Diehl (1992) found that *successful* territorial changes were made peacefully and that the stronger the international norm in favor of decolonization the less likely it was for decolonization to be resisted militarily.

Odell (1980) found that the best strategy for Latin American countries in trade disputes with the United States was to argue based on the facts of the case and relevant U.S. policy norms and rules. In his analysis of 25 cases of trade dispute Latin American countries received favorable (7 cases) or more favorable (6–8 cases) outcomes when using the norm strategy. Of course an examination of relative

TABLE 11.3: Norm Violation and Sanction Initiation

|  | High GATT Utility | Low GATT Utility |
|---|---|---|
| High Competitiveness | 27 | 6 |
| Low Competitiveness | 4 | 0 |

*Source*: Ryan 1995, 45

power would never predict this kind of success rate. As he says in the conclusion "the approach policymakers [Latin American] have been employing most often, and one of the more successful, has been the use of economic and legal norms, interpretations, and research to persuade U.S. administrators to adopt proposals favorable to the state in question" (227). Odell admits that it was only during the gathering of the empirical data that he discovered this strategy; this illustrates how often norm effects cannot be seen since many researchers are not looking for them. Odell's results all make sense within the organizational decision-making model presented in part II where bureaucrats decide based on the substance of policy, which does not necessarily mean the interests of U.S. trade lobbies.

Lipson (1985) found similar results in his analysis of British sanctions of violations of property rules in the nineteenth century. The British foreign office hestitated to intervene in favor of British investors unless there was clear evidence of malfeasance and fraud: *"In general, the more direct and clear the rule violation [of international rules about expropriation of foreign property], the more likely an overt, forceful, and purposive British response* (49, emphasis in the original). In cases of clear public fraud such as Peru's default in 1879 Britain did not hestitate to intervene. But intervention rarely occurred if *only* the interests of investors' were at stake; there had to be in addition a justification based on accepted property rules.

Ryan found analogous results when examining U.S. sanctions in trade disputes. Table 11.3 reproduces his findings. The USTR was unlikely to initiate an action that did not have high "GATT utility."[4] At the same time the U.S. government undertook cases that in areas where favorable outcomes would result in increased U.S. exports, i.e., areas where U.S. industries were competitive. The vast majority of the cases had *both* GATT and export utility. Not surprisingly many of

---

[4]U.S. trade law Section 301 says: "If USTR determines that (A) the rights of the United States under any trade agreement are being denied; or (B) a, policy, or practice of a foreign country (i) violates, or is inconsistent with, the provisions of, or otherwise denies benefits to the United States under, any trade agreement, or (ii) is unjustifiable and burdens or restricts United States commerce, then the USTR must take action" (Committee on Ways and Means 1989, cited in Ryan 1995, 336). Notice that this law is a syllogism that expresses an obligation. Also the minor premise contains three "or" clauses; two of the three involve violation of treaty agreements and the third refers to harm to the United States. Hence it is not surprising that in practice we are likely to see action when rule violation and interests clauses both apply even though legally speaking one only needs one of the two.

TABLE 11.4: Norm Violation and Sanctioning Success

|  | Compliance | Noncompliance |
|---|---|---|
| Rule-Oriented Diplomacy | 5 | 0 |
| Power-Oriented Diplomacy | 1 | 2 |

*Source*: Ryan 1995, 126

the non-GATT utility cases involved sectors where the stakes were quite high (like the exception rules discussed in chapter 6) such as semiconductors, telecommunications, and pharmaceuticals. The nontrade utility cases often revolved around issues that were likely to appear on the GATT agenda and that the United States wanted to push, such as GATT norms about product standards. The results of the real data in table 11.3 confirm the hypothetical data presented in table 11.2: sanctions require both that self-interest be at stake and that norms are violated.[5]

Not only do sanctions and norm violation go together but sanctions appear to be more successful when applied to norm violations. For example, Schoppa (1999) found that "rule-oriented" U.S. trade actions against Japan were more successful than "results" oriented ones. Bayard and Elliot (1994) found evidence that successful trade cases are related to violations of clear-cut rules. Table 11.4 provides Ryan's results with regard to compliance with 301 trade settlements. Although the N is small, we see again the contrast the impact of norm violation on the success of sanctions.

The targets of U.S. action respond in a very different manner in the norm-violation case. If the United States can make a good case that Japanese policy violates GATT rules then the chance that sanctions prove effective goes up dramatically, as a Japanese trade official said "GATT is key; it may determine win or lose for the US. If the U.S. has a strong GATT case, the case will go differently. The U.S. can use GATT as a very effective tool" (cited in Ryan 1995, 43).

In summary, the scattered results that one can find in the trade, finance, and territorial conflict literature support the claim that sanctions occur when *both* interests and norm violation are at stake. In addition, these sanctions are more successful when an international norm has been violated.

---

[5] Ryan's results are subject to the objection that he has selected on the dependent variable of USTR action. It would be nice to have systematic data on cases the USTR considered acting but did not. Ryan does provide various ancedotal evidence that the USTR often did not pursue claims presented to it because it felt there was no violation of GATT norms. However, selecting on the dependent variable is acceptable when dealing with necessary conditions which is how I have interpreted Ryan's data (Dion 1998; Braumoeller and Goertz 2000; Ragin 2000).

# Conclusion

This chapter on sanctioning has illustrated stark differences between a norm-based approach and a purely state-centric, instrumental view. The contrast could not be greater between norms which often include sanctions in their very definition (the exclusion of sanctions in my conceptualization of a norm is fairly idiosyncratic) and the virtual absence of the sanctions in expected utility frameworks. If sanctions exist then expected utility analysis builds them into the payoff structure, after which they disappear from view. By way of comparison one of the ways we observe a norm is via the sanctions associated with its violation.

The major hypothesis of this chapter claims that governments will sanction only if (1) their interests are involved, and (2) some norm has been violated. If one only looks at cases where sanctions have occurred then it is easy to make a realist claim (in fact it is just as easy to make a norm-based claim) about interests driving actions. But if we realize that in many other cases harm to interests occurs without action because norms are followed then our perspective on sanctions changes dramatically. In the trade context it becomes crucial to analyze cases in which the United States has suffered because of trade but has taken no action. Tannenwald finds the same thing with respect to nuclear weapons: "the military results achieved by atomic bombardment may be *identical* to those attained by conventional weapons, [but] the effect on world opinion will be vastly different" (U.S. State Department official in 1950, cited in Tannenwald 1999, 444). Mitchell (1994, 452) argues that without the international treaty the United States would never have detained ships for oil pollution violations, it waited ten years until the MARPOL institution took effect in 1983 to start doing so. Finally, John Jay in the *Federalist* Number 3 argues that reasons for war include (1) self-defense in case of agression or (2) violation of treaty obligations. Most of his discussion focuses on not on threats to national security but the violation of treaty obligations.

I used the literature on economic sanctions to illustrate how a normative approach to sanctions has been overshadowed by instrumental concerns. The questions of "why sanction?" has been ignored in benefit of "does it work?" To the extent international institutions become involved, one may suspect that some norm constituting the institution is involved: the United States looks for UN approval when it attacks Iraq but not Grenada or Panama. In many cases sanctions only make sense in relation to a norm, but since expected utility models take goals as exogenous the economic sanctions literature can completely ignore the "why" question. The instrumental approach says economic sanctions should be used when they are effective. The opposing hypothesis from the norms perspective is that sanctions are more likely when a widely held norm is violated. Such hypotheses remain to be investigated. More generally the expected utility literature on institutions has ignored the issue of sanctions as an important part of what an institution does.

For example, Koremenos, Lipson, and Snidal (2001) consider five dependent variables as issues in international institution design: (1) membership, (2) scope, (3) centralization, (4) control, and (5) flexibility. In contrast with this chapter and the last one, sanctions does not appear on their agenda.[6] Also, the issue of sanctions does seem important to most contributors to that special issue (i.e., Kydd 2001; Mattli 2001; Morrow 2001; Oatley 2001; Pahre 2001; Rosendorff and Milner 2001; Wendt 2001); in only a couple cases do contributors devote any real attention to this topic (i.e., Mitchell and Keilbach 2001; Richards 2001).

In part I of this essay I argued that decision making standardly uses both instrumental and moral values. The same basic argument has resurfaced in this chapter. Sanctioning responds to both instrumental—efficiency—concerns and norm violation. It is at the intersection of the two where we are likely to find sanctioning behavior; just like it is the intersection of rules (moral and instrumental) that defines fuzzy decision making. As illustrated by trade policy—U.S., Japanese, and South American—British financial policy in the nineteenth century, and decolonization cases, sanctions occur when interests are harmed *and* when international norms are violated.

---

[6]The closest thing the Koremenos, et al. get to a real discussion of sanctions is the clear emphasis on "enforcement problems." However, this is most often taken to mean that the existence of violations and not how to sanction violators. This is slightly more than Keohane (1984) which has no index entry for "sanctions" or "enforcement," but these results hardly indicate that sanctions are a central concern for this group of scholars.

# References

Adler, E. 1992. The emergence of cooperation: National epistemic communities and the international evolution of the idea of nuclear arms control. *International Organization* 46:101–46.

Ainslie, G. 1992. *Picoeconomics.* Cambridge: Cambridge University Press.

Alchourrón, C., and E. Bulygin. 1971. *Normative systems.* New York: Springer.

Alexander, C. 1964. *Notes on the synthesis of form.* Cambridge: Harvard University Press.

Allais, M., and O. Hagen (eds.). 1979. *Expected utility hypotheses and the Allais paradox.* Dordrecht, the Netherlands: Reidel.

Allison, G. 1969. Conceptual models and the Cuban Missile Crisis. *American Political Science Review* 63:689–718.

———. 1971. *The essence of decision: Explaining the Cuban missile crisis.* Boston: Little, Brown.

Anderson, P. 1981. Justifications and precedents as constraints in foreign policy decision-making. *American Journal of Political Science* 25:738–61.

Arce M., D. 2000. The evolution of heterogeneity in biodiversity in an era of globalization. *Journal of Conflict Resolution* 44:753–72.

Arend, A., and R. Beck. 1993. *International law and the use of force: Beyond the U.N. Charter paradigm.* London: Routledge.

Arrow, K., et al. 1961. Capital-labor substitution and economic efficiency. *The Review of Economics and Statistics* 43:225–50.

Ascher, W. 1983. New development approaches and the adaptability of international agencies: The case of the World Bank. *International Organization* 37:415–39.

Axelrod, R. 1984. *The evolution of cooperation.* New York: Basic Books.

———. 1986. An evolutionary approach to norms. *American Political Science Review* 80:1095–111.

Axelrod, R. (ed.). 1976. *Structure of decision: The cognitive maps of political elites.* Princeton: Princeton University Press.

Babcock, L., et al. 1995. Biased judgments of fairness in bargaining. *American Economic Review* 85:1337–43.

Bailey, K. 1993. *Strengthening nuclear non-proliferation.* Boulder, Colo.: Westview Press.

Baily, J. 1997. *Utilitarianism, institutions, and justice.* Oxford, U.K.: Oxford University Press.

Baldus, D. 1980. *Statistical proof of discrimination.* Colorado Springs, Colo.: Sherad's Inc.

Baldwin, D. 1985. *Economic statecraft.* Princeton: Princeton University Press.

Barry, B. 1978. *Sociologists, economists and democracy.* Chicago: University of Chicago Press.

Bates, R. 1996. *Open-economy politics: The political economy of the world coffee trade.* Princeton: Princeton University Press.

——. 1998. The international coffee organization: An international institution. In R. Bates et al. (eds.) *Analytic narratives.* Princeton: Princeton University Press.

Bates, R., et al. (eds.). 1998. *Analytic narratives.* Princeton: Princeton University Press.

Baumgartner, F., and B. Jones. 1993. *Agendas and instability in American politics.* Chicago: University of Chicago Press.

Baumol, W., and R. Quandt. 1964. Rules of thumb and optimally imperfect decisions. *American Economic Review* 54:23–46.

Bayard, T., and K. Elliot. 1994. *Reciprocity and retaliation in U.S. trade policy.* Washington, D.C.: Institute for International Economics.

Becker, L. 1986. *Reciprocity.* Chicago: University of Chicago Press.

Beitz, C. 1979. *Political theory and international relations.* Princeton: Princeton University Press.

Bell, D., et al. 1988. Decision making: Description, normative, and prescriptive interactions in decision making. In D. Bell et al. (eds.) *Decision making: Description, normative, and prescriptive interactions.* Cambridge: Cambridge University Press.

Benedick, R. 1998. *Ozone diplomacy,* 2nd edition. Cambridge: Harvard University Press.

Benedict, R. 1934. *Patterns of culture.* Boston: Houghton Mifflin.

Blalock, H. 1969. *Theory construction: from verbal to mathematical formulation.* Englewood Cliffs, N.J.: Prentice Hall.

——. 1982. *Conceptualization and measurement in the social sciences.* Beverly Hills, Calif.: Sage Publications.

Boehm, C. 1984. *Blood revenge: The anthropology of feuding in Montenegro and other tribal societies.* Lawrence: University Press of Kansas.

Brady, D. 1988. *Critical elections and congressional policy making.* Palo Alto, Calif.: Stanford University Press.

Brandt, R. 1979. *A theory of the good and the right.* Oxford, U.K.: Oxford University Press.

Braumoeller, B., and G. Goertz. 2000. The methodology of necessary conditions. *American Journal of Political Science* 44:844–58.

Braüninger, T., and T. König. 2000. Making rules for governing global commons: The case of deep-sea mining. *Journal of Conflict Resolution* 44:580–604.

Bray, M. 1990. Rational expectations, information, and asset market. In F. Hahn (ed.) *The economics of missing markets, information, and games.* Oxford, U.K.: Oxford University Press.

Braybrooke, D., and C. Lindbolm. 1963. *A strategy of decision: Policy evaluation as a social process.* New York: Free Press.

Brehm, J., and S. Gates. 1977. *Working, shirking, and sabotage: Bureaucratic response to a democratic public.* Ann Arbor: University of Michigan Press.

Brunk, G., D. Secrest, and H. Tamashiro. 1996. *Understanding attitudes about war: Modeling moral judgments.* Pittsburgh: University of Pittsburgh Press.

Bueno de Mesquita, B., and D. Lalman. 1992. *War and reason: Domestic and international imperatives.* New Haven, Conn.: Yale University Press.

Bull, H. 1977. *The anarchical society: A study of order in world politics.* New York: Columbia University Press.

Burgess, A. 1972. *A clockwork orange.* New York: Ballentine.

Buzan, B. 1993. From international system to international society: Structural realism and regime theory meet the English school. *International Organization* 47:327–52.

Byer, M. 1999. *Custom, power and the power of rules: International relations and customary international law.* Cambridge: Cambridge University Press.

Casstevens, T. 1980. Birth and death processes of governmental bureaus in the United States. *Behavioral Science* 25:161–65.

Chambers, R. 1988. *Applied production analysis: A dual approach.* Cambridge: Cambridge University Press.

Chayes, A., and A. Chayes. 1993. On compliance. *International Organization* 47:175–205.

———. 1995. *The new sovereignty: Compliance with international regulatory agreements.* Cambridge: Harvard University Press.

Checkel, J. 1998. The constructivist turn in international relations theory. *World Politics* 50:324–48.

Cioffi-Revilla, C. 1981. Fuzzy sets and models of international relations. *American Journal of Political Science* 25:129–59.

———. 1998. *Politics and uncertainty: Theory, models, and applications.* Cambridge: Cambridge University Press.

Cioffi-Revilla, C., and H. Starr. 1995. Opportunity, willingness, and political uncertainty: Theoretical foundations of politics. *Journal of Theoretical Politics* 7:447–76.

Clarke, H., et al. 1996. *Absent mandate.* Toronto: Gage Educational Publishing.

Clarkson, K., and T. Muris. 1981. *The Federal Trade Commision since 1970.* Cambridge: Cambridge University Press.

Claude, I. 1971. *Swords into plowshares: The problems and progress of international organization,* 4th edition. New York: Random House.

Cobb, C., and P. Douglas. 1928. A theory of production. *American Economic Review* 18:139–65.

Cohen, M., J. March, and J. Olson. 1972. A garbage can model of organizational choice. *Administrative Science Quarterly* 17:1–25.

Cohen, R. 1980. Rules of the game in international politics. *International Studies Quarterly* 24:129–50.

Coleman, J. 1990. *Foundations of social theory.* Cambridge: Harvard University Press.

Conybeare, J., et al. 1994. Alternative collective goods models of military alliances: Theory and empirics. *Economic Inquiry* 32:525–42.

Cornes, R. 1993. Dyke maintenance and other stories: Some neglected types of public goods. *Quarterly Journal of Economics* 108:259–71.

Cornes, R., and T. Sandler. 1996. *The theory of externalities, public goods, and club goods,* 2nd edition. Cambridge: Cambridge University Press.

Corrales, J., and R. Feinberg. 1999. Regimes of cooperation in the western hemisphere: Power, interests, and intellectual tradition. *International Studies Quarterly* 43:1–36.

Crawford, S., and E. Ostrom. 1995. A grammar of institutions. *American Political Science Review* 89:582–600.

Creveld, M. van. 1982. *Fighting power: German and U.S. army performance, 1939–1945.* Westport, Conn.: Greenwood Press.

Dam, K. 1979. *The GATT – law and international economic organization.* New York: Midway Reprint.

Dawkins, R. 1989. *The selfish gene,* revised edition. Oxford, U.K.: Oxford University Press.

Day, R., S. Morley, and K. Smith. 1974. Myopic optimizing and rules of thumb in a micromodel of industrial growth. *American Economic Review* 64:11–23.

Deutsch, K., et al. 1957. *Political community and the North Atlantic area: International organization in the light of historical experience.* Princeton: Princeton University Press.

Diehl, P. 1993. *International peacekeeping.* Baltimore: Johns Hopkins University Press.

———. 1994. Substitutes or complements? The effects of alliances on military spending in major power rivalries. *International Interactions* 19:159–76.

Diehl, P., and G. Goertz. 1985. Trends in military allocation since 1816: What goes up does not always come down. *Armed Forces and Society* 12:134–44.

———. 2000. *War and peace in international rivalry.* Ann Arbor: University of Michigan Press.

Dion, D. 1998. Evidence and inference in the comparative case study. *Comparative Politics* 30:127–45.

Downs, G. 1989. The rational deterrence debate. *World Politics* 41:225–37.

Downs, G., and K. Iida. 1994. Assessing the theoretical case against collective security. In G. Downs (ed.) *Collective security beyond the Cold War.* Ann Arbor: University of Michigan Press.

Doxey, M. 1987. *International sanctions in contemporary perspective.* London: Macmillan.

Drezner, D. 2000. Bargaining, enforcement, and multilateral sanctions: When is cooperation counterproductive? *International Organization* 54:73–102.

Durant, R., and P. Diehl. 1989. Agendas, alternatives, and public policy: Lessons from the U.S. foreign policy arena. *Journal of Public Policy* 9:179–205.

Durkheim, E. 1953 (1906). The determination of moral facts. In *Sociology and philosophy.* New York: Free Press.

Dworkin, R. 1986. *Law's empire.* Cambridge: Harvard University Press.

Easton, D. 1965. *A framework for political analysis.* Englewood Cliffs, N.J.: Prentice Hall.

Eayrs, J. 1957. Canadian policy and opinion during the Suez crisis. *International Journal* 12:97–108.

Eldredge, N. 1985. *Time frames: The evolution of punctuated equilibria.* Princeton: Princeton University Press.

———. 1995. *Reinventing Darwin: The great evolutionary debate.* New York: John Wiley & Sons.

Ellickson, R. 1991. *Order without law: How neighbors settle disputes.* Cambridge: Harvard University Press.

Ellsberg, D. 1972. *Papers on the war.* New York: Simon & Schuster.

Elster, J. 1978. *Logic and society: Contradictions and possible worlds.* New York: John Wiley & Sons.

———. 1982. *Explaining technical change.* Cambridge: Cambridge University Press.

———. 1989. *The cement of society: A study of social order.* Cambridge: Cambridge University Press.

———. 1990. Norms of revenge. *Ethics* 100:862–85.

Fearon, J. 1998. Bargaining, enforcement, and international cooperation. *International Organization* 52:269–306.

Feldman, M. 1989. *Order without design: Information, production, and policymaking.* Palo Alto, Calif.: Stanford University Press.

Ferejohn, J., and C. Shipan. 1990. Congressional influence on bureaucracy. *Journal of Law, Economics, and Organzation* 6:1–20.

Finnemore, M. 1996. *National interests in international society.* Ithaca, N.Y.: Cornell University Press.

Finnemore, M., and K. Sikkink. 1998. International norm dynamics and political change. *International Organization* 52:887–918.

Foucault, M. 1972. *Histoire de la folie à l'âge classique.* Paris: Gallimard.

Frank, R. 1985. *Choosing the right pond: Human behavior and the quest for status.* Oxford, U.K.: Oxford University Press.

———. 1988. *Passions within reason: The strategic role of the emotions.* New York: Norton.

Friedman, M. 1953. The methodology of positive economics. In M. Friedman (ed.) *Essays in positive economics.* Chicago: University of Chicago Press.

Gardner, R. 1969. *Sterling-dollar diplomacy.* New York: McGraw-Hill.

Garrett, G., and B. Weingast. 1993. Ideas, interests, and institutions: constructing the European Community's internal market. In J. Goldstein and R. Keohane (eds.) *Ideas and foreign policy: Belief institutions and political change.* Ithaca, N.Y.: Cornell University Press.

Gauthier, D. 1986. *Morals by agreement.* Oxford, U.K.: Oxford University Press.

Geertz, C. 1964. Ideology as a cultural system. In D. Apter (ed.) *Ideology and discontent.* New York: Free Press.

Gelpi, C. 1997. Crime and punishment: The role of norms in crisis bargaining. *American Political Science Review* 91:339–60.

Genschel, P. 1997. The dynamics of inertia: Institutional persistence and change in telecommunications and health care. *Governance: International Journal of Public Administration* 10:43–66.

George, A. 1986. U.S.-Soviet global rivalry: Norms of competition. *Journal of Peace Research* 23:247–62.

Gibbard, A. 1990. *Wise choices, apt feelings: A theory of normative judgment.* Cambridge: Harvard University Press.

Gibbs, J. 1975. *Crime, punishment, and deterrence.* Amsterdam: Elsevier.

———. 1981. *Norms, deviance, and social control: Conceptual matters.* New York: Elsevier.

Gilbert, M. 1989. *On social facts.* Princeton: Princeton University Press.

Gilpin, R. 1987. *The political economy of international relations.* Princeton: Princeton University Press.

Goertz, G. 1994. *Contexts of international politics.* Cambridge: Cambridge University Press.

Goertz, G., and P. Diehl. 1992. Towards a theory of international norms: Some conceptual and measurement issues. *Journal of Conflict Resolution* 36:634–64.

———. 1995. The initiation and termination of enduring rivalries: The impact of political shocks. *American Journal of Political Science* 39:30–52.

Goertz, G., and H. Starr (eds.). 2002. *Necessary conditions: Theory, methodology, and applications.* Lanham, Md.: Rowman & Littlefield.

Goldstein, J. 1989. The impact of ideas on trade policy: The origins of U.S. agricultural and manufacturing policies. *International Organization* 43:31–71.

———. 1996. International law and domestic institutions: Reconciling North American "unfair" trade laws. *International Organization* 50:541–64.

Gould, S. 1980. The panda's thumb. In *The panda's thumb.* New York: W.W. Norton.

———. 1983. *Hen's teeth and horse's toes: Further reflections in natural history.* New York: W.W. Norton.

———. 1987. *An urchin in the storm: Essays about books and ideas.* New York: W.W. Norton.

Gould, S. J., and N. Eldredge. 1993. Punctuated equilibrium comes of age. *Nature* 366:223–27.

Granatstein, J. 1968. Canada: Peacekeeper—a survey of Canada's participation in peacekeeping operations. In A. Taylor et al. (eds.) *Peacekeeping: International challenge and Canadian response.* Toronto: Canadian Institute of International Affairs.

Greene, W. 1991. *Econometric analysis.* London: Macmillan.

Haas, P. 1992. *Saving the Mediterranean: The politics of international environmental cooperation.* New York: Columbia University Press.

Haas, P. 1993. Epistemic communities and the dynamics of international environmental cooperation. In V. Rittberger (ed.) *Regime theory and international relations.* Oxford, U.K.: Oxford University Press.

Haggard, S., and B. Simmons. 1987. Theories of international regimes. *International Organization* 41:491–517.

Halperin, M. 1974. *Bureaucratic politics and foreign policy.* Washington, D.C.: Brookings Institution.

Hamilton, A., J. Jay, and J. Madison. 2000 (1788). *The federalist.* New York: Prometheus Books.

Hannan, M., and J. Freeman. 1984. Structural inertia and organizational change. *American Sociological Review* 49:149–64.

———. 1989. *Organizational ecology.* Cambridge: Harvard University Press.

Hare, R. M. 1952. *The language of morals.* Oxford, U.K.: Oxford University Press.

———. 1963. *Freedom and reason.* Oxford, U.K.: Oxford University Press.

Hargreaves-Heap, S., et al. 1992. *Choice: A critical guide.* Oxford, U.K.: Basil Blackwell.

Harman, G. 1977. *The nature of morality.* Oxford, U.K.: Oxford University Press.

Harsanyi, J. 1969. Rational-choice models of political behavior vs. functionalist and conformist theories. *World Politics* 21:513–38.

———. 1975. *Essays in ethics, social behavior and scientific explanation.* Dordrecht, the Netherlands: Reidel.

———. 1976. Can the maximin principle serve as a basis for morality? A critique of John Rawl's theory. *American Political Science Review* 69:594–606.

Hart, H. L. A. 1961. *The concept of law.* Oxford, U.K.: Oxford University Press.

———. 1968. *Punishment and responsibility.* Oxford, U.K.: Oxford University Press.

Harvey, F. 1998. Rigor mortis or rigor, more tests: Necessity, sufficiency, and deterrence logic. *International Studies Quarterly* 42:675–707.

———. 1999. Practicing coercion: Revisiting successes and failures using Boolean logic and comparative methods. *Journal of Conflict Resolution* 43:840–71.

Hasenclever, A., P. Mayer, and V. Rittberger. 1997. *Theories of international regimes.* Cambridge: Cambridge University Press.

Hausken, K., and T. Plümper. 1999. The impact of actor heterogeneity on the provision of international public goods. *International Interactions* 25:61–94.

Hayek, F. 1973. *Law, legislation, and liberty,* vol. 1, *Rules and order.* Chicago: Chicago University Press.

Heclo, H. 1972. Review article: Policy analysis. *British Journal of Political Science* 2:83–108.

Helm, C., and D. Sprinz. 2000. Measuring the effectiveness of international environmental regimes. *Journal of Conflict Resolution* 44:630–52.

Hempel, C. 1965. *Aspects of scientific explanation.* New York: Free Press.

Herek, G., I. Janis, and P. Huth. 1987. Decision making during international crises: Is quality of process related to outcome. *Journal of Conflict Resolution* 31:203–26.

Hermann, R., and V. Shannon. 2001. Defending international norms: The role of obligation, material interest, and perception in decision-making. *International Organization* 55:621–54.

Herrmann, R., P. Tetlock, and M. Diascro. 2001. How Americans think about trade: Reconciling conflicts among money, power, and principles. *International Studies Quarterly* 45:191–218.

Hill, K. 1993. The domestic sources of foreign policymaking: Congressional voting and American mass attitudes toward South Africa. *International Studies Quarterly* 37:195–214.

Hirschman, A. 1970. *Exit, voice, and loyalty: Responses to decline in firms, organizations, and states.* Cambridge: Harvard University Press.

———. 1991. *The rhetoric of reaction: Perversity, futility, and jeopardy.* Cambridge: Harvard University Press.

Hirshleifer, J. 1983. From weakest link to best shot: The voluntary provision of public goods. *Public Choice* 41:371–86.

———. 1985. From weakest link to best shot: Correction. *Public Choice* 46:221–23.

Hoffmann, S. 1968. *Gulliver's troubles: Or, the setting of American foreign policy.* New York: McGraw-Hill.

———. 1987. Superpower ethics: The rules of the game. *Ethics and International Affairs* 1:37–51.

Holland, J., et al. 1986. *Induction: Processes of inference, learning, and discovery.* Cambridge, Mass.: MIT Press.

Hollis, M. 1977. *Models of man.* Cambridge: Cambridge University Press.

Hollis, M., and S. Smith. 1986. Roles and reasons in foreign policy decision-making. *British Journal of Political Science* 16:269–86.

———. 1990. *Explaining and understanding international relations.* Oxford, U.K.: Oxford University Press.

Homans, G. 1961. *Social behavior: Its elementary forms.* New York: Harcourt Brace Jovanovich.

Hook, S. 1995. *National interest and foreign aid.* Boulder, Colo.: Lynne Rienner.

Hudson, V. (ed.). 1991. *Artificial intelligence and international politics.* Boulder, Colo.: Westview Press.

Hufbauer, G., et al. 1990. *Economic sanctions reconsidered: History and current policy,* 2nd edition. Washington, D.C.: Institute for International Economics.

Hume, D. 1888 (1749). *A treatise of human nature.* Oxford, U.K.: Oxford University Press.

Hurley, S. 1989. *Natural reasons: Personality and polity.* Oxford, U.K.: Oxford University Press.

Hürni, B. 1980. *The lending policy of the World Bank in the 1970s.* Boulder, Colo.: Westview Press.

Huth, P. 1996. *Standing your ground: Territorial disputes and international conflict.* Ann Arbor: University of Michigan Press.

Hybel, A. 1990. *How leaders reason.* Oxford, U.K.: Basil Blackwell.

Jackson, J. H. 1997. *The world trading system: Law and policy of international economic relations,* 2nd edition. Cambridge, Mass.: MIT Press.

Jacobson, H., and E. Weiss. 1999. Assessing the record and designing strategies to engage countries. In E. Weiss and H. Jacobson (eds.) *Engaging countries: Strengthening compliance with international environmental accords.* Cambridge, Mass.: MIT Press.

Jaggers, K., and T. Gurr. 1995. Tracking democracy's third wave with the Polity III data. *Journal of Peace Research* 32:469–82.

James, W. 1975. *Pragmatism.* Cambridge: Harvard University Press.

Jepperson, R., A. Wendt, and P. Katzenstein. 1996. Norms, identity and culture in national security. In P. Katzenstein (ed.) *The culture of national security: Norms, identity, and world politics.* New York: Columbia University Press.

Jervis, R. 1983. Security regimes. In S. Krasner (ed.) *International regimes.* Ithaca, N.Y.: Cornell University Press.

———. 1985. From balance to concert: A study of international security cooperation. *World Politics* 38:58–79.

Job, B., and D. Johnson. 1991. UNCLESAM: The application of a rule-based model of U.S. foreign policy making. In V. Hudson (ed.) *Artificial intelligence and international politics.* Boulder, Colo.: Westview Press.

Johansen, R. 1994. UN peacekeeping: How should we measure success? Book review of *International peacekeeping* by P. Diehl. *Mershon International Studies Review* 38:307–10.

Jones, B., F. Baumgartner, and J. True. 1997. Does incrementalism stem from political consensus or from institutional gridlock? *American Journal of Political Science* 41:1319–39.

Kahneman, D., J. Knetsch, and R. Thaler. 1986. Fairness and the assumptions of economics. *Journal of Business* 59:S285–300.

Kahneman, D., P. Slovic, and A. Tversky (eds.). 1982. *Judgement under uncertainty: Heuristics and biases.* Cambridge: Cambridge University Press.

Kanwisher, N. 1989. Cognitive heuristics and American security policy. *Journal of Conflict Resolution* 33:663–65.

Katzenstein, P. (ed.). 1996. *The culture of national security: Norms, identity, and world politics.* New York: Columbia University Press.

Katzmann, R. 1980. *Regulatory bureaucracy: The Federal Trade Commision and antitrust policy.* Cambridge, Mass.: MIT Press.

Kaufman, H. 1976. *Are government organizations immortal?* Washington, D.C.: The Brookings Institution.

Keating, T. 1993. *Canada and world order: The multilateralist tradition in Canadian foreign policy.* Toronto: McClelland & Stewart.

Kegley, C., and G. Raymond. 1990. *When trust breaks down: Alliance norms and world politics.* Columbia: University of South Carolina Press.

Kelsen, H. 1966. *Principles of international law,* 2nd edition. New York: Holt, Reinhardt & Winston.

————. 1967. *The pure theory of law.* Berkeley: University of California Press.

Kennan, G. 1985/1986. Morality and foreign policy. *Foreign Affairs* 64:205–18.

Keohane, R. 1980. The theory of hegemonic stability and changes in international regimes, 1967–1977. In O. Holsti, R. Siverson, and A. George (eds.) *Changes in the international system.* Boulder, Colo.: Westview.

————. 1983. The demand for international regimes. In S. Krasner (ed.) *International regimes.* Ithaca, N.Y.: Cornell University Press.

————. 1984. *After hegemony: Cooperation and discord in world political economy.* Princeton: Princeton University Press.

————. 1989. Neoliberal institutionalism: A perspective on world politics. In *International institutions and state power.* Boulder, Colo.: Westview Press.

————. 1993. The analysis of international regimes: Towards a European–American research programme. In V. Rittberger (ed.) *Regime theory and international relations.* Oxford, U.K.: Oxford University Press.

Kier, E. 1995. *Images of war: Culture, politics, and military doctrine.* Princeton: Princeton University Press.

Kingdon, J. 1984. *Agendas, alternatives, and public policies.* Boston: Little, Brown.

Klir, G., and B. Yuan. 1995. *Fuzzy sets and fuzzy logic: Theory and applications.* Englewood Cliffs, N.J.: Prentice Hall.

Klotz, A. 1995. *Protesting prejudice: Apartheid and the politics of norms in international relations.* Ithaca, N.Y.: Cornell University Press.

Koford, K., and J. Miller (eds.). 1991. *Social norms and economic institutions.* Ann Arbor: University of Michigan Press.

Koremenos, B., C. Lipson, and D. Snidal (eds.). 2001. Special issue on "The rational design of international institutions." *International Organization* 55:761–1103.

Koremenos, B., C. Lipson, and D. Snidal. 2001. The rational design of international institutions. *International Organization* 55:761–800.

Kosko, B. 1986. Fuzzy cognitive maps. *International Journal of Man-Machine Studies* 24:65–75.

————. 1993. *Fuzzy thinking: The new science of fuzzy logic.* New York: Hyperion.

Krasner, S. 1983. Structural causes and regime consequences: Regimes as intervening variables. In S. Krasner (ed.) *International regimes.* Ithaca, N.Y.: Cornell University Press.

Kratochwil, F. 1989. *Rules, norms, and decisions.* Cambridge: Cambridge University Press.

Kreps, D. 1990. Corporate culture and economic theory. In J. Alt and K. Shepsle (eds.) *Perspectives on positive political economy.* Cambridge: Cambridge University Press.

————. 1990. *Game theory and economic modelling.* Oxford, U.K.: Oxford University Press.

Kupchan, C., and C. Kupchan. 1991. Concerts, collective security, and the future of Europe. *International Security* 16:114–61.

Kydd, A. 2001. Trust building, trust breaking: The dilemma of NATO enlargement. *International Organization* 55:801–28.

Lakoff, G. 1987. *Women, fire, and dangerous things: What categories reveal about the mind.* Chicago: University of Chicago Press.

Landman, J. 1993. *Regret: The persistence of the possible.* Oxford, U.K.: Oxford University Press.

Lebow, R. 1989. Deterrence: A political and psychological critique. In P. Stern et al. (eds.) *Perspectives on deterrence.* Oxford, U.K.: Oxford University Press.

Leeds, B., A. Long, and S. McLaughlin Mitchell. 2000. Reevaluating alliance reliability: Specific threats, specific promises. *Journal of Conflict Resolution* 44:686–699.

Legro, J. 1997. Which norms matter? *International Organization* 51:31–64.

Lenat, D. 1982. The nature of heuristics. *Artificial Intelligence* 19:189–249.

Leng, R. 1983. When will they ever learn? Coercive bargaining in recurrent crises. *Journal of Conflict Resolution* 27:379–419.

Levi, E. 1948. *An introduction to legal reasoning.* Chicago: University of Chicago Press.

Levi, M. 1988. *Of rule and revenue.* Berkeley: University of California Press.

———. 1997. *Consent, dissent, and patriotism.* Cambridge: Cambridge University Press.

Levy, M., O. Young, and M. Zürn. 1995. The study of international regimes. *European Journal of International Relations* 1:267–330.

Lewis, D. 1969. *Convention: A philosophical study.* Cambridge: Harvard University Press.

Lipson, C. 1985. *Standing guard: Protecting foreign capital in the nineteenth and twentieth centuries.* Berkeley: University of California Press.

———. 1991. Why are some international agreements informal? *International Organization* 45:495–538.

List, M., and V. Rittberger. 1992. Regime theory and international environmental management. In A. Kingsbury and B. Hurrell (eds.) *The international politics of the environment.* Oxford, U.K.: Oxford University Press.

Little, D. 1991. *Varieties of social explanation: An introduction to the philosophy of social science.* Boulder, Colo.: Westview Press.

Loewenstein, G., and J. Elster (eds.). 1992. *Choice over time.* New York: Russell Sage Foundation.

Luce, R., and H. Raiffa. 1957. *Games and decisions.* New York: John Wiley & Sons.

Lumsdaine, D. 1993. *Moral vision in international politics: The foreign aid regime 1949–1989.* Princeton: Princeton University Press.

MacCormick, N. 1978. *Legal reasoning and legal theory.* Oxford, U.K.: Oxford University Press.

Malinowski, B. 1936. Anthropology. *Encyclopedia Britannica, Supplement vol. I.* London: Encyclopedia Britannica.

Mann, M. 1988. *States, war and capitalism.* Oxford, U.K.: Basil Blackwell.

Mansfield, E., and H. Milner. 1999. The new wave of regionalism. *International Organization* 53:589–628.

March, J., and H. Simon. 1993 (1958). *Organizations,* 2nd edition. Oxford, U.K.: Basil Blackwell.

Marinoff, L. 1999. The tragedy of the coffeehouse: Costly riding and how to avert it. *Journal of Conflict Resolution* 43:434–50.

Martin, L. 1992. *Coercive cooperation: Explaining multilateral economic sanctions.* Princeton: Princeton University Press.

Martin, P., and M. Fortmann. 1995. Canadian public opinion and peacekeeping in a turbulent world. *International Journal* 50:370–400.

Mastunduno, M. 1991. Do relative gains matter? America's response to Japanese industrial policy. *International Security* 16:73–113.

Mattli, W. 2001. Private justice in a global economy: From litigation to arbitration. *International Organization* 55:919–47.

Mayhew, D. 1991. *Divided we govern.* New Haven, Conn.: Yale University Press.

Mayr, E. 1970. *Populations, species and evolution.* Cambridge: Harvard University Press.

McElroy, R. 1992. *Morality and American foreign policy: The role of ethics in international affairs.* Princeton: Princeton University Press.

McLin, J. 1967. *Canada's changing defense policy, 1957–63: The problem of a middle power in alliance.* Baltimore: Johns Hopkins University Press.

McNeill, D., and P. Freiberger. 1994. *Fuzzy logic.* New York: Simon & Schuster.

McNeill, F., and E. Thro. 1994. *Fuzz logic: A practical approach.* New York: Academic Press.

Mearsheimer, J. 1993. The case for a Ukrainian nuclear deterrent. *Foreign Affairs* 72:50–66.

Milgrom, P., et al. 1990. The role of institutions in the revival of trade: The law merchant, private judges, and the Champagne Fairs. *Economics and Politics* 2:1–23.

Mill, J. S. 1979 (1861). *Utilitarianism.* Indianapolis: Hackett Publishing Company.

Miller, D., and N. Vidmar. 1981. The social psychology of punishment reactions. In M. Lerner and S. Lerner (eds.) *The justice motive in social behavior.* New York: Plenum Press.

Mintz, A. 1993. The decision to attack Iraq: A noncompensatory theory of decision-making. *Journal of Conflict Resolution* 37:595–618.

Mitchell, R. 1994. Regime design matters: Intentional oil pollution and treaty compliance. *International Organization* 48:425–58.

Mitchell, R., and P. Keilbach. 2001. Situation structure and institutional design: Reciprocity, coercion, and exchange. *International Organization* 55:891–917.

Montesquieu, Charles-Louis de Secondat, baron de. 1899. *Pensées et fragments inédits de Montesquieu.* Bordeaux, France: Gounouilhou.

Mor, B., and Z. Maoz. 1998. Learning, preference change, and evolution of enduring rivalries. In P. Diehl (ed.) *The dynamics of enduring rivalries.* Urbana: University of Illinois Press.

Morgan, T., and G. Palmer. 2000. A model of foreign policy substitutability: Selecting the right tools for the job(s). *Journal of Conflict Resolution* 44:11–32.

Morgan, T., and S. Campbell. 1991. Domestic structure, decisional constraints, and war. *Journal of Conflict Resolution* 35:187–211.

Morgan, T., and V. Schwebach. 1995. Economic sanctions as an instrument of foreign policy: The role of domestic politics. *International Interactions* 21:247–64.

Morrow, J. 1993. Arms versus allies: Trade-offs in the search for security. *International Organization* 47:207–34.

———. 1994. *Game theory for political scientists.* Princeton: Princeton University Press.

———. 1994. Modeling the forms of international cooperation: Distribution versus information. *International Organization* 48:387–424.

———. 2001. The institutional features of the prisoners of war treaties. *International Organization* 55:971–91.

Most, B., and H. Starr. 1989. *Inquiry, logic, and international politics.* Columbia: University of South Carolina Press.

Müller, H. 1989. Regimeanalyse und Sicherheitspolitik: Das Beispiel Nonproliferation. In B. Kohler-Koch (ed.) *Regime in den internationalen Beziehungen.* Baden-Baden, Germany: Nomos.

———. 1993. *Die Chance der Kooperation: Regime in den internationalen Beziehungen.* Darmstadt, Germany: Wissenschaftliche Buchgesellschaft.

Murray, G. 1973–74. Glimpses of Suez 1956. *International Journal* 29:46–66.

Murray, S. 1997. *Anchors against change: American opinion leaders' beliefs after the Cold War.* Ann Arbor: University of Michigan Press.

Nadelmann, E. 1990. Global prohibition regimes: The evolution of norms in international society. *International Organization* 44:479–526.

Nagel, E. 1961. *The structure of science: Problems in the logic of scientific explanation.* New York: Harcourt, Brace & World.

Nardin, T. 1983. *Law, morality, and the relations of states.* Princeton: Princeton University Press.

Neumann, J. von, and O. Morgenstern. 1944. *Theory of games and economic behavior.* New York: John Wiley & Sons.

Nietzsche, F. 1964. *Jenseits von Gut und Böse.* Stuttgart, Germany: Alfred Kröner Verlag.

Ninkovich, F. 1994. *Modernity and power: A history of the domino theory in the 20th century.* Chicago: University of Chicago Press.

Niou, E., and P. Ordeshook. 1994. "Less filling, tastes great": The realist neoliberal debate. *World Politics* 46:209–34.

North, D. 1984. Government and the cost of exchange in history. *Journal of Economic History* 44:255–64.

———. 1990. *Institutions, institutional change, and economic performance.* Cambridge: Cambridge University Press.

Nossal, K. 1989. International sanctions as international punishment. *International Organization* 43:301–22.

Nozick, R. 1992. *The nature of rationality.* Princeton: Princeton University Press.

Nye, J. 1995. The case for deep engagement. *Foreign Affairs* 74:90–102.

Oatley, T. 2001. Multilateralizing trade and payments in postwar Europe. *International Organization* 55:949–69.

Odell, J. 1980. Latin American trade negotiations with the U.S. *International Organization* 34:207–28.

Olson, M. 1971. *Logic of collective action.* New York: Schocken Books.

O'Neill, B. 2000. *Honor, symbols, and war.* Ann Arbor: University of Michigan Press.

O'Neill, K. 2000. *Waste trading among rich nations.* Cambridge, Mass.: MIT Press.

Ortony, A., G. Clore, and A. Collins. 1988. *The cognitive structure of the emotions.* Cambridge: Cambridge University Press.

Ostrom, E. 1991. *Governing the commons: The evolution of institutions for collective action.* Cambridge: Cambridge University Press.

———. 1998. A behavioral approach to the rational choice theory of collective action. *American Political Science Review* 92:1–22.

Ostrom, E., and J. Walker. 1997. Neither markets nor states: Linking transformation processes in collective action arenas. In D. Mueller (ed.) *Perspectives on public choice.* Cambridge: Cambridge University Press.

Owen, J. 1994. How liberalism produces democratic peace. *International Security* 19:87–125.

Pahre, R. 2001. Most-favored-nation clauses and clustered negotiations. *International Organization* 55:858–90.

Parsons, T. 1948. The position of sociological theory. *American Sociological Review* 13:156–71.

Paterson, M. 1996. *Global warming and global politics.* London: Routledge.

Paul, E., F. Millet, and J. Paul (eds.). 1998. *Self-interest.* Cambridge: Cambridge University Press.

Peters, B., and B. Hogwood. 1985. In search of the issue-attention cycle. *Journal of Politics* 47:239–53.

Petroski, H. 1985. *To engineer is human: The role of failure in successful design.* New York: Saint Martin's Press.

———. 1992. *The evolution of useful things.* New York: Alfred Knopf.

Pressman, J., and A. Wildavsky. 1973. *Implementation.* Berkeley: University of California Press.

Price, R., and N. Tannenwald. 1996. Norms and deterrence: The nuclear and chemical weapons taboos. In P. Katzenstein (ed.) *The culture of national security: Norms and identity in world politics.* New York: Columbia University Press.

Przeworski, A., and F. Limongi. 1997. Modernization: Theories and facts. *World Politics* 49:155–83.

Puchala, D., and R. Hopkins. 1983. International regimes: Lessons from inductive analysis. In S. Krasner (ed.) *International regimes.* Ithaca, N.Y.: Cornell University Press.

Radcliffe-Brown, A. 1952. *Structure and function in primitive society, essays and addresses.* New York: Free Press.

Ragin, C. 1987. *The comparative method: Moving beyond qualitative and quantitative strategies.* Berkeley: University of California Press.

———. 2000. *Fuzzy-set social science.* Chicago: University of Chicago Press.

Raup, D. 1992. *Extinction: Bad genes or bad luck?* New York: W.W. Norton.

Rawls, J. 1955. Two concepts of rules. *Philosophical Review* 64:3–32.

———. 1971. *A theory of justice.* Cambridge: Harvard University Press.

Rhodes, E. 1994. Do bureaucratic politics matter? Some disconfirming findings from the case of the U.S. Navy. *World Politics* 47:1–42.

Richards, J. 2001. Institutions for flying: How states built a market in international aviation services. *International Organization* 55:993–1017.

Riker, W. 1980. Implications from the disequilibrium of majority rule for the study of institutions. *American Political Science Review* 74:432–46.

Rittberger, V. 1993. Research on international regimes in Germany: The adaptive internalization of an American social science concept. In V. Rittberger (ed.) *Regime theory and international relations.* Oxford, U.K.: Oxford University Press.

Rittberger, V. (ed.). 1990. *International regimes in East-West politics.* London: Pinter Publishers.

———. 1993. *Regime theory and international relations.* Oxford, U.K.: Oxford University Press.

Rosendorff, B., and H. Milner. 2001. The optimal design of international trade institutions: Uncertainty and escape. *International Organization* 55:829–57.

Ross, A. 1968. *Directives and norms.* London: Routledge & Kegan Paul.

Rousseau, J.-J. 1989 (1762). Du contract social. *Œuvres politiques.* Paris: Bordas.

Russett, B. 1970. *What price vigilance? The burdens of national defense.* New Haven, Conn.: Yale University Press.

———. 1985. The mysterious case of vanishing hegemony: Or, is Mark Twain really dead? *International Organization* 39:207–31.

———. 1990. *Controlling the sword: The democratic governance of national security.* Cambridge: Harvard University Press.

———. 1993. *Grasping the democratic peace: Principles for a post–Cold War world.* Princeton: Princeton University Press.

Russett, B., H. Starr, and D. Kinsella. 2000. *World politics: The menu for choice,* 6th edition. Boston: Bedford/St. Martin's.

Ryan, M. 1995. USTR's implemention of 301 policy in the Pacific. *International Studies Quarterly* 39:333–50.

———. 1995. *Playing by the rules: American trade power and diplomacy in the Pacific.* Washington, D.C.: Georgetown University Press.

Sand, P. (ed.). 1992. *The effectivenss of international environmental agreements: A survey of existing international instruments.* Cambridge: Cambridge University Press.

Sanjian, G. 1988. Fuzzy set theory and U.S. arms transfers: Modeling the decision making process. *American Journal of Political Science* 32:1018–46.

———. 1991. Great power arms transfers: Modeling the decision-making processes of hegemonic, industrial, and restrictive exporters. *International Studies Quarterly* 35:173–93.

———. 1998. A fuzzy set model of NATO decision-making: The case of short-range nuclear forces in Europe. *Journal of Peace Research* 29:271–86.

Savage, L. 1972 (1954). *The foundations of statistics,* 2nd edition. New York: Dover.

Schelling, T. 1960. *Strategy of conflict.* Cambridge: Harvard University Press.

———. 1984. *Micromotives and macrobehavior.* New York: W.W. Norton.

Schelling, T., and M. Halperin. 1985. *Strategy and arms control.* Washington D.C.: Pergamon-Brassey.

Schlesinger, A. 1971. The necessary amorality of foreign affairs. *Harper's* 243:72–73.

Schoppa, L. 1999. The social context in coercive international bargaining. *International Organization* 53:307–42.

Schotter, A. 1981. *The economic theory of social institutions.* Cambridge: Cambridge University Press.

Schroeder, P. 1994. *The transformation of European politics, 1763–1848.* Oxford, U.K.: Oxford University Press.

Schuman, H., and S. Presser. 1981. *Questions and answers in attitude surveys.* New York: John Wiley & Sons.

Schweller, R. 1992. Domestic structure and preventive war: Are democracies more pacific? *World Politics* 44:235–69.

Scott, J. 1971. *Internalization of norms: A sociological theory of moral commitment.* Englewood Cliffs, N.J.: Prentice Hall.

Searle, J. 1969. *Speech acts: An essay in the philosophy of language.* Cambridge: Cambridge University Press.

Sen, A. 1977. Rational fools: A critique of the behavioral foundations of economic theory. *Philosophy and Public Affairs* 6:317–44.

———. 1987. *On ethics and economics.* Oxford, U.K.: Basil Blackwell.

Shepsle, K., and B. Weingast. 1981. Structure-induced equilibrium and legislative choice. *Public Choice* 37:503–19.

Sikkink, K. 1993. *The power of principled ideas: Human rights policies in the United States and Western Europe.* Ithaca, N.Y.: Cornell University Press.

Simon, H. 1977. The logic of heuristic decision-making. In R. Cohen and M. Wartofsky (eds.) *Models of discovery.* Dordrecht, the Netherlands: Reidel.

———. 1979. Rational decision making in business organizations. *American Economic Review* 69:106–17.

———. 1997. *Administrative behavior,* 4th edition. New York: Free Press.

Siverson, R. 1995. Democracies and war participation. *European Journal of International Relations* 1:481–90.

Siverson, R., and H. Starr. 1991. *The diffusion of war: A study of opportunity and willingness.* Ann Arbor: University of Michigan Press.

Skocpol, T. 1986. Analyzing causal configurations: A rejoinder to Nichols. *Comparative Social Research* 9:187–94.

Smith, L. 1994. *Between mutiny and obedience: The case of the French fifth infantry division during World War I.* Princeton: Princeton University Press.

Smith, M. 1982. *Evolution and the theory of games.* Cambridge: Cambridge University Press.

Snidal, D. 1985. The limits of hegemonic stability theory. *International Organization* 39:579–614.

———. 1985. Coordination versus Prisoners' Dilemma: Implications for international cooperation and regimes. *American Political Science Review* 79:923–42.

Snyder, G. 1971. Prisoner's dilemma and chicken models in international politics. *International Studies Quarterly* 15:66–103.

Sorokin, G. 1994. Arms, alliances, and security tradeoffs in enduring rivalries. *International Studies Quarterly* 38:421–46.

Sprinz, D. 1996. Measuring the effectiveness of international environmental regimes. Paper presented at the annual meeting of the International Studies Association.

Sprinz, D., and T. Vaahtoranta. 1994. The interest-based explanation of international environmental policy. *International Organization* 48:77–106.

Stokke, O. 2000. Managing straddling stocks: The interplay of global and regional regimes. *Ocean & Coastal Management* 43:205–34.

———. 2001. The loophole of the Barents Sea fisheries regime. In O. Stokke (ed.) *Governing high seas fisheries: The interplay of global and regional regimes.* Oxford, U.K.: Oxford University Press.

———. 2001. Boolean analysis, mechanisms, and the effectiveness of international regimes. In A. Underdal and O. Young (eds.) *Regime consequences: Methodological challenges and research strategies.* Cambridge, Mass.: MIT Press.

Stokke, O., et al. 2000. The Barents sea fisheries. In O. Young (ed.) *The effectiveness of international environmental regimes: Causal connections and behavioral mechanisms.* Cambridge, Mass.: MIT Press.

Strange, S. 1983. *Cave! hic dranges*: A critique of regime analysis. In S. Krasner (ed.) *International regimes.* Ithaca, N.Y.: Cornell University Press.

———. 1987. The persistent myth of lost hegemony. *International Organization* 41:551–74.

Sugden, R. 1986. *The economics of rights, co-operation and welfare.* Oxford, U.K.: Basil Blackwell.

Sylvan, D., and S. Chan. 1984. *Foreign policy decision making: Perception, cognition, and artificial intelligence.* New York: Praeger.

Sylvan, D., and S. Majeski. 1996. Rhetorics of place characteristics in high-level U.S. foreign policy making. In F. Beer and R. Hariman (eds.) *Post-realism: The rhetorical turn in international relations.* East Lansing: Michigan State University Press.

Tannenwald, N. 1999. The nuclear taboo: The United States and the normative basis of nuclear non-use. *International Organization* 53:433–68.

Ten, C. 1987. *Crime, guilt, and punishment.* Oxford, U.K.: Oxford University Press.

Thatcher, M., (interviewed by Hugo Young). 9 July 1986. Why sanctions are ineffective and immoral. *Manchester Guardian.*

Tocqueville, A. de. 1951. *De la démocratie en Amérique.* Paris: Gallimard.

Tucker, H. 1982. Incremental budgeting: Myth or model? *Western Political Quarterly* 35:327–38.

Ullmann-Margalit, E. 1977. *The emergence of norms.* Oxford, U.K.: Oxford University Press.

Underdal, A. 1983. Causes of negotiation failure. *European Journal of Political Research* 11:183–95.

———. 1992. The concept of regime "effectiveness." *Cooperation and Conflict* 27:227–40.

Walker, J. 1969. The diffusion of innovations among the American states. *American Political Science Review* 63:880–99.

Walker, S. 1977. The interface between beliefs and behavior: Henry Kissinger's operational code and the Vietnam War. *Journal of Conflict Resolution* 21:129–68.

Waltz, K. 1979. *Theory of international relations.* Boston: Addison-Wesley.

Weber, M. 1968. *Economy and society: An outline of interpretive sociology.* Berkeley: University of California Press.

Weber, S. 1991. *Cooperation and discord in U.S.-Soviet arms control.* Princeton: Princeton University Press.

Webster, C. 1919. *The Congress of Vienna.* London: His Majesty's Stationary Office.

Weiss, E., and H. Jacobson (eds.). 1999. *Engaging countries: Strengthening compliance with international environmental accords.* Cambridge, Mass.: MIT Press.

Welch, D. 1993. *Justice and the genesis of war.* Cambridge: Cambridge University Press.

———. 1997. Remember the Falklands? *International Journal* 52:483–507.

Welles, O., and P. Bogdanovich. 1992. *This is Orson Welles.* New York: HarperCollins.

Wendt, A. 2001. Driving with the rearview mirror: On the rational science of Institutional Design. *International Organization* 55:1019–49.

White, M. 1981. *What is and what ought to be done: An essay on ethics and epistemology.* Oxford, U.K.: Oxford University Press.

Wildavsky, A. 1975. *Budgeting: A comparative theory of budgetary process.* Boston: Little, Brown.

Wilson, J. 1989. *Bureaucracy: What government agencies do and why they do it.* New York: Basic Books.

von Wright, G. 1963. *Norms and action.* London: Routledge & Kegan Paul.

Yager, R., and D. Filev. 1994. *Essentials of fuzzy modeling and control.* New York: John Wiley & Sons.

Young, O. 1989. *International cooperation: Building regimes for natural resources and the environment.* Ithaca, N.Y.: Cornell University Press.

———. 1991. Political leadership and regime formation: On the development of institutions in international society. *International Organization* 45:281–308.

———. 1998. The effectiveness of international environmental regimes: A mid-term report. *International Environmental Affairs* 10:267–89.

———. 1998. *Creating regimes: Arctic accords and international governance.* Ithaca, N.Y.: Cornell University Press.

Young, O. (ed.). 2000. *The effectiveness of international environmental regimes: Causal connections and behavioral mechanisms.* Cambridge, Mass.: MIT Press.

Young, O., and G. Osherenko (eds.). 1993. *Polar politics: Creating international environmental regimes.*

Zacher, M. 1996. *Governing global networks.* Cambridge: Cambridge University Press.

Zadeh, L. 1965. Fuzzy sets. *Information and Control* 8:338–53.

Zahariadas, N. 1997. *Markets, states, and public policy: Privatization in Britain and France.* Ann Arbor: University of Michigan Press.

Zhou, X. 1993. The dynamics of organizational rules. *American Journal of Sociology* 98:1134–66.

Zimmerman, W., E. Nikitina, and J. Clem. 1999. The Soviet Union and the Russian Federation: A natural experiment in environmental compliance. In E. Weiss and H. Jacobson (eds.) *Engaging countries: Strengthening compliance with international environmental accords.* Cambridge, Mass.: MIT Press.

# Index

# About the Author

Gary Goertz teaches political science at the University of Arizona. His books include *Contexts of International Politics*, and with Paul Diehl *Territorial Change and International Conflict* and *War and Peace in International Rivalry*. He is coeditor with Harvey Starr of *Necessary Conditions: Theory, Methodology, and Applications* (2002).